Measuring America: The Decennial Censuses From 1790 to 2000

Issued September 2002

POL/02-MA(RV)

U.S. Department of Commerce
Donald L. Evans,
Secretary

Samuel W. Bodman,
Deputy Secretary

Economics
and Statistics
Administration
Kathleen B. Cooper,
Under Secretary for
Economic Affairs

U.S. CENSUS BUREAU
Charles Louis Kincannon,
Director

For sale by the Superintendent of Documents, U.S. Government Printing Office
Internet: bookstore.gpo.gov   Phone: toll free (866) 512-1800;   DC area (202) 512-1800
Fax: (202) 512-2250 Mail: Stop SSOP, Washington, DC 20402-0001

ISBN 0-16-051209-3

CONTENTS

Individual Histories of the United States Censuses—Con.

APPENDIXES

Measuring America:
The Decennial Censuses From 1790 to 2000

CENSUS QUESTIONNAIRES AND INSTRUCTIONS: 1790 TO 2000

1790 QUESTIONNAIRE

The early census acts prescribed the inquiries in each decennial census, but the U.S. Government did not furnish uniform printed schedules until 1830. In 1790, the marshals submitted their returns in whatever form they found convenient (and sometimes with added information).

In 1790, marshals took the census in the original 13 states; plus the districts of Kentucky, Maine, and Vermont; and the Southwest Territory (Tennessee). Each household provided the name of the head of the family and the number of persons in each household of the following descriptions: Free White males of 16 years and upward (to assess the countries industrial and military potential), free White males under 16 years, free White females, all other free persons (by sex and color), and slaves.

1800 QUESTIONNAIRE

From 1800 to 1820, the states provided schedules of varying size and typeface. The 1800 schedule of inquiries called for the name of the county, parish, township, town, or city where the family resides; the name of the head of the family; a statement for each family of the number of free White males and females under 10 years of age, of 10 and under 16, of 16 and under 26, of 26 and under 45, and 45 years and upward; the number of all other free persons (except Indians not taxed); and the number of slaves.

1810 QUESTIONNAIRE

The 1810 schedule of inquiries was identical to that of 1800, collecting the name of the county, parish, township, town, or city where the family resides; the name of the head of the family; a statement for each family of the number of free White males and females under 10 years of age, of 10 and under 16, of 16 and under 26, of 26 and under 45, and 45 years and upward; the number of all other free persons (except Indians not taxed); and the number of slaves.

1820 QUESTIONNAIRE

The schedule of inquiries for 1820 called for the same age distribution of the free White population, as in 1800 and 1810, with the addition in 1820 of the number of free White males between 16 and 18 years. It also provided for a separation of the number of free colored persons and of slaves, respectively, by sex, according to the number under 14 years of age, of 14 and under 26, of 26 and under 45, and of 45 years and upward, with a statement of the number of "all other persons, except Indians not taxed." Additionally, inquiries were made to ascertain the number of foreigners not naturalized, and the number of persons (including slaves) engaged in agriculture, commerce, and manufactures.

Instructions to Marshals

The interrogatories to be put at each dwelling house, or to the head of every family are definitely marked in relation to the various classes of inhabitants discriminated in the several columns of the schedule, by the titles at the head of each column. That of the name of the head of each family, must indeed be varied according to its circumstances, as it may be that of a master, mistress, steward, overseer, or other principal person therein. The subsequent inquiries, How many free white males under 10 years there are in the family? How many of 10 and under 16? etc., will follow in the order of the columns. But, to facilitate the labor of your assistants, a printed list of all the interrogatories for enumeration, believed to be necessary, is enclosed; (No. 5) in which all the questions refer to the day when the enumeration is to commence; the first Monday in August next. Your assistants will thereby understand that

they are to insert in their returns all the persons belonging to the family on the first Monday in August, even those who may be deceased at the time when they take the account; and, on the other hand, that they will not include in it, infants born after that day. This, though not prescribed in express terms by the act, is the undoubted intention of the legislature, as manifested by the clause, providing that every person shall be recorded as of the family in which he or she shall reside on the first Monday in August.

It will be necessary to remember, that the numbers in the columns of free white males between 16 and 18—foreigners not naturalized—persons engaged in agriculture persons engaged in commerce persons engaged in manufactures must not be added to the general aggregates, of which the sum total is to be opposed. All the persons included within these columns must necessarily be included also in one of the other columns. Those, for instance, between 16 and 18, will all be repeated in the column of those between 16 and 26. The foreigners not naturalized, and those engaged in the three principal walks of life, will also be included in the columns embracing their respective ages. In the printed form of a schedule herewith enclosed, the description at the top of these columns is printed, in *italics,* and the division lines between the columns themselves are double ruled, with a view to distinguish them from the other columns, the sums of which are to go to the general aggregate. In preparing their schedules from this form, your assistants will find it useful, for convenience and accuracy, to distinguish thosecolumns, by ruling them with red ink, or in some other manner, which may keep them separate from the others, by a sensible impression constantly operating upon the mind.

The discrimination between persons engaged in agriculture, commerce, and manufactures, will not be without its difficulties. No inconsiderable portion of the population will probably be found, the individuals of which being asked, to which of those classes they belong, will answer, to all three. Yet, it is obviously not the intention of the legislature that any one individual should be included in more than one of them—of those whose occupations are exclusively agricultural or commercial, there can seldom arise a question, and in the column of manufactures will be included not only all the persons employed in what the act more specifically dominates manufacturing establishments, but all those artificers, handcraftsmen, and mechanics whose labor is preeminently of the hand, and not upon the field.

By persons engaged in agriculture, commerce, or manufactures, your assistants will understand that they are to insert in those columns, not whole families, including infants and superannuated persons, but only those thus engaged by actual occupation. This construction is given to the act, because it is believed to be best adapted to fulfill the intentions of the legislature, and because, being susceptible of the other, it might be differently construed by different persons employed in the enumeration and thus destroy the uniformity of returns, essential to a satisfactory result.

Besides this enumeration of manufactures, the marshals and their assistants are required, by the tenth section of the act to take an account of the several *manufacturing establishments and their manufactures,* within their several districts, territories, and divisions; and the meaning of the legislature, by this provision, is illustrated by the clause in the oaths of the marshals and assistants, that they will take an account of the manufactures, *except household manufactures,* from which it seems fairly deducible, that, in the intention of the legislature, persons employed only upon household manufactures are not to be included in the column of persons bearing that denomination, the occupation of manufacturing being, in such cases, only incidental, and not the profession properly marking the class of society to which such individual belongs.

This then, offers a criterion by which your assistants may select the column of occupation to which each individual may be set down; namely, to that which is the principal and not the occasional, or incidental, occupation of his life.

The more particular the account of manufactures can be made, the more satisfactory will the returns prove. Among the papers enclosed is an alphabetical list of manufactures (No. 6), which may facilitate the labor of your assistants, but which they will not consider as complete. It is intended merely to give a direction to their inquiries, and each of them will add to it every manufacture not included in it and of which he takes an account within his division. A printed form (No. 7) is likewise enclosed, of inquiries to be made in relation to manufacturing establishments, on a sheet of paper, upon which the information requested may be written and returned. In every case when it can be conveniently done, your assistant will do well to give this form to some person principally concerned in the manufacturing establishment, requesting him to give the information desired himself.

The execution of the fifth section of the act requires the further interrogatories, whether any person, whose usual abode was in the family on the first Monday of August, 1820, be absent therefrom at the time of the inquiry made: and, if so, the sex, age, color, and condition, of such person are to be asked, and marked in the proper column, in the return of the family. It follows, of course, that any person who, at the time of taking the number of any family, has his usual abode in it, is, nevertheless, not to be included in the return of that family, if his usual place of abode was, on the first Monday of August, in

another family. The name of every person having no settled place of residence, is to be inserted in the columns of the schedule allotted for the heads of families in the division where such person shall be on the first Monday of August.

1830 QUESTIONNAIRE

The 1830 Census was the first enumeration in which a uniform schedule was used to enumerate the inhabitants of the United States (previously, individual marshals or the states supplied the schedules). The questionnaire used measured 18 1/2" X 16'", and was printed on both sides of the form. The enumeration consisted of inquiries dividing the free White population of each sex according to the number under 5 years of age, 5 to 10, 10 to 15, 15 to 20, 20 to 30, 30 to 40, 40 to 50, 50 to 60, 60 to 70, 70 to 80, 80 to 90, 90 to 100, and 100 years and upward; a classification of slaves and free colored persons, respectively, according to the number of each sex under 10 years of age, 10 to 24, 24 to 36, 36 to 55, 55 to 100, and 100 years and upward; the number of White persons and of "slaves and colored persons," aged under 14 years, 14 and under 25, and 25 years and upward, who were deaf and dumb, but without distinction of sex in either case, and also the number of each of these two classes named who were blind, but without distinction of sex or age; and a statement, of White persons only, who were aliens, i.e., foreigners not naturalized.

Instructions to Marshals

The execution of the fifth section of the act requires the further interrogatories, whether any person, whose usual abode was in the family on the 1st day of June, 1830, be absent therefrom at the time of making the inquiry, and if so, the sex, age, color, and condition, are to be asked and marked in the proper column, in the return of the family. It follows, of course, that any person, who, at the time of taking the enumeration of any family, has his abode in it, is, nevertheless, not to be included in the return of that family, *if his usual place of abode, was, on the 1st day of June, in another Family.* The name of every person, having no settled place of residence, is to be inserted in the column of the schedule, allotted for the heads of families, in the division where such person shall be on the 1st day of June, and of course, also in one of the other columns, according to the age and condition of such person.

To facilitate the labor of your assistants, a printed list of all the interrogatories for enumeration is enclosed (No. 3), in which all the questions refer to the day when the enumeration is to commence—the 1st day of next June. Your assistants will also bear in mind to include all persons of a family (except Indians not taxed) who were members thereof on the 1st day of June, 1830, whether present or not, and not to include any person whose usual abode was not in the family they are enumerating on the said 1st day of June. They will, of course, include such persons as may have deceased after that day, and will not include in it infants born after that day. This, though not prescribed in express terms by the act, is the undoubted intention of the legislature, as manifested by the clause, providing that every person shall be recorded as of the family in which he or she shall reside on the 1st day of June, 1830.

1840 QUESTIONNAIRE

The instructions to enumerators were consistent with those used during the 1830 census.

SCHEDULE I.—Free Inhabitants in _District Nº 2_ in the County of _Fayette_ of _Kentucky_ enumerated by me, on the _7th_ day of _Augt_ 1850. _Jno. M. Monroe_

1	2	3	4	5	6	7	8	9	10	11	12	13	
Dwelling-houses numbered in the order of visitation.	Families numbered in the order of visitation.	The Name of every Person whose usual place of abode on the first day of June, 1850, was in this family.	Age.	Sex.	White, black, or mulatto.	Profession, Occupation, or Trade of each Male Person over 15 years of age.	Value of Real Estate owned.	Place of Birth. Naming the State, Territory, or Country.	Married within the year.	Attended School within the year.	Persons over 20 y'rs of age who cannot read & write.	Whether deaf and dumb, blind, insane, idiotic, pauper, or convict.	
		Nancy Wheatley	59	F				Maryland					1
		Walter S. Wheatley	17	M		Printer		Kentucky					2
408	429	John McCracken	71	M		Farmer	8,000	Ireland					3
		Emily McCracken	54	F				Ireland					4
		Frederic Myers	35	M		Gardener		Germany					5
409	430	C. McFarland	44	M		None		Massachusetts					6
		T. J. Moore	29	M		None		Maryland					7
410	431	Augustus Moseback	24	M		Baker		Germany					8
		Charles Kanz	35	M		Baker		Germany					9
		James Hanna	40	M		None		Ireland					10
411	432	Henry Clay	73	M		Statesman	50,000	Virginia					11 X

Instructions to Marshals and Assistants (Explanation of Schedule NO. 1.—Free Inhabitants)

This schedule is to be filled up in the following manner:

Insert in the heading the name or number of the district, town, or city of the county or parish, and of the state, and the day of the month upon which the enumeration was taken. This is to be attested on each page of each set, by the signature of the assistant.

The several columns are to be filled as follows:

1. Under heading 1, entitled "_Dwelling houses numbered in the order of visitation,_" insert the number of dwelling houses occupied by free inhabitants, as they are visited. The first house visited to be numbered 1; the second one visited, 2; the third one visited, 3; and so on to the last house visited in the subdivision. By a dwelling house is meant a separate inhabited tenement, containing one or more families under one roof. Where several tenements are in one block, with walls either of brick or wood to divide them, having separate entrances, they are each to be numbered as separate houses; but where not so divided, they are to be numbered as one house.

If a house is used partly for a store, shop, or for other purposes, and partly for a dwelling house, it is to be numbered as a dwelling house. Hotels, poorhouses, garrisons, hospitals, asylums, jails, penitentiaries, and other similar institutions, are each to be numbered as a dwelling house; where the house is of a public nature, as above, write perpendicularly under the number, in said column, the name or description, as "hotel," "poorhouse," etc.

2. Under heading 2, entitled "_Family numbered in the order of visitation,_" insert the number of the families of free persons, as they are visited. The first family visited by the assistant marshal is to be numbered 1; the second one visited, 2; and so on to the last one visited in his district.

By the term family is meant, either one person living separately in a house, or a part of a house, and providing for him or herself, or several persons living together in a house, or in part of a house, upon one common means of support, and separately from others in similar circumstances. A widow living alone and separately providing for herself, or 200 individuals living together and provided for by a common head, should each be numbered as one family.

The resident inmates of a hotel, jail, garrison, hospital, an asylum, or other similar institution, should be reckoned as one family.

3. Under heading 3, entitled "_The name of every person whose usual place of abode on the 1st day of June,_

1850, was in this family," insert the name of every free person in each family, of every age, including the names of those temporarily absent, as well as those that were at home on that day. The name of any member of a family who may have died *since the 1st day of June* is to be entered and described as if living, but the name of any person born since the 1st day of June is to be omitted. The names are to be written, beginning with the father and mother; or if either, or both, be dead, begin with some other ostensible head of the family; to be followed, as far as practicable, with the name of the oldest child residing at home, then the next oldest, and so on to the youngest, then the other inmates, lodgers and borders, laborers, domestics, and servants.

All landlords, jailors, superintendents of poorhouses, garrisons, hospitals, asylums, and other similar institutions, are to be considered as heads of their respective families, and the inmates under their care to be registered as members thereof, and the details concerning each designated in their proper columns.

Indians not taxed are not to be enumerated in this or any other schedule.

By place of abode is meant the house or usual lodging place of a person. Anyone who is temporarily absent on a journey, or for other purposes, without taking up his place of residence elsewhere, and with the intention of returning again, is to be considered a member of the family which the assistant marshal is enumerating.

Students in colleges, academies, or schools, when absent from the families to which they belong, are to be enumerated only as members of the family in which they usually boarded and lodged on the 1st day of June.

Assistant marshals are directed to make inquiry at all stores, shops, eating houses, and other similar places, and take the name and description of every person who usually slept there, provided such person is not otherwise enumerated.

Inquiries are to be made at every dwelling house, or of the head of every family. Those only who belong to such family, and consider it their home or usual place of abode, whether present or temporarily absent on a visit, journey, or a voyage, are to be enumerated. Persons on board of vessels accidentally or temporarily in port, those whose only habitation was the vessel to which they belong, those who are temporarily boarding for a few days as a sailors' boarding or lodging house, if they belong to other places are not to be enumerated as the population of a place.

The sailors and hands of a revenue cutter which belongs to a particular port should be enumerated as of such port. A similar rule will apply to those employed in the navigation of the lakes, rivers, and canals. All are to be taken at their homes or usual places of abode, whether present or absent; and if any live on board of vessels or boats who are not so enumerated, they are to be taken as of the place where the vessel or boat is owned, licensed, or registered. And the assistant marshals are to make inquiry at every vessel and boat employed in the internal navigation of the United States, and enumerate those who are not taken as belonging to a family on shore; and all persons of such description in any one vessel are to be considered as belonging to one family and the vessel their place of abode. The assistants in all seaports will apply at the proper office for lists of all persons on a voyage at sea and register all citizens of the United States who have not been registered as belonging to some family.

Errors necessarily occurred in the last census in enumerating those employed in navigation, because no uniform rule was adopted for the whole United States. Assistant marshals are required to be particular in following the above directions, that similar errors may now be avoided.

4. Under heading 4, entitled "*Age,*" insert in figures what was the specific age of each person at his or her last birthday previous to the 1st of June, opposite the name of such person. If the exact age in years can not be ascertained, insert a number which shall be the nearest approximation to it.

    The age, either exact or estimated, of everyone, is to be inserted.

    If the person be a child under 1 year old, the entry is to be made by the fractional parts of a year, thus: One month, one-twelfth; two months, two-twelfths; three months, threetwelfths, and so on to eleven months, eleven-twelfths.

5. Under heading 5, entitled "*Sex,*" insert the letter M for male, and F for female, opposite the name, in all cases, as the fact may be.

6. Under heading 6, entitled "*Color,*" in all cases where the person is white, leave the space blank; in all cases where the person is black, insert the letter B; if mulatto, insert M. It is very desirable that these particulars be carefully regarded.

7. Under head 7, entitled "*Profession, occupation, or trade of each person over 15 years of age,*" insert opposite the name of each male the specific profession, occupation, or trade which the said person is known and reputed to follow in the place where he resides—as clergyman, physician, lawyer, shoemaker, student, farmer, carpenter, laborer, tailor, boatman, sailor, or otherwise, as the fact may be. When more convenient, the name of the article he produces may be substituted.

When the individual is a clergyman, insert the initials of the denomination to which he belongs before his profession—as Meth. for Methodist, R.C. for Roman Catholic, O.S.P. for Old School Presbyterian, or other appropriate initials, as the fact may be. When a person follows several professions or occupations the name of the principal one only is to be given. If a person follows no particular occupation, the space is to be filled with the word "none."

8. Under the heading 8 insert the value of real estate owned by each individual enumerated. You are to obtain the value of real estate by inquiry of each individual who is supposed to own real estate, be the same located where it may, and insert the amount in dollars. No abatement of the value is to be made on account of any lien or encumbrance thereon in the nature of debt.

9. Under the heading 9, "*Place of birth.*" The marshal should ask the place of birth of each person in the family. If born in the State or Territory where they reside, insert the name or initials of the State or Territory, or the name of the government or country if without the United States. The names of the several States may be abbreviated.

    Where the place of birth is unknown, state "unknown."

10. Under heading No. 10 make a mark, or dash, opposite the name of each person married during the year previous to the 1st of June, whether male or female.

11. Under heading 11, entitled "*At school within the last year.*" The marshal should ask what member of this family has been at school within the last year; he is to insert a mark, thus, (1), opposite the names of all those, whether male or female, who have been at educational institutions within that period. Sunday schools are not to be included.

12. Under the heading 12, entitled "*Persons over 20 years of age who can not read and write.*" The marshal should be careful to note all persons in each family, over 20 years of age, who can not read and write, and opposite the name of each make a mark, thus, (1). The spaces opposite the names of those who can read and write are to be left blank. If the person can read and write a foreign language, he is to be considered as able to read and write.

13. Heading 13, entitled "*Deaf and dumb, blind, insane, idiotic, pauper, or convict.*" The assistant marshal should ascertain if there be any person in the family deaf, dumb, idiotic, blind, insane, or pauper. If so, who? And insert the term "deaf and dumb," "blind," "insane," and idiotic," opposite the name of such persons, as the fact may be. When persons who had been convicted of crime within the year reside in families on the 1st of June, the fact should be stated, as in the

other cases of criminals; but as the interrogatory might give offence, the assistants had better refer to the county record for information on this head, and not make the inquiry of any family. With the county record and his own knowledge he can seldom err. Should a poorhouse, asylum for the blind, insane or idiotic, or other charitable institution, or a penitentiary, a jail, house of refuge, or other place of punishment, be visited by the assistant marshal, he must number such building in its regular order, and he must write after the number, and perpendicularly in the same column (No. 1) the nature of such institution—that it is a penitentiary, jail, house of refuge, as the case may be; and in column 13, opposite the name of each person, he must state the character of the infirmity or misfortune, in the one case, and in the other he must state the crime for which each inmate is confined, and of which such person was convicted; and in column No. 3, with the name, give the year of conviction, and fill all the columns concerning age, sex, color, etc., with as much care as in the case of other individuals.

1850 QUESTIONNAIRE—SLAVE INHABITANTS

(12 1/2" X 17 1/2," printed on two sides with space for 40 entries on each side)
The 1850 questionnaire relating to slave inhabitants collected the names of slave owners; number of slaves; the slaves color, sex, age, and whether deaf and dumb, blind, insane, or idiotic; the numbers of fugitives from the state; and the number manumitted.

Explanation of Schedule 2—Slave Inhabitants

This schedule is to be filled up in the following manner:

Insert in the heading the number or name of the district, town, city, and the county or parish, and of the state in which the slave inhabitants enumerated reside, and the day of the month upon which the enumeration was taken. This is to be attested on each page of each set, by the signature of the assistant marshal. The several columns are to be filled up as follows:

1. Under heading 1, entitled "*Name of slave holders,*" insert, in proper order, the names of the owners of slaves. Where there are several owners to a slave, the name of one only need be entered, or when owned by a corporation or trust estate, the name of the trustee or corporation.

2. Under heading 2, entitled "*Number of slaves,*" insert, in regular numerical order, the number of all slaves of both sexes and of each age, belonging to such owners. In the case of slaves, numbers are to be substituted for names. The number of every slave who usually resides in the district enumerated is to be entered, although he may happen to be temporarily absent.

The slaves of each owner are to be numbered separately, beginning at No. 1, and a separate description of each is to be given. The person in whose family, or on whose plantation, the slave is found to be employed, is to be considered the owner—the principal object being to get the number of slaves, and not that of masters or owners.

3. Under heading 3, entitled "*Age,*" insert, in figures, the specific age of each slave opposite the number of such slave. If the exact age can not be ascertained, insert a number which shall be the nearest approximation to it. The age of every slave, either exact or estimated, is to be inserted. If the slave be a child which, on the 1st of June, was under 1 year old, the entry is to be made by fractional parts of a year; thus, one month old, one-twelfth; two months, two-twelfths; three months, three-twelfths; eleven months, eleven-twelfths; keeping ever in view, in all cases, that the age must be estimated at no later period than the 1st of June.

4. Under heading 4, entitled "*Sex,*" insert the letter M for male, and F for female opposite the number in all cases, as the fact may be.

5. Under heading 5, entitled "*Color,*" insert in all cases, when the slave is black, the letter B; when he or she is mulatto, insert M. The color of all slaves should be noted.

6. Under heading 6 insert, in figures, opposite the name of the slave owner, the number of slaves who, having absconded within the year, have not been recovered.

7. In column 7, insert opposite the name of the former owner thereof, the number of slaves manumitted within the year. The name of the person is to be given, although at the time of the enumeration such person may not have held slaves on the 1st of June. In such case, no entry is to be made in column No. 2.

8. Under heading 8, entitled "*Deaf and dumb, blind, insane, or idiotic,*" the assistant should ascertain if any of these slaves be deaf and dumb, blind, insane, or idiotic; and if so, insert opposite the name or number of such slave, the term deaf and dumb, blind, insane, or idiotic, as the fact may be. If slaves be found imprisoned convicts, mention the crime in column 8, and the date of conviction before the number in vacant space below the name of the owner. The convict slaves should be numbered with the other slaves of their proper owner.

1860 QUESTIONNAIRE

(12 1/2" X 17 1/2", printed on both sides with space for
40 entries on each side)

Dwelling Houses—numbered in the order of visitation.	Families numbered in the order of visitation.	The name of every person whose usual place of abode on the first day of June, 1860, was in this family.	DESCRIPTION.			Profession, Occupation, or Trade of each person, male and female, over 15 years of age.	VALUE OF ESTATE OWNED.		Place of Birth, Naming the State, Territory, or Country.	Married within the year.	Attended School within the year.	Persons over 20 years of age who can not read and write.	Whether deaf and dumb, blind, insane, idiotic, pauper, or convict.	
			Age.	Sex.	Color, (White, Black, or Mulatto.)		Value of Real Estate.	Value of Personal Estate.						
1	2	3	4	5	6	7	8	9	10	11	12	13	14	
1														1
2														2
3														3

Additional questionnaires were used to collect data on slave inhabitants, mortality, agriculture, products of industry, and social statistics. These questionnaires collected the same information as those in 1850, with a few exceptions.

Instructions to Marshals and Assistants

The instructions to marshals and assistant marshals were virtually identical to those for the 1850 census, with the exception of guidelines for collecting information on a few additional/modified inquiries. There were slight changes in the instructions' wording; however, these served only to clarify the 1850 instructions.

1870 QUESTIONNAIRE

(12 1/2" X 17 1/2", printed on two sides, space for 40 entries on each side)

Dwelling-houses, numbered in the order of visitation.	Families, numbered in the order of visitation.	The name of every person whose place of abode on the first day of June, 1870, was in this family.	DESCRIPTION.			Profession, Occupation, or Trade of each person, male or female.	VALUE OF REAL ESTATE OWNED.		Place of Birth, naming State or Territory of U. S.; or the Country, if of foreign birth.	PARENTAGE.		If born within the year, state month (Jan., Feb., &c.)	If married within the year, state month (Jan., Feb., &c.)	Attended school within the year.	EDUCATION.		Whether deaf and dumb, blind, insane, or idiotic.	CONSTITUTIONAL RELATIONS.	
			Age at last birthday. If under 1 year, give months in fractions, thus ⅓.	Sex—Males (M.), Females (F.)	Color—White (W.), Black (B.), Mulatto (M.), Chinese (C.), Indian (I.)		Value of Real Estate.	Value of Personal Estate.		Father of foreign birth.	Mother of foreign birth.				Cannot read.	Cannot write.		Male Citizens of U. S. of 21 years of age and upwards.	Male Citizens of U. S. of 21 years of age and upwards, whose right to vote is denied or abridged on other grounds than rebellion or other crime.
1.	2	3	4	5	6	7	8	9	10	11	12	13	14	15	16	17	18	19	20
1																				1
2																				2
3																				3

Instructions to Marshals and Assistants (Schedule 1—Inhabitants)

Numbering.—Dwelling houses and families will be numbered consecutively, in order as visited, until the township, borough, or parish (or ward or a city) is completed, when a new numbering will begin, as is the case with the numbering of pages.

Dwelling houses.—By "dwelling house" is meant a house standing alone, or separated by walls from other houses in a block. Only such buildings are to be reckoned as dwelling houses as have been used as the entire habitation of a family. But houses only temporarily uninhabited are to be returned and numbered in order. In that case a dash, thus (—), will be drawn through column No. 2, and the remaining spaces on the line be left blank. Hotels, poorhouses, garrisons, asylums, jails, and similar establishments, where the inmates live habitually under a single roof, are to be regarded as single dwelling houses for the purpose of the census. The character of such establishments should be written longitudinally in the columns.

Eating houses, stores, shops, etc.—Very many persons, especially in cities, have no other place of abode than stores, shops, etc.; places which are not primarily intended for habitation. Careful inquiry will be made to include this class and such buildings will be reckoned as dwelling houses within the intention of the census law; but a watchman, or clerk belonging to a family resident in the same town or city, and sleeping in such store or shop merely for purposes of security, will be enumerated as of his family.

Families.— By "family" (column 2) is meant one or more persons living together and provided for in common. A single person, living alone in a distinct part of a house, may constitute a family; while, on the other hand, all the inmates of a boarding house or a hotel will constitute but a single family, though there may be among them many husbands with wives and children. Under whatever circumstances, and in whatever numbers, people live together under one roof, and are provided for at a common table, there is a family in the meaning of the law.

Names of individuals.—In column 3 will be entered the name of every person in each family, of whatever age, including the names of such as were temporarily absent on the 1st day of June, 1870. The name of any member of the family who may have died between the 1st day of June, 1870, and the day of the assistant marshal's visit is be entered, and the person fully described, as if living; but the name of any person born during that period is to be omitted. The name of the father, mother, or other ostensible head of the family (in the case of hotels, jails, etc., the landlord, jailor, etc.) is to be entered first of the family. The family name is to be written first in the column, and the full *first or characteristic* Christian or "given" name of each member of the family in order thereafter. So long as the family name remains the same for the several members it need not be repeated, provided a clear horizontal line be drawn in the place it would occupy, thus:

Smith, John

_____ Elizabeth.

Place of abode.—By "place of abode" is meant the house or usual lodging place. All persons temporarily absent on journey or visit are to be counted as of the family; but children and youth absent for purposes of education on the 1st of June, and having their home in a family where the school or college is situated, will be enumerated at the latter place.

Seafaring men are to be reported at their land homes, no matter how long they may have been absent, if they are supposed to be still alive. Hence, sailors temporarily at a sailors' boarding or lodging house, *if they acknowledge any other home within the United States,* are not to be included in the family of the lodging or boarding house. Persons engaged in internal transportation, canal men, expressmen, railroad men, etc., if they habitually return to their home in the intervals of their occupation, will be reported as of their families, and not where they may be temporarily staying on the 1st of June.

Personal Description

Columns 4, 5, and 6 must, in every case, be filled with the age, sex, or color of the person enumerated. No return will be accepted when these spaces are left blank.

Ages.—The exact age, in figures, will be inserted in column 4, wherever the same can be obtained; otherwise, the nearest approximation thereto. Where the age is a matter of considerable doubt, the assistant marshal may make a note to that effect. Children, who, on the 1st of June, 1870, were less than a year old, will have their age stated by the fractional part of the year, as (1 month) 1-12, (3 months) 3-12, (9 months) 9-12, etc. In all other cases, months will be omitted. The age taken is the age at last birthday.

Color.—It must not be assumed that, where nothing is written in this column, "White" is to be understood. The column is always to be filled. Be particularly careful in reporting the class *Mulatto*. The word is here generic, and includes quadroons, octoroons, and all persons having any perceptible trace of African blood. Important scientific results depend upon the correct determination of this class in schedules 1 and 2.

(For reporting occupation, see remarks at the close of the instructions in regard to this schedule.)

Property.—Column 8 will contain the value of all real estate owned by the person enumerated, without any deduction on account of mortgage or other encumbrance, whether within or without the census subdivision or the county. The value meant is the full market value, known or estimated.

"Personal estate," column 9, is to be inclusive of all bonds, stocks, mortgages, notes, live stock, plate, jewels, or furniture, but exclusive of wearing apparel. No report will be made when the personal property is under $100.

Column 10 will contain the "Place of birth" of every person named upon the schedule. If born within the United States, the State or Territory will be named, whether it be the State or Territory in which the person is at present residing or not. If of foreign birth, the country will be named as specifically as possible. Instead of writing "Great Britain" as the place of birth, give the particular country, as England, Scotland, Wales. Instead of "Germany," specify the State, as Prussia, Baden, Bavaria, Wurttemburg, Hesse, Darmstadt, etc.

The inquiries in columns numbered 11, 12, 15, 16, 17, 19, and 20 are of such a nature that these columns only require to be filled when the answer to the inquiry is "Yes." If the person being enumerated had a father or mother of foreign birth; if he or she attended school during the year; if he or she can not read or can not write; if he is a citizen of the United States above the age of 21 years, and if, being such citizen, his right to vote is denied or abridged on other grounds than participation in rebellion or other crime, then an affirmative mark, thus (/), will be drawn in each of the above columns opposite the name.

Education.—It will not do to assume that, because a person can read, he can, therefore, write. The inquiries contained in columns 16 and 17 must be made separately. Very many persons who will claim to be able to read, though they really do so in the most defective manner, will frankly admit that they can not write. These inquiries will be asked of children under 10 years of age. In regard to all persons above that age, children or adults, male and female, the information will be obtained.

At school.—It is not intended to include those whose education has been limited to Sunday or evening schools.

Deaf and dumb, Blind, Insane, or Idiotic.—Great care will be taken in performing this work of enumeration, so as at once to secure completeness and avoid giving offense. Total blindness and undoubted insanity only are intended in this inquiry. Deafness merely, without the loss of speech, is not to be reported. The fact of idiocy will be better determined by the common consent of the neighborhood, than by attempting to apply any scientific measure to the weakness of the mind or will.

Constitutional Relations

Upon the answers to the questions under this head will depend the distribution of representative power in the General Government. It is therefore imperative that this part of the enumeration should be performed with absolute accuracy. Every male person born within the United States, who has attained the age of 21 years, is a citizen of the United States by the force of the Fourteenth Amendment to the Constitution; also, all persons born out of the limits and jurisdiction of the United States, whose fathers at the time of their birth were citizens of the United States (act of February 10, 1855); also, all persons born out of the limits and jurisdiction of the United States, who have been declared by judgment of court to have been duly naturalized, having taken out *both* "papers."

The part of the enumerator's duty which relates to column 19 is therefore easy, but it is none the less of importance. It is a matter of more delicacy to obtain the information required by column 20. Many persons never try to vote, and therefore do not know whether their right to vote is or is not abridged. It is not only those whose votes have actually been challenged, and refused at the polls for some disability or want of qualification, who must be reported in this column; but all who come within the scope of any State law denying or abridging suffrage to any class or individual on any other ground than the participation in rebellion, or legal conviction of crime. Assistant marshals, therefore, will be required carefully to study the laws of their own States in these respects, and to satisfy themselves, in the case of each male citizen of the United States above the age of 21 years, whether he does not, come within one of these classes.

As the fifteenth amendment to the Constitution, prohibiting the exclusion from the suffrage of any person on account of race, color, or previous condition of servitude, has become the law of the land, all State laws working such exclusion have ceased to be of virtue. If any person is, in any State, still practically denied the right to vote by reason of any such State laws not repealed, that denial is merely an act of violence, of which the courts may have cognizance, but which does not come within the view of marshals and their assistants in respect to the census.

Indians.—"Indians not taxed" are not to be enumerated on schedule 1. Indians out of their tribal relations, and exercising the rights of citizens under state or Territorial laws, will be included. In all cases write "Ind." in the column for "*Color.*" Although no provision is made for the enumeration of "Indians not taxed," it is highly desirable, for statistical purposes, that the number of such persons not living upon reservations should be known. Assistant marshals are therefore requested, where such persons are found within their subdivisions, to make a separate memorandum of names, with sex and age, and embody the same in a special report to the census office.

Occupation.—The inquiry, "Profession, occupation, or trade," is one of the most important questions of this schedule. Make a study of it. Take special pains to avoid unmeaning terms, or such as are too general to convey a definite idea of the occupation. Call no man a "factory hand" or a "mill operative." State the kind of a mill or factory. The better form of expression would be, "works in cotton mill," "works in paper mill," etc. Do not call a man a "shoemaker," "bootmaker," unless he makes the entire boot or shoe in a small shop. If he works in (or for) a boot and shoe factory, say so.

Do not apply the word "jeweler" to those who make watches, watch chains, or jewelry in large manufacturing establishments.

Call no man a "commissioner," a "collector," an "agent," an overseer," a "professor," a "treasurer," a "contractor," or a "speculator," without further explanation.

When boys are entered as apprentices, state the trade they are apprenticed to, as "apprenticed to carpenter," "apothecary's apprentice."

When a lawyer, a merchant, a manufacturer, has retired from practice or business, say "retired lawyer," "retired merchant," etc. Distinguish between fire and life insurance agents.

When clerks are returned, describe them as "clerk in store," "clerk in woolen mill," "R.R. clerk," "bank clerk," etc.

Describe no man as a "mechanic" if it is possible to describe him more accurately.

Distinguish between stone masons and brick masons.

Do not call a bonnet maker a bonnet manufacturer, a lace maker a lace manufacturer, a chocolate maker a chocolate manufacturer. Reserve the term manufacturer for proprietors of establishments; always give the *branch* of manufacture.

Whenever merchants or traders can be reported under a single word expressive of their special line, as "grocer," it should be done. Otherwise, say dry goods merchant, coal dealer, etc.

Add, in all cases, the class of business, as wholesale (wh.), retail (ret.), importer (imp.), jobber, etc.

Use the word huckster in all cases where it applies.

Be very particular to distinguish between farmers and farm laborers. In agricultural regions this should be one of the points to which the assistant marshal should especially direct his attention.

Confine the use of words "glover," hatter," and "furrier" to those who *actually make*, or make up, in their own establishments, all, or a part, of the gloves and hats or furs which they sell. Those who only sell these articles should be characterized as "glove dealer," "hat and cap dealer," "fur dealer."

Judges (state whether federal or state, whether probate, police, or otherwise) may be assumed to be lawyers, and that addition, therefore, need not be given; but all other *officials* should have their profession designated, it they have any, as "retired merchant, governor of Massachusetts," "paper manufacturer, representative in legislature." If anything is to be omitted, leave out the office, and put in the occupation.

As far as possible distinguish machinists as "locomotive builders," "engine builders," etc.

Instead of saying "packers," indicate whether you mean "pork packers" or "crockery packers," or "mule packers."

The organization of domestic service has not proceeded so far in this country as to render it worth while to make distinction in the character of work. Report all as "domestic servants."

Cooks, waiters, etc., in hotels and restaurants will be reported separately from domestic servants.

The term "housekeeper" will be reserved for such persons as receive distinct wages or salary for the service. Women keeping house for their own families or for themselves, without any other gainful occupation, will be entered as "keeping house." Grown daughters assisting them will be reported without occupation.

You are under no obligation to give any man's occupation just as he expresses it. If he can not tell intelligibly what it *is,* find out what he *does,* and characterize his profession accordingly.

The inquiry as to occupation will not be asked in respect to infants or children too young to take any part in production. Neither will the doing of domestic errands or family chores out of school be considered an occupation. "At home" or "attending school" will be the best entry in the majority of cases. But if a boy or girl, whatever the age, is earning money regularly by labor, contributing to the family support, or appreciably assisting in mechanical or agricultural industry, the occupation should be stated.

1880 QUESTIONNAIRE-SCHEDULE 1, "INHABITANTS"

(15" X 20 1/2", printed on two sides with space for 50
entries on each side)

In Cities.		Dwelling houses numbered in order of visitation.	Families numbered in order of visitation.	The Name of each Person whose place of abode, on 1st day of June, 1880, was in this family.	Personal Description.				Relationship of each person to the head of this family—whether wife, son, daughter, servant, boarder, or other.	Civil Condition.				Occupation.	
Name of Street.	House Number.				Color—White, W; Black, B; Mulatto, Mu; Chinese, C; Indian, I.	Sex—Male, M; Female, F.	Age at last birthday prior to June 1, 1880. If under 1 year, give months in fractions, thus: ¾.	If born within the Census year, give the month.		Single, /.	Married, /.	Widowed, D.	Married during Census year, /.	Profession, Occupation or Trade of each person, male or female.	Number of months this person has been unemployed during the Census year.
		1	2	3	4	5	6	7	8	9	10	11	12	13	14
1															
2															
3															

Health.						Education.			Nativity.		
Is the person [on the day of the Enumerator's visit] sick or temporarily disabled, so as to be unable to attend to ordinary business or duties? If so, what is the sickness or disability?	Blind, /.	Deaf and Dumb, /.	Idiotic, /.	Insane, /.	Maimed, Crippled, Bedridden, or otherwise disabled, /.	Attended school within the Census year, /.	Cannot read, /.	Cannot write, /.	Place of Birth of this person, naming State or Territory of United States, or the Country, if of foreign birth.	Place of Birth of the FATHER of this person, naming the State or Territory of United States, or the Country, if of foreign birth.	Place of Birth of the MOTHER of this person, naming the State or Territory of United States, or the Country, if of foreign birth.
15	16	17	18	19	20	21	22	23	24	25	26

Instructions to Enumerators
(Duties of Enumerators)

It is by law made the duty of each enumerator, after being duly qualified as above to visit personally each dwelling in his subdivision, and each family therein, and each individual living out of a family in any place of abode, and by inquiry made of the head of such family, or of the member thereof deemed most credible and worthy of trust, or of such individual living out of a family, to obtain each and every item of information and all the particulars required by the act of March 3, 1879, as amended by act of April 20, 1880.

By individuals living out of families is meant all persons occupying lofts in public buildings, above stores, warehouses, factories, and stables, having no other usual place of abode; persons living solitary in cabins, huts, or tents; persons sleeping on river boats, canal boats, barges, etc., having no other usual place of abode, and persons in police stations having no homes. Of the classes just mentioned, the most important, numerically, is the first, viz: those persons, chiefly in cities, who occupy rooms in public buildings, or above stores, warehouses, factories, and stables. In order to reach such persons, the enumerator will need not only to keep his eyes open to all indications of such casual residence in his enumeration district, but to make inquiry both of the parties occupying the business portion of such buildings and also of the police. A letter will be addressed from this office to the mayor of every large city of the United States, requesting the cooperation of the police, so far as it may be necessary to prevent the omission of the classes of persons herein indicated.

It is further provided by law that in case no person shall be found at the usual place of abode of such family, or individual living out of a family, competent to answer the inquiries made in compliance with the requirements of the act, then it shall be lawful for the enumerator to obtain the required information, as nearly as may be practicable, from the family or families, or person or persons, living nearest to such place of abode.

It is the prime object of the enumeration to obtain the name, and the requisite particulars as to personal descriptions, of every person in the United States, of whatever age, sex, color, race, or condition, with this single exception, viz: that "Indians not taxed" shall be omitted from the enumeration.

INDIANS

By the phrase "Indians not taxed" is meant Indians living on reservations under the care of Government agents, or roaming individually, or in bands, over unsettled tracts of country.

Indians not in tribal relations, whether full-bloods or half-breeds, who are found mingled with the white population, residing in white families, engaged as servants or laborers, or living in huts or wigwams on the outskirts of towns or settlements are to be regarded as a part of the ordinary population of the country for the constitutional purpose of the apportionment of Representatives among the states, and are to be embraced in the enumeration.

SOLDIERS

All soldiers of the United States Army, and civilian employees, and other residents at posts or on military reservations will be enumerated in the district in which they reside, equally, with other elements of the population.

COURTESY ON THE PART OF ENUMERATORS

It is the duty of an enumerator, in the exercise of his authority to visit houses and interrogate members of families resident therein as provided by law, to use great courtesy and consideration. A rude peremptory, or overbearing demeanor would not only be a wrong to the families visited, but would work an injury to the census by rendering the members of those families less disposed to give information with fullness and exactness. It would doubtless be found in the long run to be an injury to the enumerator himself and to retard his work.

By the above remark it is not intended to imply that the enumerator need enter into prolix explanations, or give time to anything beyond the strictly necessary work of interrogation. It is entirely possible for the enumerator to be prompt, rapid, and decisive in announcing his object and his authority, and in going through the whole list of questions to be proposed, and at the same time not to arouse any antagonism or give any offense.

THE OBLIGATION TO GIVE INFORMATION

It is not within the choice of any inhabitant of the United States whether he shall or shall not communicate the information required by the census law. By the fourteenth section of the act approved March 3, 1879, it is provided:

"That each and every person more than 20 years of age, belonging to any family residing in any enumeration district, and in case of the absence of the heads and other members of any such family, then any agent of such family, shall be, and each of them hereby is, required, if thereto requested by the superintendent, supervisor, or enumerator, to render a true account, to the best of his or her knowledge, of every person belonging to such family in the various particulars required by law, and whoever shall willfully fail or refuse shall be guilty of a misdemeanor, and upon conviction thereof shall forfeit and pay a sum not exceeding one hundred dollars."

Enumerators will, however, do well not unnecessarily to obtrude the compulsory feature of the enumeration. It will be found in the vast majority of cases that the persons called upon to give information will do so without objection or delay. No people in the world are so favorably disposed toward the work of the census as the people of the United States. With the high degree of popular intelligence here existing, the importance of statistical information is very generally appreciated; and if the enumerator enters upon his work in a right spirit, he will generally meet with a favorable and even cordial response.

It is only where information required by law is refused that the penalties for noncompliance need be adverted to. The enumerator will then quietly, but firmly, point out the consequences of persistency in refusal. It will be instructive to note that at the census of 1870 the agents of the census in only two or three instances throughout the whole United States found it necessary to resort to the courts for the enforcement of the obligation to give information as required by the census act.

It is further to be noted that the enumerator is not required to accept answers which he knows, or has reason to believe, are false. He has a right to a true statement on every matter respecting which he is bound to inquire; and he is not concluded by a false statement. Should any person persist in making statements which are obviously erroneous, the enumerator should enter upon the schedule the facts as nearly as he can ascertain them by his own observation or by inquiry of credible persons.

The foregoing remark is of special importance with reference to the statements of the heads of families respecting afflicted members of their households. The law requires a return in the case of each blind, deaf and dumb, insane or idiotic, or crippled person. It not infrequently happens that fathers and mothers, especially the latter, are disposed to conceal, or even to deny, the existence of such infirmities on the part of children. In such cases, if the fact is personally known to the enumerator, or shall be ascertained by inquiry from neighbors, it should be entered on the schedules equally as if obtained from the head of the family.

A second class of cases under this head concerns the reporting of the values produced in agricultural or other occupations. The enumerator is not bound by any statement which he knows or has reason to believe to be false. His duty is to report the actual facts as nearly as he can ascertain them.

The enumerator is prohibited by law from delegating to any other person his authority to enter dwellings and to interrogate their inhabitants. The work of enumeration must be done by the enumerator in person, and can not be performed by proxy.

SCHEDULE NO. 1 [7-296]—POPULATION

This is the population or family schedule. Upon it is to be entered, as previously noted, the name of every man, woman, and child, who, on the 1st day of June, 1880,

shall have his or her "usual place of abode" within the enumerator's districts . No child born between the 1st day of June, 1880, and the day of the enumerator's visit (say June 5 or 15 or 25) is to be entered upon the schedule. On the other hand, every person who was a resident of the district upon the 1st day of June, 1880, but between that date and the day of the enumerator's visit shall have died, should be entered on the schedule precisely as if still living. The object of the schedule is to obtain a list of the inhabitants on the *1st day of June,* 1880, and all changes after that date, whether in the nature of gain or of loss, are to be disregarded in the enumeration.

DWELLING HOUSES

In column No. 1 of this schedule is to be entered the number of the dwelling house in the order of visitation. A dwelling house, for the purpose of the census, means any building or place of abode, of whatever character, material, or structure, in which a person is at the time living, whether in a room above a warehouse or factory, a loft above a stable or a wigwam on the outskirts of a settlement, equally with a dwelling house in the usual, ordinary sense of that term. Wholly uninhabited dwellings are not to be taken notice of.

FAMILIES

In the column numbered 2 is to be entered the number, in the order of visitation, of each family residing in the district. The word family, for the purposes of the census, includes persons living alone, as previously described, equally with families in the ordinary sense of that term, and also all larger aggregations of people having only the tie of a common roof and table. A hotel, with all its inmates, constitutes but one family within the meaning of this term. A hospital, prison, an asylum is equally a family for the purposes of the census. On the other hand, the solitary inmate of a cabin, a loft, or a room finished off above a store constitutes a family in the meaning of the census act. In the case, however, of tenement houses and of the so-called "flats" of the great cities, as many families are to be recorded as there are separate tables.

NAMES

In column numbered 3 is to be entered the name of every person whose "usual place of abode" on the 1st day of June, 1880, was in that family.

The census law furnishes no definition of the phrase, "usual place of abode," and it is difficult, under the American system of a protracted enumeration, to afford administrative directions which will wholly obviate the danger that some persons will be reported in two places and others not reported at all. Much must be left to the judgment of the enumerator, who can, if he will take the pains, in the great majority of instances satisfy himself as to the propriety of including or not including doubtful cases in his enumeration of any given family. In the cases of boarders at hotels or students at schools or colleges, the enumerator can, by one or two well directed inquiries, ascertain whether the person concerning whom the question may arise has, at the time, any other place of abode within another district at which he is likely to be reported. Seafaring men are to be reported at their land homes, no matter how long they may have been absent, if they are supposed to be still alive. Hence, sailors temporarily at a sailors' boarding or lodging house, if they *acknowledge any other home within the United States*, are not to be included in the family of the lodging or boarding house. Persons engaged in internal transportation, canal men, express men, railroad men, etc., if they habitually return to their homes in the intervals of their occupations, will be reported *as of their families*, and not where they may be temporarily staying on the 1st of June, 1880.

In entering names in column 3, the name of the father, mother, or other ostensible head of the family (in the case of hotels, jails, etc., the landlord, jailer, etc.) is to be entered first of the family. The family name is to be written first in the column, and the full *first or characteristic* Christian or "given" name of each member of the family in order thereafter. It is desirable that the children of the family proper should follow in the order of their ages, as will naturally be the case. So long as the family name remains the same for the several members, it need not be repeated, provided a distinct horizontal line or dash be drawn in the place it would occupy, thus:

Smith, John.
_____, Elizabeth.
_____, J. Henry.

Personal Description

The columns 4, 5, and 6, which relate to age, sex, and color, must in every case be filled. No returns will be accepted where these spaces are left blank.

Ages.—The exact age in figures will be inserted in column 6 whenever the same can be obtained; otherwise, the nearest approximation thereto. Children who, on the 1st of June, 1880, were less than a year old, will have their age stated by the fractional part of the year, as (1 month), 1/12; (3 months), 3/12; (9 months), 9/12, etc. In all other cases months will be omitted.

Color.—It must not be assumed that, where nothing is written in this column, "white" is to be understood. The column is always to be filled. Be particularly careful in reporting the class *mulatto*. The word is here generic, and includes quadroons, octoroons, and all persons having any perceptible trace of African blood. Important scientific results depend upon the correct determination of this class in schedules 1 and 5.

OCCUPATION

In the column number 13 is to be reported the occupation of each person 10 years of age and upward. (See instructions for 1870, col. 7.)

PLACE OF BIRTH
(SEE INSTRUCTIONS FOR 1870, COL. 10.)

1880 QUESTIONNAIRE-SCHEDULE 1, "INDIAN DIVISION"

(27" X 11", folded to provide cover and three pages, 9" X 11"). The annual *Report of the Superintendent of the Census...1889* (p.26), states, "An attempt was made...to enumerate [Indians living on reservations] upon a very elaborate plan, and of many of the tribes, particularly those on the west coast, a full enumeration was obtained; but the investigation was stopped by the failure of the appropriation, and was not resumed."

The manuscript consists of four volumes in Record Group 29 in the National Archives (*Preliminary Inventory 161,* page 101, item 298): I and II, schedules for Indians near Fort Simcoe and at Tulalip, Washington Territory; III, Indians near Fort Yates, Dakota Territory; and IV, Indians in California. All schedules are arranged within the volumes by name of tribe.

The 1880 Indian schedule made the following inquiries: Name (Indian name, English translation of Indian name, other name habitually used); relationship to head of household; civil condition (single, married, widowed/divorced, whether a chief or war chief); whether Indian of full or mixed blood; whether adopted into the tribe; time in years and fractions person has lived on a reservation; time in years and fractions person has worn "citizen's dress"; language spoken; sex; age; occupation; whether sick or disabled (if so, what is the sickness or disability); whether vaccinated; whether maimed, crippled, bedridden, or otherwise disabled; whether blind, deaf and dumb, idiotic, or insane; whether attending school; literacy; number of livestock owned (horses, cattle, sheep, swine, dogs); whether the household possess a firearm; acreage owned and type of ownership; time cultivating land; whether self-supporting or supported by other entity (self, family, or government) or occupation (hunting, fishing, or "natural products of the soil," i.e. roots, berries, etc.).

U.S. Census Bureau

1890 QUESTIONNAIRE

(11 1/2″ X 18″, printed on both sides)

FAMILY SCHEDULE—I TO IO PERSONS.

	[7—556 b.]	Eleventh Census of the United States.

Supervisor's District No. _____

Enumeration District No. _____

SCHEDULE No. 1.

POPULATION AND SOCIAL STATISTICS.

Name of city, town, township, precinct, district, beat, or other minor civil division. _____ ; County : _____ ; State : _____ ;

Street and No.: _____ ; Ward : _____ ; Name of Institution : _____ .

Enumerated by me on the _____ day of June, 1890.   _____ , Enumerator.

A.—Number of Dwelling-house in the order of visitation.	B.—Number of families in this dwelling-house.	C.—Number of persons in this dwelling-house.	D.—Number of Family in the order of visitation.	E.—No. of Persons in this family.

	INQUIRIES.	1	2	3	4	5
1	Christian name in full, and initial of middle name.					
	Surname.					
2	Whether a soldier, sailor, or marine during the civil war (U. S. or Conf.), or widow of such person.					
3	Relationship to head of family.					
4	Whether white, black, mulatto, quadroon, octoroon, Chinese, Japanese, or Indian.					
5	Sex.					
6	Age at nearest birthday. If under one year, give age in months.					
7	Whether single, married, widowed, or divorced.					
8	Whether married during the census year (June 1, 1889, to May 31, 1890).					
9	Mother of how many children, and number of these children living.					
10	Place of birth.					
11	Place of birth of Father.					
12	Place of birth of Mother.					
13	Number of years in the United States.					
14	Whether naturalized.					
15	Whether naturalization papers have been taken out.					
16	Profession, trade, or occupation.					
17	Months unemployed during the census year (June 1, 1889, to May 31, 1890).					
18	Attendance at school (in months) during the census year (June 1, 1889, to May 31, 1890).					
19	Able to Read.					
20	Able to Write.					
21	Able to speak English. If not, the language or dialect spoken.					
22	Whether suffering from acute or chronic disease, with name of disease and length of time afflicted.					
23	Whether defective in mind, sight, hearing, or speech, or whether crippled, maimed, or deformed, with name of defect.					
24	Whether a prisoner, convict, homeless child, or pauper.					
25	Supplemental schedule and page.					

TO ENUMERATORS.—See inquiries numbered 26 to 30, inclusive, on the second page of this schedule. These inquiries must be made concerning each family and each farm visited.

(19279—1,780,000.) I b   34

SCHEDULE No. 1.—POPULATION AND SOCIAL STATISTICS.

	INQUIRIES.	6	7	8	9	10
1	Christian name in full, and initial of middle name.					
	Surname.					
2	Whether a soldier, sailor, or marine during the civil war (U. S. or Conf.), or widow of such person.					
3	Relationship to head of family.					
4	Whether white, black, mulatto, quadroon, octoroon, Chinese, Japanese, or Indian.					
5	Sex.					
6	Age at nearest birthday. If under one year, give age in months.					
7	Whether single, married, widowed, or divorced.					
8	Whether married during the census year (June 1, 1889, to May 31, 1890).					
9	Mother of how many children, and number of these children living.					
10	Place of birth.					
11	Place of birth of **Father.**					
12	Place of birth of **Mother.**					
13	Number of years in the United States.					
14	Whether naturalized.					
15	Whether naturalization papers have been taken out.					
16	Profession, trade, or occupation.					
17	Months unemployed during the census year (June 1, 1889, to May 31, 1890).					
18	Attendance at school (in months) during the census year (June 1, 1889, to May 31, 1890).					
19	Able to **Read.**					
20	Able to **Write.**					
21	Able to speak English. If not, the language or dialect spoken.					
22	Whether suffering from **acute** or **chronic** disease, with name of disease and length of time afflicted.					
23	Whether defective in mind, sight, hearing, or speech, or whether crippled, maimed, or deformed, with name of defect.					
24	Whether a prisoner, convict, homeless child, or pauper.					
25	Supplemental schedule and page.					
26	Is the home you live in hired, or is it owned by the head or by a member of the family?					
27	If owned by head or member of family, is the home free from mortgage incumbrance?					
28	If the head of family is a farmer, is the farm which he cultivates hired, or is it owned by him or by a member of his family?					
29	If owned by head or member of family, is the farm free from mortgage incumbrance?					
30	If the home or farm is owned by head or member of family, **and mortgaged,** give the post-office address of owner.					

TO ENUMERATORS.—The inquiries numbered 26 to 30, inclusive, must be made concerning each family and each farm visited.

(19279—1,780,000.) **2 b**

THE PLAN OF ENUMERATION IN INSTITUTIONS.

Instructions to Enumerators

The statistics of population and other special data concerning persons residing in institutions will be taken by institution enumerators; that is, some official or other trustworthy person connected with the institution, who will be appointed specially for the purpose.

This plan of enumeration will not be extended to all institutions, but the appointment of special institution enumerators will be determined partly by the size of the institution and partly by its nature.

For those institutions where this plan of enumeration is to be carried out the enumerators for the districts in which such institutions are located will have no responsibility.

Each enumerator will receive in advance of the enumeration due notification from the supervisor for his district as to the institutions which are not to be taken by him. It should be the duty of the enumerator, however, if there is any institution in his district, whatever may be its size or character, to satisfy himself by personal inquiry of the officer in charge whether a special institution enumerator has been appointed, and if not, to proceed to enumerate the population as in the case of all other houses visited by him. On the other hand, if a special institution enumerator has been appointed for it, then it has been withdrawn from his district, and he will leave it to be enumerated by the special institution enumerator.

SOLDIERS AND SAILORS

All soldiers of the United States Army, civilian employees, and other residents at posts or on military reservations, will be enumerated in the same manner as has been provided for institutions, by the appointment of a special resident enumerator; and in all such cases where the district enumerator has been so notified such posts or military reservations should not be included as a part of his district. For posts not garrisoned, and any other posts not so withdrawn, the district enumerator will make the necessary inquiries, and if no special enumerator has been appointed he will include the residents of such posts as a part of his district equally with other elements of the population.

In a similar way all sailors and marines stationed on vessels, and at the United States navy yards, as well as resident officers, with their families, will be specially enumerated, and need not be taken by the district enumerator if, upon inquiry or by notification, he knows that such special provision has been made.

SPECIAL ENUMERATION OF INDIANS

The law provides that the Superintendent of Census may employ special agents or other means to make an enumeration of all Indians living within the jurisdiction of the United States, with such information as to their condition as may be obtainable, classifying them as to Indians taxed and Indians not taxed.

By the phrase "Indians not taxed" is meant Indians living on reservations under the care of Government agents or roaming individually or in bands over unsettled tracts of country.

Indians not in tribal relations, whether full-bloods or half-breeds, who are found mingled with the white population, residing in white families, engaged as servants or laborers, or living in huts or wigwams on the outskirts of towns or settlements, are to be regarded as a part of the ordinary population of the country, and are to be embraced by the enumeration.

The enumeration of Indians living on reservations will be made by special agents appointed directly from this office, and supervisors and enumerators will have no responsibility in this connection.

Many Indians, however, have voluntarily abandoned their tribal relations or have quit their reservations and now sustain themselves. When enumerators find Indians off of or living away from reservations, and in no [ways] dependent upon the agency or Government, such Indians, in addition to their enumeration on the population and supplemental schedules, in the same manner as for the population generally, should be noted on a special schedule [7-917] by name, tribe, sex, age, occupation, and whether taxed or not taxed.

The object of this is to obtain an accurate census of all Indians living within the jurisdiction of the United States and to prevent double enumeration of certain Indians.

Where Indians are temporarily absent from their reservations the census enumerators need not note them, as the special enumeration for Indian reservation will get their names.

SCHEDULE NO. 1—POPULATION

The schedule adopted for the enumeration of the population is what is known as the family schedule; that is, a separate schedule for each family, without regard to the number of persons in the family. Three forms of this schedule are provided for the use of enumerators, according as the families to be enumerated are made up of a large or small number of persons.

The single-sheet schedules [7-566a] are provided for use in enumerating families containing from 1 to 10 persons, the double-sheet schedules [7-556b] for use in enumerating families containing more than 10 but not over 20 persons, and the additional sheets [7-556C] for use in enumerating families containing more than 20 persons. In the case of large families, boarding houses, lodging houses, hotels, institutions, schools, etc., containing more than 20 persons use the double sheet for 1 to 20 persons, and such number of the additional sheets as may be necessary. Wherever the additional sheets are used, be careful to write on each sheet, in the spaces provided therefor, the number of the supervisor's district, enumeration district, dwelling house, and family, and also the name of the institution, school, etc., as the case may be. Also, at the heads of the columns in which the information concerning the several persons enumerated is entered, fill in the "tens" figures on the dotted lines preceding the printed unit figures, and continue to number the columns consecutively, as 21, 22, etc., until all persons in the family have been enumerated.

Upon one or the other of these forms of the population schedule, according to the size of the family to be enumerated, is to be entered the name of every man, woman, and child who *on the 1st day of June,* 1890, shall have his or her usual place of abode within the enumerator's district. No child born between the 1st day of June, 1890, and the day of the enumerator's visit (say June 5, June 15, etc., as the case may be) is to be entered upon the schedule. On the other hand, every person who was a resident of the district upon the 1st day of June, 1890, but between that date and the day of the enumerator's visit shall have died, should be entered on the schedule precisely as if still living. The object of the schedule is to obtain a list of the inhabitants *on the 1st of June,* 1890, and all changes after that date, whether in the nature of gain or loss, are to be disregarded in the enumeration.

In answering the several inquiries on the population and other schedules the space provided for each answer should be filled by a definite statement or a symbol used to denote either that the inquiry is not applicable to the person for whom the answers are being made or that the information can not be obtained. In all cases where the inquiry is not applicable use the following symbol: (X). If for any reason it is not possible to obtain answers to inquiries which are applicable to the person enumerated, use the following symbol to denote this fact: (=). The enumerator must bear in mind, however, that where he has every reason to suppose that he can supply the answer himself it is better than the symbol; and in any case the symbol should not be used until he has made every effort to ascertain the proper answer from the persons in the family or in the neighborhood, as required by law.

Illustrative examples of the manner of filling the population and the use of these symbols are contained in printed sheets which are supplied to enumerators.

SUPERVISORS' AND ENUMERATION DISTRICTS

The first thing to be entered at the head of each schedule is the number of the supervisor's district and of the enumeration district in which the work is performed. These numbers must be repeated for each family enumerated,

and where additional sheets are used these numbers are to be carried to those sheets, as already stated.

CIVIL DIVISIONS

Be careful to enter accurately the name of the city, town, township, precinct, etc., and distinguish carefully between the population of villages within townships and the remainder of such townships. The correct enumeration of the population of these minor civil divisions is especially important, and is of interest in the presentation in the printed reports of details concerning these small bodies of population. So far as possible, also, the population of small unincorporated villages and hamlets should be separately reported. Also enter at the head of each schedule, in the spaces provided therefor, the name of the county and State or Territory in which the minor subdivision is located. In cities the street, street number, and ward should be entered in the proper spaces, and in those cities where special sanitary districts have been established for the purposes of the census enumeration the letters used to designate them should be added in some convenient space at the head of each schedule and encircled thus: (A), (B), (C), etc., according to the special letters used to distinguish these sanitary districts.

Institutions

Whenever an institution is to be enumerated, as, a hospital, asylum, almshouse, jail, or penitentiary, the full name and title of the institution should be entered, and all persons having their usual place of abode in such institution, whether officers, attendants, inmates, or persons in confinement, should then be entered consecutively on the schedules as one family. If, as sometimes may be the case, a sheriff, warden, or other prison official may live in one end of the prison building, but separated by a partition wall from the prison proper, his family (including himself as its head) should be returned on a separate schedule, and should not be returned on the schedule upon which the prisoners are entered. Where the officers or attendants, or any of them, do not reside in the institution buildings, but live with their families in detached dwellings, no matter whether the houses are owned by the institutions or located in the same grounds, they should be reported on separate schedules, but should be included as a part of the work of the special institution enumerator, where one is appointed, and should not be left to be taken by the district enumerator. It may happen also that some of the officers or attendants may reside wholly outside of the institution precincts, either in rented houses or houses owned by the institution, or by themselves, and in such cases they should be enumerated by the district enumerator and not by the special institution enumerator. The tour of duty of the special institution enumerator should not extend beyond the boundaries of the institution grounds, but should include all those persons and inmates whose usual places of abode are clearly within the territory controlled by the institutions.

U.S. Census Bureau

Persons, Families, and Dwellings

A. *Number of dwelling house in the order of visitation.*

In the space against the inquiry marked A is to be entered the number of the dwelling house in the order of visitation. The object of this inquiry is to ascertain the total number of dwelling houses. A dwelling house for the purposes of the census means any building or place of abode, of whatever character, material, or structure, in which any person is living at the time of taking the census. It may be a room above a warehouse or factory, a loft above a stable, a wigwam on the outskirts of a settlement, or a dwelling house in the ordinary sense of that term. A tenement house, whether it contains two, three, or forty families, should be considered for the purposes of the census as one house. A building under one roof suited for two or more families, but with a dividing partition wall and separate front door for each part of the building, should be counted as two or more houses. A block of houses under one roof, but with separate front doors, should be considered as so many houses, without regard to the number of families in each separate house in the block. Wholly uninhabited dwellings are not to be counted.

B. *Number of families in this dwelling house.*

The inquiry marked B calls for the number of families, whether one or more, in each dwelling house. *Where there is more than one family in a dwelling house, this inquiry should be answered only on the schedule for the first family enumerated and omitted on the schedules for the second and subsequent families enumerated in the same house,* to avoid duplication of results; the space on the schedules for the second and subsequent families should be filled, however, by an X, as not being applicable. An example of this character is given on the printed sheets illustrative of the manner of filling schedules.

C. *Number of persons in this dwelling house.*

The inquiry marked C calls for the number of persons in each dwelling house, and where there is more than one family in the house the answer should represent the total number of persons included in the several families occupying the same house. Where there is but a single family to a house, the answer to this inquiry should be the same as for Inquiry E. *Where there is more than one family in a dwelling house, this inquiry, as in the case of Inquiry B, should be answered only on the schedule for the first family enumerated.*

D. *Number of family in the order of visitation.*

In answer to the inquiry marked D enter the number, in the order of visitation, of each family residing in the district. The fact that more than one family is often found in a house makes the family number exceed, necessarily, the house number, as called for by Inquiry A.

The word family, for the purposes of the census, includes persons living alone, as well as families in the ordinary sense of that term, and also all larger aggregations of people having only the tie of a common roof and table. A hotel, with all its inmates, constitutes but one family within the meaning of this term. A hospital, a prison, an asylum is equally a family for the purposes of the census. On the other hand, the solitary inmate of a cabin, a loft, or a room finished off above a store, and indeed, all individuals living out of families, constitute a family in the meaning of the census act.

By "individuals living out of families" is meant all persons occupying lofts in public buildings, above stores, warehouses, factories, and stables, having no other usual place of abode; persons living solitary in cabins, huts, or tents; persons sleeping on river boats, canal boats, barges, etc., having no other usual place of abode, and persons in police stations having no homes. Of the classes just mentioned the most important numerically, is the first viz: Those persons, chiefly in cities, who occupy rooms in public buildings, or above stores, warehouses, factories, and stables. In order to reach such persons, the enumerator will need not only to keep his eyes open to all indications of such casual residence in his enumeration district, but to make inquiry both of the parties occupying the business portion of such buildings and also of the police. In the case, however, of tenement houses and of the so-called "flats" of the great cities as many families are to be recorded as there are separate tables.

A person's home is where he sleeps. There are many people who lodge in one place and board in another. All such persons should be returned as members of that family with which they lodge.

E. *Number of persons in this family.*

The answer to this inquiry should correspond to the number of columns filled on each schedule, and care should be taken to have all the members of the family included in this statement and a column filled for each person in the family, including servants, boarders, lodgers, etc. Be sure that the person answering the inquiries thoroughly understands the question, and does not omit any person who should be counted as a member of the family.

Names, Relationship to Head of Family, and Whether Survivors of the War of the Rebellion

1. *Christian name in full, initial of middle name, and surname.*

Opposite to the inquiry numbered 1 on the schedule are to be entered the names of all persons whose usual place of abode on the 1st day of June, 1890, was in the family enumerated.

The census law furnishes no definitions of the phrase "usual place of abode;" and it is difficult, under the American system of protracted enumeration, to afford administrative directions which will wholly obviate the danger that some persons will be reported in two places and others not reported at all. Much must be left to the judgment of the enumerator, who can, if he will take the pains, in the great majority of instances satisfy himself as to the propriety of including or not including doubtful cases in his enumeration of any given family. In the cases of boarders at hotels or students at schools or colleges the enumerator can by one or two well directed inquiries ascertain whether the person concerning whom the question may arise has at the time any other place of abode within another district at which he is likely to be reported. Seafaring men are to be reported at their land homes, no matter how long they may have been absent, if they are supposed to be still alive. Hence, sailors temporarily at a sailors' boarding or lodging house, *if they acknowledge any other home within the United States,* are not to be included in the family of the lodging or boarding house. Persons engaged in internal transportation, canal men, expressmen, railroad men, etc., if they habitually return to their homes in the intervals of their occupations, will be reported *as of their families,* and not where they may be temporarily staying on the 1st of June, 1890.

In entering the members of a family the name of the father, mother, or other ostensible head of the family (in the case of hotels, jails, etc., the landlord, jailor, etc.) is to be entered in the first column. It is desirable that the wife should be enumerated in the second column, and the children of the family proper should follow in the order of their ages, as will naturally be the case. The names of all other persons in the family, whether relatives, boarders, lodgers, or servants, should be entered successively in subsequent columns.

The Christian name in full and initial of middle name of each person should be first entered and the surname immediately thereunder, as shown in the illustrative example.

1. *Whether a soldier, sailor, or marine during the civil war (United States or Confederate), or widow of such person.*

   Write "Sol" for soldier, "Sail" for sailor, and "Ma" for marine. If the person served in the United States forces add "U.S." in parentheses, and if in the Confederate forces add "Conf." in parentheses, thus: Sol (U.S.); Sail (U.S.); Sol (Conf.), etc. In the case of a widow of a deceased soldier, sailor, or marine, use the letter "W" in addition to the above designations, as W. Sol (U.S.), W. Sol (Conf.), and so on.

   The enumeration of the survivors of the late war, including their names, organizations, length of service, and the widows of such as have died, is to be taken on a special schedule prepared for the purpose, as provided for by the act of March 1, 1889, and *relates only to those persons, or widows of persons, who served in the Army, Navy, or Marine Corps of the United States in the late war.* The inquiry concerning the survivors of both the United States and Confederate forces is made on the population schedule so as to ascertain the *number* now living and the *number* who have died and have left widows.

2. *Relationship to head of family.*

   Designate the head of a family, whether a husband or father, widow or unmarried person of either sex, by the word "*Head;*" other members of a family by *wife, mother, father, son, daughter, grandson, daughter-in-law, aunt, uncle, nephew, niece, servant,* or other properly distinctive term, according to the particular relationship which the person bears to the head of the family. Distinguish between *boarders,* who sleep and board in one place, and lodgers, who room in one place and board in another. If an inmate of an institution or school, write *inmate, pupil, patient, prisoner,* or some equivalent term which will clearly distinguish inmates from the officers and employees and their families. But all officers and employees of an institution who reside in the institution building are to be accounted, for census purposes, as one family, the head of which is the superintendent, matron, or other officer in charge. If more than one family resides in the institution building, group the members together and distinguish them in some intelligible way. In addition to defining their natural relationship to the head of the institution or of their own immediate family, their official position in the institution, if any, should be also noted, thus: *Superintendent, clerk, teacher, watchman, nurse,* etc.

COLOR, SEX, AND AGE

4. *Whether white, black, mulatto, quadroon, octoroon, Chinese, Japanese, or Indian.*

   Write *white, black, mulatto, quadroon, octoroon, Chinese, Japanese,* or *Indian,* according to the color or race of the person enumerated. Be particularly careful to distinguish between blacks, mulattoes, quadroons, and octoroons. The word "black" should be used to describe those persons who have three-fourths or more black blood; "mulatto," those persons who have from three-eighths to five-eighths black blood; "quadroon," those persons who have one-fourth black blood; and "octoroon," those persons who have one-eighth or any trace of black blood.

5. **Sex.**

Write *male* or *female,* as the case may be.

6. *Age at nearest birthday. If under one year, give age in months.*

Write the age in figures at nearest birthday in whole years, omitting months and days, for each person of one year of age or over. For children who on the 1st of June, 1890, were less than one year of age, give the age in months, or twelfths of a year, thus: 3/12, 7/12, 10/12. For a child less than one month old, state the age as follows: 0/12. The exact years of age for all persons one year old or over should be given whenever it can be obtained. In any event, do not accept the answer "Don't know," but ascertain as nearly as possible the approximate age of each person. The general tendency of persons in giving their ages is to use the round numbers, as 20, 25, 30, 25, 40, etc. If the age is given as "about 25," determine, if possible, whether the age should be entered as 24, 25, or 26. Particular attention should be paid to this, otherwise it will be found when the results are aggregated in this office that a much more than normal number of persons have been reported as 20, 25, 30, 35, 40, etc., years of age , and a much less than normal at 19, 21, 24, 26, 29, 31, etc.

CONJUGAL CONDITION AND CHILDREN AND CHILDREN LIVING

7. *Whether single married, widow, or divorced.*

Write *single, married, widowed,* or *divorced,* according to the conjugal condition of the person enumerated. No matter how young the person may be, the conjugal condition, if "single," should be always stated.

8. *Whether married during the census year (June 1, 1889, to May 31, 1890).*

Write *yes* or *no,* as the case may be.

9. *Mother of how many children, and number of these children living.*

This inquiry is to be made concerning all women who are or have been married, including those widowed or divorced. The answers should be given in figures, as follows: 6 5; that is, mother of six (6) children, of which five (5) are living. If a woman who is or has been married has had no children, or if none are living, state the fact thus: 0 0 or 3 0, as the case may be.

Place of Birth and Parent Nativity

10. *Place of birth.*

Give the place of birth of the *person* whose name appears at the head of the column opposite inquiry 1, and for whom the entries are being made.

11. *Place of birth of father.*

Give the place of birth of the *father* of the person for whom the entries are being made.

12. *Place of birth of mother.*

Give the place of birth of the *mother* of the person for whom the entries are being made.
If the person (inquiry 10), or father (inquiry 11), or mother (inquiry 12) were born in the United States, name the state or territory, or if of foreign birth name the country. The names of countries, and not of cities, are wanted. In naming the country of foreign birth, however, do not write, for instance, "Great Britain," but give the particular country, as *England, Scotland,* or *Wales.*

If the person, or father, or mother were born in a foreign country of American parents, write the name of the country and also the words *"American citizen."* If born at sea write the words "At sea;" if in the case of the father or mother the words "At sea" be used, add the nationality of the father's father or mother's father.

If born in Canada or Newfoundland, write the word "English" or "French" after the particular place of birth, so as to distinguish between persons born in any part of British America of French and English extraction respectively. *This is a most important requirement, and must be closely observed in each case and the distinction carefully made.*

NATURALIZATION

Inquiries 13, 14, and 15 should be made concerning only those adult males of foreign birth who are 21 years of age or over.

13. *Number of years in the United States.*

Give the answer in figures as 1, 2, 3, 6, 10, etc., according to the number of years such person (as stated above) may have resided in the United States.

14. *Whether naturalized.*

Write "Yes" or "No," as the case may be.

15. *Whether naturalization papers have been taken out.*

If naturalized (Inquiry 14), use the symbol X; if not naturalized (Inquiry 14), write "Yes" or "No," as the case may be, in answers to this inquiry (15).

Profession, Trade, or Occupation, and Months Employed

16. *Profession, trade, or occupation.*

This is a most important inquiry. Study these instructions closely, and in reporting occupations avoid the use of unmeaning terms. A person's occupation is the profession, trade, or branch of work upon which he chiefly depends for support, and in which he would ordinarily be engaged during the larger part of the year. General or indefinite terms which do not indicate the kind of work done by each person must not be used. You are under no obligation to give a person's occupation just as he expresses it. If he can not tell intelligibly what he is, find out what he does, and describe his occupation accordingly. The name of the place worked in or article made or worked upon should not be used as the sole basis of the statement of a person's occupation. Endeavor to ascertain always *the character of the service rendered or kind of work done,* and so state it.

The illustrations given under each of the general classes of occupations show the nature of the answers which should be made to this inquiry. They are not intended to cover all occupations, but are indicative of the character of the answers desired in order to secure, for each person enumerated, properly descriptive designations of service rendered or work done by way of occupation and as the means of gaining a livelihood.

AGRICULTURAL PURSUITS.—Be careful to distinguish between the *farm laborer,* the *farmer,* and *farm overseer;* also between the *plantation laborer,* the *planter,* and *plantation overseer.* These three classes must be kept distinct, and each occupation separately returned.

Do not confuse the *agricultural laborer,* who works on the farm or plantation, with the general or day laborer, who works on the road or at odd jobs in the village or town. Distinguish also between *woodchoppers* at work regularly in the woods or forests and the laborer, who takes a job occasionally at chopping wood.

Make a separate return for *farmers* and *planters* who own, hire, or carry on a farm or plantation, and for *gardeners, fruit growers, nurserymen, florists, vine growers,* etc., who are engaged in raising vegetables for market or in cultivation of fruit, flowers, seeds, nursery products, etc. In the latter case, if a man combines two or more of these occupations, be careful to so state it, as *florist, nurseryman, and seed grower.*

Avoid the confusion of the *garden laborer, nursery laborer,* etc., who hires out his services, with the proprietor gardener, florist, nurseryman, etc., who carries on the business himself or employs others to assist him.

Return as *dairymen* or *dairywoman* those persons whose occupation in connection with the farm has to do chiefly with the dairy. Do not confuse them with employees of butter and cheese or condensed milk factories, who should be separately returned by some distinctive term.

Return *stock herders* and *stock drovers* separately from stock raisers.

Do not include *lumbermen, raftsmen, log drivers,* etc., engaged in hauling or transporting lumber (generally by water) from the forest to the mill, with the employees of lumber yards or lumber mills.

FISHING.—For *fishermen* and *oystermen* describe the occupation as accurately as possible. Be careful to avoid the return of fishermen on vessels as sailors. If they gain their living by fishing, they should be returned as "fishermen," and not as sailors.

MINING AND QUARRYING.—Make a careful distinction between the *coal miners* and *miners of ores;* also between miners generally and *quarrymen.* State the *kind* of ore mined or stone quarried.

Do not return proprietors or officials of mining or quarrying companies as miners or quarrymen, but state their business or official position accurately.

PROFESSIONAL PURSUITS.—This class includes *actors, artists* and *teachers of art, clergymen, dentists, designers, draftsmen, engravers, civil engineers,* and *surveyors, mechanical* and *mining engineers, government clerks* and *officials, journalists, lawyers, musicians* and *teachers of music, physicians, surgeons, professors* (in colleges and universities), *teachers* (in schools), and other pursuits of a professional nature. Specify each profession in detail, according to the fact. These are cited simply as illustrations of these classes of pursuits.

Distinguish between *actors, theatrical managers,* and *showmen.*

Make a separate return for *government clerks* occupying positions under the National, State, county, city, or town governments from clerks in offices, stores, manufacturing establishments, etc.; also distinguish *government officials.*

Return *veterinary surgeons* separately from other surgeons.

Distinguish *journalists, editors,* and *reporters* from *authors and other literary persons* who do not follow journalism as a distinct profession.

Return separately *chemists, assayers, metallurgists,* and other scientific persons.

DOMESTIC AND PERSONAL SERVICE.—Among this class of occupations are comprised *hotel keepers, boarding-house keepers, restaurant keepers, saloon keepers,* and *bartenders; housekeepers, cooks,* and *servants* (in hotels, boarding houses, hospitals, institutions, private families, etc.); *barbers* and *hairdressers; city, town,* and *general day laborers; janitors, sextons,* and *undertakers; nurses* and *midwives; watchmen, policemen,* and *detectives.* Specify each occupation or kind of service rendered in detail, according to the fact. The above are given only as examples of the occupations which would naturally be included under this general class of work.

Distinguish carefully between *housekeepers,* or women who receive a stated wage or salary for their services, and *housewives,* or women who keep house for their own families or for themselves, without any gainful occupation. The occupation of grown daughters who assist in the household duties without fixed remuneration should be returned as "Housework—without pay."

As stated under agricultural pursuits, do not confuse *day laborers,* at work for the city, town, or at odd jobs, with agricultural laborer, at work on the farm or plantation or in the employ of gardeners, nurserymen, etc. State specifically the *kind* of work done in every instance.

Clerks in hotels, restaurants, and saloons should be so described and carefully distinguished from *bartenders.* In many instances bartenders will state their occupation as "clerk" in wine store, etc., but the character of the service rendered by such persons will readily determine whether they should be classed as "bartenders" or not.

Stationary engineers and *firemen* should be carefully distinguished from *engineers* and *firemen* employed on locomotives, steamboats, etc.

Soldiers, sailors, and *marines* enlisted in the service of the United States should be so returned. Distinguish between officers and enlisted men, and for civilian employees return the kind of service performed by them.

PURSUITS OF TRADE AND TRANSPORTATION.—Distinguish carefully between *real estate agents, insurance agents, claim agents, commission agents,* etc. If a person is a real estate agent and also an auctioneer, as is often the case, return his occupation as *real estate agent* and *auctioneer.*

Return accountants, bookkeepers, clerks, cashiers, etc., separately, and state the kind of service rendered, as *accountant—insurance; bookkeeper—wholesale dry goods; clerk—gas company; cashier—music store.*

Do not confound a clerk with a salesman, as is often done, especially in dry goods stores, grocery stores, and provision stores. Generally speaking, the persons so employed are to be considered as salesmen, unless the bulk of their service is in the office on the books and accounts; otherwise they should be returned as *salesman—dry goods; salesman—groceries,* etc.

Stenographers and *typewriters* should be reported separately, and should not be described simply as "clerks." Distinguish carefully between *bank clerks, cashiers in banks,* and *bank officials,* describing the particular position filled in each case. In no case should a *bank cashier* be confounded with cashiers in stores, etc.

Distinguish between foremen and overseers, packers and shippers, porters and helpers, and errand, office, and messenger boys in stores, etc., and state in each case the character of the duties performed by them, as *foreman wholesale wool house; packer—crockery; porter—rubber goods; errand boy—dry goods; messenger boy—telegraph.*

State the kind of merchants and dealers, *as dry goods merchant, wood and coal dealer,* etc. Whenever a single word will express the business carried on, as *grocer,* it should be so stated.

In the case of hucksters and peddlers also state the kind of goods sold, as *peddler—tinware.*
Distinguish *traveling salesmen* from salesmen in stores, and state the kind of goods sold by them.

Return *boarding* and *livery stable keepers* separately from the *hostlers* and other stable employees.

Distinguish also between *expressmen, teamsters, draymen,* and *carriage and hack drivers.*

Steam railroad employees should be reported separately, according to the nature of their work, as *baggagemen, brakemen, conductors, laborers on railroad, locomotive engineers, locomotive firemen, switchmen, yardmen,* etc.

Officials of railroad, telegraph express, and *other companies* should be separately returned and carefully distinguished from the employees of such companies.

Boatmen, canal men, pilots, longshoremen, stevedores, and *sailors* (on steam or sailing vessels) should be separately returned.

Telegraph operators, telephone operators, telegraph linemen, telephone linemen, electric-light men, etc., should be kept distinct, and a separate return made for each class.

MANUFACTURING AND MECHANICAL PURSUITS.—In reporting occupations pertaining to manufactures there are many difficulties in the way of showing the kind of work done rather than the article made or the place worked in. The nature of certain occupations is such that it is well nigh impossible to find properly descriptive terms without the use of some expression relating to the article made or place in which the work is carried on.

Do not accept "maker" of an article or "works in" mill, shop, or factory, but strive always to find out the particular work done.
Distinguish between persons who tend machines and the unskilled workman or laborer in mills, factories, and workshops.

Describe the proprietor of the establishment as a "manufacturer," and specify the branch of manufacture, as *cotton manufacturer*, etc. In no case should a manufacturer be returned as a "maker" of an article.

In the case of apprentices, state the trade to which apprenticed, as *apprentice-carpenter*, etc.

Distinguish between *butchers*, whose business is to slaughter cattle, swine, etc., and *provisions dealers*, who sell meats only.

Distinguish also between *glover*, *hatter*, or *furrier* who actually make or make up in their own establishments all or part of the gloves, hats, or furs which they sell, and the person who simply deals in but does not make these articles.

Do not use the words "factory operative," but specify in every instance the kind of work done, as *cotton mill spinner*; *silk mill weaver*, etc.

Do not describe a person in a printing office as a "printer" where a more expressive term can be used, as *compositor*, *pressman*, *press feeder*, etc.

Make the proper distinction between a *clock* or *watch* "maker" and a *clock* or *watch* "repairer." Do not apply the word "jeweler" to those who make watches, watch chains, or jewelry in large establishments.

Avoid in all cases the use of the word "mechanic," and state whether a *carpenter, mason, house painter, machinist, plumber*, etc.

Do not say "finisher," "molder," "polisher," etc., but state the article finished, molded, or polished, as *brass finisher, iron molder, steel polisher*, etc.

Distinguish between *cloakmakers, dressmakers, seamstresses, tailoresses*, etc. In the case of *sewing-machine operators*, specify the work done.

OTHER OCCUPATIONS.—When a lawyer, merchant, manufacturer, etc., has retired from practice or business, say *retired lawyer, retired merchant*, etc.

The distinction to be made between *housewives, housekeepers*, and those assisting in *housework* has already been stated under "Domestic and Personal Service." For the large body of persons, particularly young women, who live at home and do nothing, make the return as "No occupation." With respect to infants and children too young to take any part in production or to be engaged in any state occupation, distinguish between those at home and those attending school. For those too young to go to school, or who for some reason did not attend school during the census year, write the words "At home," and for those who attended school during some part of the school year write the words, "At school—public," or "At school—private," according to the kind of school. If taught by a governess or tutor, it should be so stated. The *student* at college or engaged in special studies should be reported separately from *scholars in public or private schools*.

The doing of domestic errands or family chores out of school hours, where a child regularly attends school, should not be considered an occupation. But if a boy or girl, whatever the age, is earning money regularly by labor, contributing to the family support, or appreciably assisting in mechanical or agricultural industry, the kind of work performed should be stated.

17. *Months unemployed during the census year (June 1, 1889, to May 31, 1890).*

If a person having a gainful occupation was unemployed during any part of the census year it should be so stated in months and parts of months. If, as may often happen, a person was unemployed at his usual occupation for some time during the census year and yet found other temporary employment for some part or the whole of the time, this fact should be clearly stated. For instance, a person's occupation may be that of "farm laborer," at which he may have had no employment for three months during the census year. During two of these three months, however, he may have worked in a shoe shop, so that, so far as actual idleness is concerned, he was only out of work one month. In all such cases, where the nonemployment returned in answer to inquiry 17 does not represent actual idleness as regards the person's usual actual occupation given in answer to inquiry 16, indicates the number of months unemployed at occupation by inserting the figures, in parenthesis, after the name of the occupation itself. In the case just cited, and as shown in the "illustrative example," the answer to inquiry 16 would appear as "Farm laborer (3)" and the answer to inquiry 17 as "1." For all persons not engaged in gainful occupation the symbol "X" should be used.

SCHOOL ATTENDANCE, ILLITERACY, AND LANGUAGE SPOKEN

18. *Attendance at school (in months) during the census year (June 1, 1889, to May 31, 1900).*

For all persons between the ages of 5 and 17, inclusive, the attendance at school during the census year should be in all cases stated in months and parts of months. Where a person within the above ages did not attend school at all during the census year write "0," and for all other persons to whom the inquiry is not applicable use the symbol "X."

Inquiries numbered 19 and 20 relate to illiteracy, and are to be made only of or concerning persons 10 years of age or over.

19. Able to read.

Write "Yes" or "No," as the case may be.

20. *Able to write.*

    Write *"Yes"* or *"No,"* as the case may be.

    A person may not be able to read or write the English language, and yet may be able to read or write (or both) their native language, as French, Spanish, Italian, etc. If in such cases a person can read or write (or both) some language, the answer to Inquiry 19 and Inquiry 20 should be "Yes," according to the fact. If not able to so read or write the answer should be "No." For all persons *under* 10 years of age use the symbol "X."

21. *Able to speak English. If not, the language or dialect spoken.*

    This inquiry should also be made of or concerning every person 10 years of age or over. If the person is able to speak English so as to be understood in ordinary conversation, write "English;" otherwise, write the name of the language or dialect in which he usually expresses himself, as *"German," "Portuguese," "Canadian French," "Pennsylvania Dutch,"* etc. For all persons *under* 10 years of age use the symbol "X."

MENTAL AND PHYSICAL DEFECTS, ETC.

22. *Whether suffering from acute or chronic disease, with name of disease and length of time afflicted.*

    If a person is suffering from acute or chronic disease so as to be unable to attend to ordinary business or duties, give the name of the disease and the length of time that it has lasted.

23. *Whether defective in mind, sight, hearing, or speech, or whether crippled, maimed, or deformed, with name of defect.*

    If a person is mentally or physically defective, state the nature of the defect.

24. *Whether a prisoner, convict, homeless child, or pauper.*

    If the person is a prisoner, convict, homeless child, or pauper, be careful to so state, as *"prisoner," "pauper,"* etc.

25. *Supplemental schedule and page.*

    If answers are required to inquiries 22, 23, or 24, indicate in this space the number of the supplemental schedule and page of schedule on which the special inquiries relating to such person have been answered. (See instructions concerning supplemental schedules.)

OWNERSHIP OF HOMES AND FARMS

26. *Is the home you live in hired, or is it owned by the head or by a member of the family?*

    If hired, say "Hired;" if owned, say "Owned," and indicate whether owned by *head, wife, son, daughter,* or other member of family, as "Owned—head;"

"Owned— wife;" "Owned—son," etc. If there is more than one son or daughter in the family, and the home is owned by one of them, indicate which one by using the figure at the head of the column in which the name, etc., of the person is entered, as "Owned—son (4)."

27. *If owned by head or member of family, is the home free from mortgage encumbrance?*

    If free from encumbrance, say "Free;" if mortgaged, say "Mortgaged."

28. *If the head of family is a farmer, is the farm which he cultivates hired, or is it owned by him or by a member of his family?*

    To be answered in the same manner as for inquiry 26.

29. *If owned by head or member of family, is the farm free from mortgage encumbrance?*

    To be answered in the same manner as for inquiry 27.

30. *If the home or farm is owned by head or member of family, and mortgaged, give the post-office address of owner.*

In answer to this inquiry the post-office address of the owner of a mortgaged home or farm must be correctly stated; that is, the post office at which the owner (whether head of family, wife, son, daughter, etc.) usually receives his or her mail.

In all cases where it can not be definitely ascertained whether the home or farm is mortgaged or not return the post-office address of the owner, so that this office can communicate with such persons.

In connection with the definition of mortgage encumbrance it should be stated that judgment notes or confessions of judgment, as in Pennsylvania and Virginia, the deeds of trust of many States, deeds with vendor's lien clause, bonds or contracts for title that are virtually mortgages, crop liens or mortgages upon crops, and all other legal instruments that partake of the nature of mortgages upon real estate, are to be regarded as such; but mechanics' liens are not to be regarded as mortgage encumbrances upon homes or farms.

The enumerator should be careful to use the local name for the mortgage encumbrance when making the inquiries, and should not confine himself to the word "mortgage" when it will be misunderstood.

Some of the difficulties which will arise in connection with the prosecution of the inquiries concerning homes and farms, and how they are to be treated, may be mentioned, as follows:

1. A house is not necessarily to be considered as identical with a home and to be counted only once as a

home. If it is occupied as a home by one or more tenants, or by owner and one or more tenants, it is to be regarded as a home to each family.

2. If a person owns and cultivates what has been two or more farms and lives on one, they are not to be taken as more than one farm.

3. If a person owns and cultivates what has been two or more farms and all are not mortgaged, the several farms are to be counted as one farm and as mortgaged.

4. If a person hires both the farm he cultivates and the home he lives in, or owns both, the home is to be considered as part of the farm.

5. If a person owns the home he lives in and hires the farm he cultivates, or owns the farm he cultivates and hires the home he lives in, both farm and home are to be entered upon the schedule, and separately.

6. If the tenant of a farm and its owner live upon it, either in the same house or in different houses, the owner is to be regarded as owning the home he lives in and the tenant as hiring the farm he cultivates. If the owner simply boards with the tenant, no account is to be made of the owner.

7. If the same person owns and cultivates one farm and hires and cultivates another farm, he is to be entered upon the schedule as owning the farm he cultivates.

8. The head of a family may own and cultivate a farm and his wife may own another farm which is let to tenant, perhaps to her husband. In such case only the farm which is owned by the head of the family is to be considered, but the rented farm is to be taken account of when its tenant's family is visited.

9. A person who cultivates a farm is not to be regarded as hiring it if he works for a definite and fixed compensation in money or fixed quantity of produce, but he is to be regarded as hiring it if he pays a rental for it or is to receive a share of the produce, even though he may be subject to some direction and control by the owner.

U.S. Census Bureau

1900 QUESTIONNAIRE—POPULATION

(19 1/2" X 18 5/8", printed on two sides, space for 50
entries on each side; reverse side was identical except for
line numbers).

LOCATION			NAME	RELATION	PERSONAL DESCRIPTION									NATIVITY		
IN CITIES			of each person whose place of abode on June 1, 1900, was in this family	Relationship of each person to the head of the family			DATE OF BIRTH							Place of birth of each person and parents of each person enumerated. If born in the United States, give the *State or Territory*; if of foreign birth, give the *Country* only		
Street	House Number	Number of dwelling house, in the order of visitation	Enter surname first, then the given name and middle initial, if any		Color or race	Sex	Month	Year	Age at last birthday	Whether single, married, widowed, or divorced	Number of years married	Mother of how many children	Number of these children living	Place of birth of this PERSON	Place of birth of FATHER of this person	Place of birth of MOTHER of this person
		Number of family, in the order of visitation	INCLUDE every person living on June 1, 1900 OMIT children born *since* June 1, 1900													
	1	2	3	4	5	6	7		8	9	10	11	12	13	14	15
1																
2																
3																

CITIZENSHIP			OCCUPATION, TRADE, OR PROFESSION		EDUCATION				OWNERSHIP OF HOME				
Year of immigration to the United States	Number of years in the United States	Naturalization	of each person TEN YEARS of age and over		Attended school (in months)	Can read	Can write	Can speak English	Owned or rented	Owned free or mortgaged	Farm or house	Number of farm schedule	
			OCCUPATION	Months not employed									
16	17	18	19	20	21	22	23	24	25	26	27	28	
													1
													2
													3

Instructions to Enumerators
(Name and Relationship)

108. Column 3. Name of each person enumerated.—Enter the name of every person whose usual place of abode (see paragraph 111) is in the family or dwelling place for which the enumeration is being made. The census day, that is, the day as of which the enumeration is made, is June 1, 1900. Include, therefore, every person living on June 1, 1900, or during any part of that day, and omit children born after that date.

109. It is intended that the name of every man, woman, and child whose usual place of abode *on the first day of June,* 1900, was within your district shall be entered on the population schedule, but no entry is to be made of a child born between the first day of June, 1900, and the day of your visit, say June 5, June 15, etc., as the case may be.

110. On the other hand, every person who was a resident of your district upon the first day of June, 1900, but between that date and the day of your visit shall have died, should be entered on the schedule precisely as if still living. The object of the schedule is to obtain a list of the inhabitants *on the first day of June,* 1900, and all changes after that date, whether in the nature of gain or loss, are to be disregarded.

111. The census law furnishes no definitions of the phrase "usual place of abode;" and it is difficult to guard against the danger that some persons will be reported in two places and others not reported at all. Much must be left to the judgement of the enumerator, who, if he will take the pains, can satisfy himself, in the great majority of instances, as to the propriety of including or not including doubtful cases in his enumeration of any given family.

112. In the case of boarders at hotels, students at schools or colleges, and inmates of institutions, ascertain whether the person concerning whom the question may arise has at the time any other place of abode within another district at which he is likely to be reported. Seafaring men are to be reported at their land homes, no matter how long they may have been absent, if they are supposed to be still alive. Hence, sailors temporarily at a sailors' boarding or lodging house, *if they acknowledge any other home within the United States,* are not to be included in the family of the lodging or boarding house.

113. Persons engaged in internal transportation, canal men, expressmen, railroad men, etc., if they habitually return to their homes in the intervals of their occupations, will be reported *as of their families,* and not where they may be temporarily staying on June 1, 1900.

114. The transient guests of a hotel are not to be enumerated as of the hotel, unless they are likely otherwise to be omitted from the enumeration; but the proprietor and his family, and those boarders, employees, and servants who regularly sleep there are to be so included.

115. The inmates of transient lodging-houses are to be so enumerated, if they claim no other home or have no other place of abode.

116. All inmates of hospitals or other institutions are to be enumerated; but if they have some other permanent place of residence, write it in the margin of the schedule on the left-hand side of the page.

117. If a soldier, sailor, or marine (officer or enlisted man), or civilian employee in the service of the United States at a station at home or abroad, is a member of a family living in your district, he should be enumerated as a member of that family, even though he may be absent on duty at the time of the enumeration.

118. Summer boarders at hotels or country houses and persons temporarily residing in foreign lands should be enumerated as part of their family at their home or usual place of abode.

119. The floating population in vessels, steamboats, and house boats at wharves and piers or river landings should be enumerated on the morning of June 1, as far as possible, by the enumerators of the districts contiguous to the water front, including in the enumeration all persons who claim to be residents of the United States, even though they have no other home than on board the craft where they are found; but the officers and crew of a foreign ship only temporarily in the harbor are not to be enumerated.

120. It is important to ascertain beyond a doubt whether the information given by the person supplying the same covers all the persons in the family, including not only the immediate members of the family, as the head, wife, and children, but also other relatives living with the family, servants (if they sleep in the house), and persons who live with the family, as boarders, lodgers, etc.

121. In the case of families reported "out" at the first visit, but enumerated at a later visit, no spaces should be left blank on the population schedule for the entries concerning the members of such a family, as you can have no knowledge, in most cases, of the number of members constituting the family, and hence of the number of lines to be left blank. The enumeration of the family is to be made on that sheet of the population schedule on which you are at work on the day when the information concerning such family is finally obtained by you.

122. In the case, however, of boarders, lodgers, or other persons living in a family, for whom no information can be obtained at the first visit, but which is supplied later, either in person or through the lady of the house, you should duly enter the name of such person as a member of the family so enumerated, and arrange to secure by a second or third visit, if necessary, the information needed to complete the record for such person. It is important that the person should be recorded by name at least as a member of the family with whom he resides, as otherwise the enumeration of that family will be incomplete, and if omitted from its proper place on the population schedule, such person is likely to be counted, when finally enumerated, as a family of one, which is not the fact.

123. Enter the members of each family in the following order, namely: Head first, wife second, children (whether sons or daughters) in the order of their ages, and all other persons living with the family, whether relatives, boarders, lodgers, or servants.

124. Enter first the surname, then the given name in full, and the initial of the middle name, if any. Where the surname is the same as, that of the person on the preceding line indicate this by drawing a horizontal line (___) thereunder, as shown in illustrative example.

125. Column 4. Relationship to head of family. Designate the head of the family, whether a husband or father, widow or unmarried person of either sex, by the word "Head;" for other members of a family write *wife, mother, father, son, daughter, grandson, daughter-in-law, aunt, uncle, nephew, niece, boarder, lodger, servant*, etc., according to the particular relationship which the person bears to the head of the family. Occupants of an institution or school, living under a common roof, should be designated as *officer, inmate, pupil, patient, prisoner*, etc., and in case of the chief officer his title should be used, as *warden, principal, superintendent*, etc. Institutions whose inmates occupy different buildings should be enumerated as though they occupied one institution building. If more than one family resides in the institution building or buildings, group the members together and distinguish them in some intelligible way. If two or more persons share a common abode as partners, write "head" for one and "partner" for the other or others.

PERSONAL DESCRIPTION

126. Column 5. Color or race. Write "W" for white; "B" for black (negro or negro descent); "Ch" for Chinese; "Jp" for Japanese, and "In" for Indian, as the case may be.

127. Column 6. Sex. Write "M" for male and "F" for female, as the case may be.

128. Column 7. Date of birth. The object of this question is to help in getting the exact age in years of each person enumerated. Many a person who can tell the month and year of his birth will be careless or forgetful in stating the years of his age, and so an error will creep into the census. This danger can not be entirely avoided, but asking the question in two forms will prevent it in many cases.

129. Enter in the first division of column 7 the name or abbreviation of the month in which the person was born, thus: Jan., Feb., Mar., Apr., May, June, July, Aug., Sept., Oct., Nov., or Dec.

130. Enter in the second division the year in which the person was born, thus: 1841, 1897, etc.

131. Column 8. Age at last birthday. The object of this question is to get the age of each person in completed years, or in the case of a child under one year of age in completed months.

132. For each person of one year of age or over, enter the age at *last* birthday in whole years, omitting months and days. For children who, on the first day of June, 1900, were less than one year of age, enter the age in months, or twelfths of a year, thus 3/12, 7/12, 8/12. For a child less than one month old, enter the age as follows: 0/12.

133. Endeavor to ascertain in each case the month and year of birth called for in column 7, but where this is impossible get as nearly as possible the exact years of age. An answer given in round numbers, such as "about 30," "about 45," is likely to be wrong. In such cases endeavor to get the exact age.

134. Column 9. Whether single, married, widowed, or divorced. Write "S" for single or unmarried persons, "M" for married, "Wd" for widowed (man or woman), and "D" for divorced.

135. Column 10. Number of years married. Enter in this column for all persons reported as married (column 9) the number of years married (to present husband or wife), as 5, 9, 29, etc.; for person married during the census year, that is, from June 1, 1899, to May 31, 1900, write "0;" for all other persons leave the column blank. Notice that this question can not be answered for single persons and need not be for widowed or divorced persons.

136. Columns 11 and 12. Mother of how many children and number of these children living. This question applies only to women, and its object is to get the number of children each woman has had, and whether the children are or are not living on the census day. Stillborn children are not to be counted.

137. Enter in column 11 the figure showing the number of children born to this woman, as 1, 2, 3, 6, 10, etc. If she has had none, write "0." Enter in column 12 the figure showing the number of these children living on the census day. Whether the children are living in your district or elsewhere makes no difference. If the woman has had no children, or if they are all dead, write "0."

NATIVITY

138. Column 13. Place of birth of person. The object of this question is to get the birthplace of every person living in your district. If the person was born in the United States, enter in column 13 the state or territory (not city or town) of the United States in which he was born. A person born in what is now West Virginia, North Dakota, South Dakota, or Oklahoma should be reported as so born, although at the time of his birth the particular region may have had a different name.

139. If the person was born outside the United States, enter in column 13 the country (not city or district) in which he was born. By country is meant usually a region whose people have direct relation with other countries. Thus, do not write Prussia or Saxony, but Germany. To this rule, however, note the following exceptions.

140. Write Ireland, England, Scotland, or Wales rather than Great Britain. Write Hungary or Bohemia rather than Austria for persons born in Hungary or Bohemia, respectively. Write Finland rather than Russia for persons born in Finland.

141. Note, also, that the language spoken is not always a safe guide to the birthplace. This is especially true of Germans, for over one-third of the Austrians and nearly three-fourths of the Swiss speak German. In case a person speaks German, therefore, inquire carefully whether the birthplace was Germany, Austria, or Switzerland.

142. In case the person speaks Polish, as Poland is not now a country, inquire whether the birthplace was what is now known as German Poland or Austrian Poland or Russian Poland, and enter the answer accordingly as Poland (Ger.), Poland (Aust.), or Poland (Russ.).

143. If the birthplace reported is Canada or Newfoundland, ask whether the person is of English or French decent. Write Canada English or Canada French, according to the answer.

144. If the person was born abroad of American parents, write in column 13 both the birthplace and "Am. Cit.;" that is, American citizen.

145. If the person was born at sea, write "at sea."

146. Spell out the names of states, territories, and countries, and do not abbreviate, except for American Citizen, as mentioned in paragraph 144.

147. Columns 14 and 15. Place of birth of father and mother. Apply the instructions for filling column 13 to these two columns; but where either the father or mother was born at sea, write in the proper column, besides the words "at sea," the birthplace of the father's father or mother's mother.

CITIZENSHIP

148. Column 16. Year of immigration to the United States.—If the person is a native of the United States, leave the column blank. If he was born abroad, enter the year in which he arrived in the United States.

149. Column 17. Number of years in the United States.—If the person is a native of the United States, leave the column blank. If he was born abroad, enter the number of years since his arrival in the United States. Disregard all fractions of a year. If the time is less than one year, write "0." Endeavor to get the exact number of years in all cases.

150. The question of immigration (columns 16 and 17) applies to all foreign-born persons, male and female, of whatever age. It does not apply to persons born in the United States.

151. Column 18. Naturalization.—If the person is a native of the United States, leave the column blank. If he was born abroad, and has taken no steps toward becoming an American citizen, write "Al" (for alien). If he has declared his intention to become an American citizen and taken out his "first" papers, write "Pa" (for papers). If he has become a full citizen by taking out second or final papers of naturalization, write "Na" (for naturalized).

152. The question of naturalization (column 18) applies only to foreign-born males 21 years of age and over. It does not apply to foreign-born minors, to foreign-born females, or to any person, male or female, who was born in the United States, either of native or foreign parentage.

OCCUPATION, TRADE, OR PROFESSION

153. NOTE.—The following instructions concerning the return of the occupation, trade, or profession in column 19 do not, in the main, form a part of the instructions contained in the portfolio or the

instructions printed at the bottom of the illustrative example. These instructions are very important, however, and must be not only read but studied carefully.

154. Column 19. Occupation.—This question applies to every person 10 years of age and over who is at work, that is, occupied in gainful labor, and calls for the profession, trade, or branch of work upon which each person depends chiefly for support, or in which he is engaged ordinarily during the larger part of the time. (See paragraph 223.)

155. This is a most important question. In reporting occupations avoid the use of general or indefinite terms which do not indicate the kind of work done. You need not give a person's occupation just as he expresses it. If he can not tell intelligibly what he is, find out what he does, and describe his occupation accordingly. Endeavor to ascertain always *the kind of work done,* and so state it.

156. Indicate in every case the kind of work done or character of service rendered. Do not state merely the article made or worked upon, or the place where the work is done. For example, the reply "carriage builder," or "works in carriage factory," is unsatisfactory, because men of different trades, such as blacksmiths, joiners, wheelwrights, painters, upholsterers, work together in building carriages. Such an answer, therefore, does not show what kind of work the person performs.

157. Return every person according to his own occupation, not that of his employer. For example, describe a blacksmith employed by a manufacturer of carriages as a carriage blacksmith and not as a carriage builder, or a cooper employed by a brewery as a cooper and not a brewer, etc.

158. If a person has two occupations, enter the more important one, that is, the one from which he gets the more money. If you can not learn that, enter the one in which he spends the more time. For example, describe a person who gets most of his income by managing a farm, but also preaches, as a "farmer," but if he gets more income from his preaching, describe him as a "preacher" and not as a farmer.

159. Sometimes you will find a person engaged in one occupation, but claiming a different one. This will be common in certain resorts for invalids. Such persons often take up for the time occupations different from those followed at home. For example, you may find a clergyman canvassing for books or a physician herding cattle. In such a case ask from which occupation the person gets the more money or to which he gives more time during the year.

160. If a married woman has a gainful occupation, return the occupation accordingly, whether she does the work at her home or goes regularly to a place of employment, and whether she is regularly or only occasionally so employed. For example, "milliner," "dressmaker," "nurse," etc.

161. In farming sections, where a farm is found that is under the management or supervision of a woman as owner or tenant, return the occupation of such woman as "farmer" in all cases.

162. Report a student who supports himself by some occupation according to the occupation, if more time is given to that, but as a student, if more time is given to study. Thus report a student who does stenographic work as a student unless more of his time is spent in stenography. Report a salesman in a grocery store, who attends a night school as "salesman, groceries," because most of his day is spent in the store. (See paragraph 219.)

163. Many a person who does not follow any occupation still has an income. In that case indicate the source of the income. Report a person whose income comes from the rent of lands or buildings as "landlord." Report a person who receives his income, or most of it, from money loaned at interest, or from stocks, bonds, or other securities, as a "capitalist."

164. Abbreviations.—The space in column 19 is somewhat narrow, and it may be necessary to use the following abbreviations (but no others):

Agric.	agriculture
Mfr.	manufacturer
Agt.	agent
Prest.	president
Asst.	assistant
R.R.	railroad or railway
Co.	company
Sch.	school
Comsn.	commission
Secy.	secretary
Dept.	department
Supt.	superintendent
Fcty.	factory
Teleg.	telegraph
Insur.	insurance
Telph.	telephone
Merch.	merchant
Trav.	traveling, or traveler
Mfg.	manufacturing
Treas.	treasurer

165. The illustrations given under this head show the nature of the answers which should be made to this inquiry. They are not intended to cover all occupations, but are merely examples of the answers

desired in order to secure a proper description of the character of the service rendered or kind of work done by each and every person engaged in gainful labor.

Agricultural Pursuits

166.   Do not confuse a *farmer* with a *farm laborer*. If a person works on a farm for a stated wage (in money or its equivalent), even though he may be a son or other relative of the person who conducts the farm, he should be entered as a *farm laborer*, and not as a farmer. On the other hand, if a person owns or rents a farm, or operates it with or for another person, for a fixed share of the products, he should be entered as a *farmer*, and not as a farm laborer. Enter the older children of a farmer (who work on the farm) as farm laborers, except when a father and son (or sons) jointly operate the farm for fixed shares of the product.

167.   Do not confuse a *day laborer* at work for the city, town, or at odd jobs with a *farm laborer* at work on the farm or plantation or in the employ of gardeners, nurserymen, etc. Do not say simply "*laborer*," but state in every case the *kind* of work done as *day laborer, farm laborer, garden laborer*, etc. If a person is a *laborer* in a mill, workshop, or factory, specify the fact, in addition to the word laborer, as *laborer (cement works)*, etc.

168.   Distinguish between a *woodchopper* at work regularly in the woods or forests and an ordinary laborer who takes a job occasionally at chopping wood.

169.   Distinguish between a *farmer* or a *planter* who owns, hires, or carries on a farm or plantation, and a *gardener, fruit grower, nurseryman, florist, or vine grower*, etc., who is engaged in raising vegetables for market or in the cultivation of fruit, flowers, seeds, nursery products, etc.

170.   Avoid the confusion of the *garden laborer, nursery laborer*, etc., who hires out his services, with the proprietor gardener, florist, nurseryman, etc., who carries on the business himself or employs others to assist him.

171.   Return as a *dairyman* or *dairywoman* any person whose occupation in connection with the farm has to do chiefly with the dairy. Do not confuse such a person with an employee of a butter and cheese or condensed milk factory, who should be separately returned by some distinctive term.

172.   Return a *stock herder* or *stock drover* separately from a stock raiser.

173.   Do not include a *lumberman, raftsman, log driver*, etc., engaged in hauling or transporting lumber (generally by water) from the forest to the mill with an employee of a lumber yard or a lumber mill.

Fishing

174.   For a *fisherman* or *oysterman* describe the occupation as accurately as possible. Be careful to avoid the return of a fisherman on a vessel as a sailor. If he gains his living by fishing, he should be returned as a "fisherman," and not as a sailor.

Mining and Quarrying

175.   Make a careful distinction between a *coal miner* and a *miner of ores*; also between a miner and a *quarryman*. State the *kind* of ore mined or stone quarried.

176.   Do not return a *proprietor* or *official* of a mining or quarrying company as a miner or quarryman, but state his business or official position accurately.

Professional Pursuits

177.   Specify each profession in detail, according to the fact, as follows: *actor, artist or teacher of art, clergyman, dentist, designer, draftsman, engraver, civil engineer or surveyor, mechanical or mining engineer, government clerk or official, journalist, lawyer, librarian, musician or teacher of music, physician, surgeon, professor* (in college or university), *teacher* (in school), or other pursuits of a professional nature.

178.   Distinguish between an *actor*, a *theatrical manager*, and a *showman*.

179.   Return a *government official*, in the service of the national, state, county, city, or town government, by the title of his office, if that is the occupation upon which he depends chiefly for a livelihood; otherwise by his usual trade or profession.

180.   Distinguish between a *government clerk* occupying a position under the national, state, county, city, or town government and a clerk in an office, store, manufacturing establishment, etc.

181.   Return a *veterinary surgeon* separately from another surgeon.

182.   Distinguish a *journalist editor*, or *reporter* from an *author* or other literary person who does not follow journalism as a distinct profession.

183.   Return a *chemist, assayer, metallurgist*, or other scientific person by his distinctive title.

Domestic and Personal Service

184.   Specify each occupation or kind of service rendered in detail, according to the fact, as *hotel keeper, boarding-house keeper, restaurant keeper, saloon keeper*, or *bartender; housekeeper, cook*, or *servant* (in hotel, boarding-house, hospital, institution, private family, etc.); *barber* or *hairdresser; janitor*,

sexton, or *undertaker; nurse* or *midwife; watchman, policeman,* or *detective. The above are given only as examples of the occupations which would naturally be included under this general class of work.*

185. Return as a *housekeeper* a woman who receives a stated wage or salary for her services, and do not confuse her with a woman who keeps house for her own family or for herself, without any gainful occupation, or with a grown daughter who assists in the household duties without pay. A wife or daughter who simply keeps house for her own family should not be returned as a housekeeper in any case. (See paragraph 218.)

186. A *clerk* in a hotel, restaurant, or saloon should be so described and carefully distinguished from a bartender. In many instances a bartender will state his occupation as "clerk" in wine store, etc., but the character of the service rendered by such a person will readily determine whether he should be classed as a "bartender," or as a "clerk."

187. A *stationary engineer* or *fireman* should be carefully distinguished from a *locomotive engineer* or *fireman.*

188. A *soldier, sailor,* or marine enlisted in the service of the United States should be so returned. Distinguish between an officer and an enlisted man, and for a civilian employee state the kind of service performed by him.

Pursuits of Trade and Transportation

189. Distinguish carefully between a *real estate agent, insurance agent, claim agent,* or *commission agent,* etc.

190. If a person combines two or more of these occupations, as is often the case, return the occupation from which he derives the larger share of his income.

191. Return an accountant, bookkeeper, clerk, cashier, etc., according to his distinctive occupation, and state the kind of service rendered, as *accountant—insurance; bookkeeper—wholesale dry goods; clerk—gas company; cashier—music store.*

192. Do not confound a clerk with a salesman, as is often done, especially in dry goods stores, grocery stores, and provision stores. Generally speaking, a person so employed is to be considered as a salesman, unless most of his service is in the office on the books and accounts; otherwise he should be returned as *salesman—dry goods; salesman—groceries,* etc.

193. A *stenographer* or *typewriter* should be reported as such, and should not be described simply as a "clerk."

194. Distinguish carefully between a *bank clerk in bank, cashier in bank,* or *bank official,* describing the particular position filled in each case. In no case should a *bank cashier* be confounded with a cashier in a store, etc.

195. Distinguish between a foreman and overseer, a packer and shipper, a porter and helper, and an errand, office, and messenger boy in a store, etc., and state in each case the character of the duties performed by him, as *foreman—wholesale wool; packer—crockery; porter—rubber goods; errand boy—dry goods; messenger boy—telegraph.*

196. State the kind of merchant or dealer, as *dry goods merchant, wood and coal dealer,* etc. Whenever a single word will express the business carried on, as *grocer,* it should be used.

197. In the case of a *huckster* or *peddler* also state the kind of goods sold, as *peddler—tinware.*

198. Distinguish a traveling salesman from a salesman in a store, return the former as a "*commercial traveler,*" and state the kind of goods sold by him.

199. Return a *boarding* or *livery stable keeper* separately from a *hostler* or other stable employee.

200. Distinguish also between an *expressman, teamster, drayman,* and *carriage and hack driver.*

201. A steam railroad employee should be reported according to the nature of his work, as *baggageman, brakeman, conductor, railroad laborer, locomotive engineer, locomotive fireman, switchman, yardman,* etc.

202. An *official of a railroad, telegraph, express,* or *other company* should be returned by his title and carefully distinguished from an employee of such company.

203. Return a *boatman, canalman, pilot, longshoreman, stevedore,* or *sailor* (on a steam or sailing vessel) according to his distinctive occupation.

204. A *telegraph operator, telephone operator, telegraph lineman, telephone lineman, electric-light man,* etc., should be reported according to the nature of the work performed.

Manufacturing and Mechanical Pursuits

205. In reporting this class of occupations there are many difficulties in the way of showing the kind of work done rather than the article made or the place worked in. The nature of certain occupations is

such that it is well-nigh impossible to find properly descriptive terms without the use of some expression relating to the article made or place in which the work is carried on.

206. Do not accept "maker" of an article or "works in" mill, shop, or factory, but strive always to find out the particular work done.

207. Do not use the words "factory operative," but specify the kind of work done, as *cotton mill—spinner; silk mill—weaver*, etc.

208. Avoid in all cases the use of the word "mechanic," and state whether a *carpenter, mason, house painter, machinist, plumber*, etc.

209. Do not say "finisher," "molder," "polisher," etc., but describe the work done as *brass finisher, iron molder, steel polisher*, etc.

210. Distinguish between a person who tends machines and the unskilled workman or laborer in mills, factories, and workshops.

211. Describe the proprietor of the establishment as a "manufacturer," and specify the branch of manufacture, as *cotton manufacturer*, etc. In no case should a manufacturer be returned as a "maker" of any article.

212. In the case of an apprentice, state the trade to which apprenticed, as *Apprentice—carpenter*, etc.

213. Distinguish between a *butcher*, whose business is to slaughter cattle, swine, etc., and a *provision dealer*, who sells meats.

214. Distinguish also between a *glover, hatter*, or *furrier* who actually makes in his own establishment all or part of the gloves, hats, or furs which he sells, and a person who simply deals in but does not make these articles.

215. Do not describe a person in a printing office as a "printer" where a more expressive term can be used, as *compositer, pressman, press feeder*, etc.

216. Make the proper distinction between a *clock or watch* "maker" and a *clock or watch* "repairer." Do not apply the word "jeweler" to those who make watches, watch chains, or jewelry in large establishments.

217. Distinguish between a *cloakmaker, dressmaker, seamstress, tailoress*, etc. In the case of a sewing-machine operator, specify the kind of work done.

Nongainful Pursuits

218. If a person is attending school write "at school." No entry in column 19 should be made, however, for a lawyer, merchant, manufacturer, etc., who has retired from practice or business; nor for a wife or daughter living at home and assisting only in the household duties without pay (see paragraph 185); nor for a person too old to work, or a child under 10 years of age not at school.

219. The doing of domestic errands or family chores out of school hours, where a child regularly attends school, is not an occupation. But if a boy or girl, above 10 years of age, is earning money regularly by labor, contributing to the family support, or appreciably assisting in mechanical or agricultural industry, the kind of work performed should be stated. (See paragraph 162.)

220. In the case of an inmate of an institution or home, such as a hospital, asylum, home for the aged, soldiers' home, penitentiary, jail, etc., no entry is required in column 19 unless the inmate is actually engaged in remunerative work for which he receives a stated wage in addition to his board. The occupation of an officer or regular employee of such institution or home, however, is to be entered in this column, the same as for all other persons having a gainful occupation.

221. Column 20.—Months not employed. The object of this question is to get the number of months (or parts of months) in the census year (June 1, 1899, to May 31, 1900) during which each person having a gainful occupation was not employed. For those who have no gainful occupation, leave the column blank.

222. The law does not contemplate that this question shall apply solely to the principal occupation in which the person may have been engaged during the year, but it is the intent to find out the number of months (or parts of months) during which a person ordinarily engaged in gainful labor was not employed at all.

223. A return is required in columns 19 and 20 for each and every person 10 years of age and over who was engaged in gainful labor during any part of the census year (June 1, 1899, to May 31, 1900, inclusive), or who is ordinarily occupied in remunerative work but during the census year was unable to secure work of any kind. In the latter case enter his customary occupation, as carpenter, bricklayer, etc., in column 19 and the figure "12" in column 20 to show that, although he had an occupation or trade, he was not employed at all during the year at that or any other kind of work.

EDUCATION

224. Column 21.—Attended school (in months). For all persons attending school during the year ending June 1, 1900, enter the number of months (or parts

of months) of school attendance, as 9, 8 , etc. If a person of school age did not attend school at all during the year, write "0." For all other persons to whom the inquiry is not applicable, leave the column blank.

225. Column 22.   Can read.—Write "*Yes*" for all persons 10 years of age and over who can read any language, and "*No*" for all other person of that age who can not read in any language. For persons under 10 years, leave the column blank.

226. Column 23. Can write.—Write "*Yes*" for all persons 10 years of age and over who can write any language, and "*No*" for all other person of that age who can not write in any language. For persons under 10 years, leave the column blank.

227. The inquiries in columns 22 and 23 are intended to show the literacy of all persons 10 years of age and over, and should be answered according as they are able to read or write the language ordinarily spoken by them.

228. Column 24. Can speak English.—Write "*Yes*" for all persons 10 years of age and over who can speak English, and "*No*" for all other persons of that age who can not speak English. For persons under 10 years, leave the column blank.

OWNERSHIP OF HOME

229. Fill columns 25, 26, and 27 for each head of family only; for every other person, leave the columns blank.

230. Column 25.—If the home is owned, write "O." If it is rented, write "R."

231. Column 26.—If the home is rented, leave the column blank. If it is owned and mortgaged, write "M." If it is owned free from mortgage encumbrance, write "F."

232. Column 27.—If the home is a farm, write "F." If it is only a house, write "H."

233. Column 28.—If the home is only a house, leave the column blank. If the home is a farm, write the number of its farm schedule; that is, the farm number as reported on Schedule No. 2, relating to agriculture. *Enter the number of each farm schedule on the line for the member of the family by whom the farm is operated.* (See paragraph 246.)

234. Definition of home.   By the word "home" in the census is meant any place of abode inhabited by any person or persons, whether it is a house, a tent, a boat, or whatever it may be. If any such place of abode is inhabited by more than one family, it is the home of each of them, and it may accordingly be counted as two or more homes instead of one. The family is the basis for all inquiries in columns 25, 26, and 27.

235. A home occupied by a family engaged in farming, gardening, or any other form of agricultural production includes the land cultivated. If occupied by a family not so engaged, it includes only the dwelling and the ground occupied by it, with the appurtenances thereto.

236. In case a family resides in a tent or boat, write in column 27 the word "tent" or "boat."

237. If a family cultivates a farm, but resides in a house detached from the farm, in a village or elsewhere, the farm and the house must jointly be considered the family home and that home a farm, unless the chief occupation of the person operating the farm is something other than farming. In the latter case, the house alone is to be regarded as the home.

238. Owned or rented.—A home is to be classed as "owned" whenever the title, in whole or in part, is vested in any member of the family (not a boarder) by which the house is occupied. It is owned if any member of the family has a life interest or estate in it; or if it is occupied by a settler on the public domain who has not "proved up;" or if it is held under a contract or bond for a deed, or occupied for redemption purposes after having been sold for debt. It is not necessary that full payment for the property should have been made. All homes not owned as herein explained are to be classed as "rented."

239. In case of a farm part of which is owned and part rented; or in case different members of the same family operate different farms, of which one is owned and the other rented; or in case of the cultivation of a farm by a family which does not reside upon the farm, but elsewhere, the dwelling being owned and the farm rented, or, on the contrary, the farm being owned and the dwelling rented, the principle applies that "part ownership is ownership." In all these and similar cases write in column 25 the letter "O."

240. Following the same general rule, if a family occupies a house upon leased land for which "ground rent" is paid, and the building is owned by any member of the family (not boarder), write "O." Ownership of the building and not the ground, or of the ground and not the building, but the occupant, is part ownership.

241. If, of two families occupying the same house, one has an interest in it, and the other not, the home occupied by the former is to be returned as "owned" but that occupied by the other as "rented."

242. **Free or mortgaged.**—The question in column 26 applies only to homes which are owned (in whole or in part, as explained above). Its aim is to ascertain whether the home, or so much of the home as is owned by the occupant, has been fully paid for and is without encumbrance of any sort, either in the form of a mortgage or otherwise. This question has no relation to rented property.

243. All homes which are not fully paid for, or upon which there is any encumbrance in the form either of a mortgage or of a lien upon which judgment has been had in a court, are to be reported as mortgaged, but not others.

244. Liabilities or encumbrances of any sort which attach to land occupied in connection with a home, but not owned by the family, are not to be regarded as mortgages upon the home. For instance, if, as mentioned in paragraphs 239 and 240, in the case of a farm partly owned and partly rented, or in that of two farms, one of which is owned and the other rented, or in that of a house erected by the occupant upon ground owned by another person, there is a mortgage upon the leased land, but not upon the farm or portion of a farm or dwelling owned by the occupant, the house is to be returned as free from mortgage.

245. **Farm or house.**—The letter "F" in column 27 means that some member of the family operates a farm, which should be separately reported on the agricultural schedule, and its number in the order of visitation entered in column 28. In all other cases enter in column 27 the letter "H." Usually a farmer resides upon his farm, and persons who reside on farms are farmers. If, however, a family resides upon a farm, but no member of the family operates it, write "H." On the other hand, if a farm is operated by any person who does not reside upon it, but off the farm, in a village, or elsewhere, enter against the name of the head of the family of which such person is a member the letter "F."

246. **Farm number.**—The serial number of each farm reported, in the order of visitation, is to be entered in column 28, precisely as the numbers of houses and families enumerated are entered in columns 1 and 2. This number should, in every instance, be the same as the number in the heading of the corresponding farm schedule. (See paragraphs 233.)

1900 QUESTIONNAIRE—INDIAN POPULATION

(19 1/2" X 18 3/4", printed on two sides, space for 20 entries on each side, reverse side contained continuation of instructions. The top of the questionnaire contained questions 1-28 which were identical with those on the general schedule)

The 1900 Indian schedule collected the following information in addition to that of the general population schedule: Other name, if any; name of Indian tribe; tribal affiliation of mother and father; whether of full or mixed blood; whether living in polygamy; whether taxed; year of acquiring citizenship and whether acquired by allotment; whether living in a fixed or moveable dwelling.

Instructions for Enumerators

This modified form of Schedule No. 1 is to be used in making the enumeration of Indians, both those on reservations and those living in family groups outside of reservations.

Detached Indians living either in white or negro families outside of reservations should be enumerated on the general population schedule (Form 7-224) as members of the family in which they are found; but detached whites or negroes living in Indian families should be enumerated on this schedule as members of the Indian families in which they are found. In other words, every family composed mainly of Indians should be reported entirely on this schedule, and every family composed mainly of persons not Indian should be reported entirely on the general population schedule.

This schedule contains on each side twenty horizontal lines, each running twice across the page, and it is consequently possible to enumerate on it only forty persons (twenty persons on the A side and twenty persons on the B side). Each Indian should be carried through from the beginning to the end of the line on which he is entered, as line 1, line 2, etc., and each inquiry from column 1 to column 38 which applies to the individual case should be answered.

COLUMNS 1 to 28.—These columns are identical with those on the general population schedule. Fill each column, so far as the inquiry applies, in accordance with the instructions for filling the corresponding columns in the general population schedule, but note the following additional instructions in relation to filling columns 1, 2, and 19.

COLUMNS 1 and 2.—If you are canvassing a given territory with both the general population schedule (Form 7-224) and this schedule for Indian population, make two independent series of numbers for these columns, one series in each kind of schedule, so that the last numbers on the two schedules when added together will correctly give the whole number of dwellings and of families visited and enumerated in your entire district.

COLUMN 19.—If the Indian has no occupation and is wholly dependent on the Government for support, write "Ration Indian." If he is partly self-supporting and partly dependent on the Government, write the occupation and then the letter "R" (for ration). If the Indian is under ten years of age and receives rations, write "Under age R."

INSTRUCTION CONTINUED ON "B" SIDE OF SHEET (INSTRUCTIONS FOR FILLING THIS SCHEDULE)

The following instructions apply to columns 29 to 38:

Column 29.—Write the Indian name, if the person has one, in addition to the English name given in column 3. If the Indian has only one name, Indian or English, repeat the name in this column.

Column 30, 31, and 32.—If the Indian was born in this country answers should be obtained, if possible, to inquiries 13, 14, and 15, relating to the state of birth of the person and of his or her parents. In any event secure the name of the tribe with which the person is connected and the name of the tribe of his or her parents, and enter the same in columns 30, 31, and 32.

Column 33.—If the Indian has no white blood, write 0. If he or she has white blood, write 1/2, 1/4, 1/8, whichever fraction is nearest the truth.

Column 34.—If the Indian man is living with more than one wife, or if the Indian woman is a plural wife or has more than one husband, write "Yes." If not, write "No." If the Indian is single, leave the column blank.

Citizenship.—If the Indian was born in this country, no entry can be made in columns 16, 17, or 18; but for columns 35, 36, and 37 answers must be obtained. If the Indian was born in another country, answers will be made both in columns 16, 17, and 18, and in columns 35, 36, and 37, in accordance with the facts.

Column 35.—An Indian is to be considered "taxed" if he or she is detached from his or her tribe and living among white people as an individual, and as such subject to taxation, whether he or she actually pays taxes or not; also if he or she is living with his or her tribe but has received an allotment of land, and thereby has acquired citizenship; in either of these two cases the answer to this inquiry is "Yes."

An Indian on a reservation, without an allotment, or roaming over unsettled territory, is considered "not taxed," and for such Indians the answer to this inquiry is "No."

Column 36.—If the Indian was born in tribal relations, but has acquired American citizenship, write the year in which it was acquired. If he or she has not acquired citizenship, leave the column blank.

Column 37.—If the Indian acquired citizenship by receiving an allotment of land from the Government, write "Yes." If he or she acquired citizenship by other means, write "No." If he or she has not acquired American citizenship, leave the column blank.

Column 38.—If the Indian is living in a tent, tepee, or other temporary structure, write "movable." If he or she is living in a permanent dwelling of any kind, write "fixed."

1910 QUESTIONNAIRE—GENERAL POPULATION

(23" X 16", printed on two sides, space for 50 entries on each side, reverse side identical except for line numbers). After the schedules were printed, a question was added concerning the "mother tongue" of the foreign born. The responses were to be entered, as appropriate, in columns 12, 13, and 14. See instructions under "Nativity and Mother Tongue."

LOCATION.				NAME	RELATION.	PERSONAL DESCRIPTION.						
Street, avenue, road, etc.	House number (in cities or towns).	Number of dwelling house in order of visitation.	Number of family in order of visitation.	of each person whose place of abode on April 15, 1910, was in this family. Enter surname first, then the given name and middle initial, if any. Include every person living on April 15, 1910. Omit children born since April 15, 1910.	Relationship of this person to the head of the family.	Sex.	Color or race.	Age at last birthday.	Whether single, married, widowed, or divorced.	Number of years of present marriage.	Mother of how many children.	
											Number born.	Number now living.
	1	2		3	4	5	6	7	8	9	10	11
1												
2												
3												

NATIVITY.			CITIZENSHIP.		
Place of birth of each person and parents of each person enumerated. If born in the United States, give the state or territory. If of foreign birth, give the country.			Year of immigration to the United States.	Whether naturalized or alien.	Whether able to speak English; or, if not, give language spoken.
Place of birth of this Person.	Place of birth of Father of this person.	Place of birth of Mother of this person.			
12	13	14	15	16	17

OCCUPATION.					EDUCATION.			OWNERSHIP OF HOME.				Whether a survivor of the Union or Confederate Army or Navy.	Whether blind (both eyes).	Whether deaf and dumb.	
Trade or profession of, or particular kind of work done by this person, as spinner, salesman, laborer, etc.	General nature of industry, business, or establishment in which this person works, as cotton mill, dry goods store, farm, etc.	Whether an employer, employee, or working on own account.	If an employee—		Whether able to read.	Whether able to write.	Attended school any time since September 1, 1909.	Owned or rented.	Owned free or mortgaged.	Farm or house.	Number of farm schedule.				
			Whether out of work on April 15, 1910.	Number of weeks out of work during year 1909.											
18	19	20	21	22	23	24	25	26	27	28	29	30	31	32	
															1
															2
															3

	Tribe of this Indian.	Tribe of Father of this Indian.	Tribe of Mother of this Indian.	PROPORTIONS OF INDIAN AND OTHER BLOOD.			Number of times married.	Whether now living in polygamy.	If living in polygamy, whether the wives are sisters.
				Indian.	White.	Negro.			
	33	34	35	36	37	38	39	40	41
1									
2									
3									

GRADUATED FROM WHAT EDUCATIONAL INSTITUTION.	Is this Indian taxed?	If Indian has received allotment, give year of allotment.	RESIDENCE AND DWELLING.	
			Residing on his own lands.	Living in civilized or aboriginal dwelling.
42	43	44	45	46

Instructions to Enumerators

92. Column 1.—Number of dwelling house in order of visitation. In this column the first dwelling house you visit should be numbered as "1," the second as "2," and so on until the enumeration of your district is completed. The number should always be *entered opposite the name of the first person enumerated in each dwelling house,* and should not be repeated for other persons or other families living in the same house.

93. Dwelling house defined.—A dwelling house, for census purposes, is a place in which, at the time of the census, one or more persons regularly sleep. It need not be a house in the usual sense of the word, but may be a room in a factory, store, or office building, a loft over a stable, a boat, a tent, a freight car, or the like. A building like a tenement or apartment house counts as only one dwelling house, no matter how many persons or families live in it. A building with a partition wall through it and a front door for each of the two parts, however, counts as two dwelling houses. But a two-apartment house with one apartment over the other and a separate front door for each apartment counts as only one dwelling house.

94. Column 2. Number of family in order of visitation.—In this column number the families in your district in the order in which they are enumerated, entering the number *opposite the name of the head of EACH family.* Thus the first family you visit should be numbered as "1," the second as "2," and so on, until the enumeration of your district is completed.

95. Family defined.—The word "family," for census purposes, has a somewhat different application from what it has in popular usage. It means a *group of persons living together in the same dwelling place.* The persons constituting this group may or may not be related by ties of kinship, but if they live together forming one household they should be considered as one family. Thus a servant who sleeps in the house or on the premises should be included with the members of the family for which he or she works. Again, a boarder or lodger should be included with the members of the family with which he lodges; but a person who boards in one place and lodges or rooms at another should be returned as a member of the family at the place where he lodges or rooms.

96. It should be noted, however, that two or more families may occupy the same dwelling house without *living together.* If they occupy separate portions of the dwelling house and their housekeeping is entirely separate, they should be returned as separate families.

97. Boarding-house families.—All the occupants and employees of a hotel, boarding house, or lodging house, if that is their usual place of abode, make up, for census purposes, a single family. But in an apartment or tenement house, there will usually be as many families as there are separate occupied apartments or tenements, even though use may be made of a common cafe or restaurant.

98. Institutional families.—The officials and inmates of an institution who live in the institution building or group of buildings form one family. But any officers or employees who sleep in detached houses or separate dwelling places containing no inmates should be returned as separate families.

99. Persons living alone.—The census family may likewise consist of a single person. Thus a clerk in a store who regularly sleeps there is to be returned as a family and the store as his dwelling place.

NAME AND RELATION

100. Column 3. Name of each person enumerated.—Enter the name of every person whose usual place of abode on April 15, 1910, waswith the family or in the dwelling place for which the enumeration is being made. In determining who is to be included with the family, follow instructions in paragraphs 95 to 99.

101. Order of entering names.—Enter the member of each family in the following order, namely: Head first, wife second, then children (whether sons or daughters) in the order of their ages, and lastly, all other persons living with the family, whether relatives, boarders, lodgers, or servants.

102. How names are to be written.—Enter first the last name or surname, then the given name in full, and the initial of the middle name, if any. Where the surname is the same as that of the person in the preceding line do not repeat the name, but draw a horizontal line (_____) under the name above.

103. Column 4. Relationship to head of family.—Designate the head of the family, whether husband or father, widow, or unmarried person of either sex, by the word "*Head;*" for other members of a family write *wife, father, mother, son, daughter, grandson, daughter-in-law, uncle, aunt, nephew, niece, boarder, lodger, servant,* etc., according to the particular relationship which the person bears to the head of the family.

104. Occupants of an institution or school, living under a common roof, should be designated as *officer, inmate, pupil, patient, prisoner,* etc.; and in the case of the *chief* officer his title should be used, as *warden, principal, superintendent,* etc., instead of the word "Head."

105. If two or more persons share a common abode as partners, write *head* for one and *partner* for the other or others.

106. In the case of a hotel or boarding or lodging house family (see paragraph 97), the *head* of the family is the manager or the person who keeps the hotel or boarding or lodging house.

PERSONAL DESCRIPTION

107. Column 5. Sex.—Write "M" for male and "F" for female.

108. Column 6. Color or race.—Write "W" for white; "B" for black; "Mu" for mulatto; "Ch" for Chinese; "Jp" for Japanese; "In" for Indian. For all persons not falling within one of these classes, write "Ot" (for other), and write on the left-hand margin of the schedule the race of the person so indicated.

109. For census purposes, the term "black" (B) includes all persons who are evidently fullblooded negroes, while the term "mulatto" (Mu) includes all other persons having some proportion or perceptible trace of negro blood.

110. Column 7. Age at last birthday.—This question calls for the age in completed years at last birthday. Remember, however, that the age question, like all other questions on the schedule, relates to April 15, 1910. Thus a person whose exact age on April 15, the census day, is 17 years, 11 months, and 25 days should be returned simply as 17, because that is his age at last birthday prior to April 15, although at the time of your visit he may have completed 18 years.

111. Age in round numbers.—In many cases persons will report the age in round numbers, like 30 or 45, or "about 30" or "about 45," when that is not the exact age. Therefore, when an age ending in 0 or 5 is reported, you should ascertain whether it is the exact age. If, however, it is impossible to get the exact age, enter the approximate age rather than return the age as unknown.

112. Ages of children.—Take particular pains to get the exact ages of children. In the case of a child not 2 years old, the age should be given in *completed months,* expressed as twelfths of a year. Thus the age of a child 3 months old should be entered as 3/12, a child 7 months old as 7/12, a child 1 year and 3 months old as 1 3/12, etc. If a child is not yet a month old, enter the age as 0/12. But note again that this question should be answered with reference to April 15. For instance, a child who is just a year old on the 17th of April, 1910, should nevertheless be returned as 11/12, because that is its age in completed months on April 15.

113. Column 8. Whether single, married, widowed, or divorced. Write "S" for single or unmarried persons; "Wd" for widowed (man or woman); "D" for divorced; for married persons, inquire whether they have been married before, and if this is the first marriage, write "M1," but if this is the second or subsequent marriage, write "M2" (meaning married more than once).

114. Persons who were single on April 15 should be so reported, even though they may have married between that date and the day of your visit; and, similarly, persons who become widowed or divorced after April 15 should be returned as married if that was their condition on that date.

115. Column 9. Number of years of present marriage.—This question applies only to persons reported as married, and the answer should give the number of years married to the present husband or wife. Thus a woman who may have been married for 10 years to a former husband, but has been married only 3 years to her present husband, should be returned as married 3 years. For instance, a person who on April 15, the census day, has been married 3 years and 11 months should be returned as married 3 years. For a person married less than 1 year, write "0" (meaning less than 1 year).

116. Column 10. Number of children born.—This question applies to women who are now married, or who are widowed, or divorced. The answer should give the total number of children that each such woman has had during her lifetime. It should include, therefore, the children by any former marriage as well as by her present marriage. It should not include the children which her present husband may have had by a former wife, even though they are members of her present family. Stillborn children should not be included. If the woman has never had any children, write "0" in this column and also in column 11.

117. Column 11. Number of children now living.—This refers again only to the children which the woman herself has had. Include all of these children that are living, no matter whether they are living in your district or somewhere else. If all the children are dead, write "0."

NATIVITY AND MOTHER TONGUE

118. Column 12. Place of birth of this person. If the person was born in the United States, give the state or territory (not county, city, or town) in which born. The words "United States" are not sufficiently definite. A person born in what is now West Virginia, North Dakota, South Dakota, or Oklahoma

should be reported as so born, although at the time of his birth the particular region may have had a different name. Do not abbreviate the names of states and territories.

119. If the person was born outside the United States, enter the country (not city or district) in which born.

120. Instead of Great Britain, write *Ireland, England, Scotland,* or *Wales.*

121. For persons born in the double Kingdom of Austria-Hungary, be sure to distinguish Austria from Hungary. For person born in Finland, write *Finland* and not "Russia." For persons born in Turkey, be sure to distinguish *Turkey in Europe* from *Turkey in Asia.*

122. Do not rely upon the language spoken to determine birthplace. This is especially true of Germans, for over one-third of the Austrians and nearly three-fourths of the Swiss speak German. In the case of persons speaking German, therefore, inquire carefully whether the birthplace was *Germany, Switzerland, Austria,* or elsewhere.

123. If the person was born abroad, but of American parents, write in column 12 both the birthplace and *Am. cit.*— that is, American citizen. If the person was born at sea, write *At sea.*

124. Mother tongue.—The question "What is your mother tongue or native language?" should be asked of all persons who were born in any foreign country, and the answer should be written in column 12, after the name of the country of birth. In order to save space, the abbreviations (indicated on separate "List of foreign countries") should be used for the country of birth, but the *language given as the mother tongue should be written out in full.* In returning the mother tongue observe the rules laid down in paragraphs 134 to 143.

125. For example, if a person reports that he was born in Russia and that his mother tongue is Lithuanian, write in column 12 *Russ.—Lithuanian;* or if a person reports that he was born in Switzerland and that his mother tongue is German, write *Switz.—German.*

126. Note that the name of the mother tongue must be given even when it is the same as the language of the country in which the person was born. Thus, if a person reports that he was born in England and that his mother tongue is English, write *Eng.—English;* or if a person reports that he was born in Germany and that his mother tongue is German, write *Ger.—German.* This is necessary to distinguish such persons from others born in the same country but having a different mother tongue.

127. The question of mother tongue should not be asked of any person born in the United States.

128. Columns 13 and 14. Place of birth of father and mother.—Enter in columns 13 and 14 the birthplace of the father and of the mother of the person whose own birthplace was entered in column 12. In designating the birthplace of the father and mother, follow the same instructions as for the person himself. In case, however, a person does not know the state or territory of birth of his father or mother but knows that he or she was born in the United States, write United States rather than "unknown."

129. Mother tongue of father and mother. Ask for the mother tongue of any parent born abroad and write down the answer in columns 13 and 14, following the instructions given for reporting the mother tongue of persons enumerated in column 12.

130. In short, *whenever a person gives a foreign country as a birthplace of himself or either of his parents, before writing down that country ask for the mother tongue and write the answer to both questions in columns 12, 13, or 14, as the case may be,* in the manner herein indicated.

CITIZENSHIP

131. Column 15. Year of immigration to the United States.—This question applies to all foreign-born persons, male and female, of whatever age. It should be answered, therefore, for every person whose birthplace as reported in column 12 was in a foreign country. Enter the year in which the person came to the United States. If he has been in the United States more than once, give the year of his first arrival.

132. Column 16. Whether naturalized or alien.—This question applies only to foreign-born males 21 years of age and over. It does not apply to females, to foreign-born minors, or to any male born in the United States. If the person was born abroad, but has become a full citizen, either by taking out a second or final papers of naturalization or through the naturalization of his parents while he was under the age of 21 years, write "Na" (for naturalized). If he has declared his intention to become an American citizen and has taken out his "first papers," write "Pa" (for papers). If he has taken no steps toward becoming an American citizen, write "Al" (for alien).

ABILITY TO SPEAK ENGLISH

133. Column 17. Whether able to speak English; or, if not, give language spoken.—This question applies to all persons 10 years of age and over. If such a person is able to speak English, write *English.* If he is not able to speak English—and in such cases only—write the name of the language which he does speak, as *French, German, Italian.* If he speaks

more than one language, but does not speak English, write the name of that language which is his native language or mother tongue. For persons under 10 years of age, leave the column blank.

134. The following is a list of principal foreign languages spoken in the United States. Avoid giving other names when one in this list can be applied to the language spoken. With the exception of certain languages of eastern Russia, the list gives a name for every European language in the proper sense of the word.

Albanian	Italian	Scotch
Armenian	Japanese	Servian or
Basque	Lappish	Croatian
Bohemian	Lettish	(including
		Bosnian,
		Dalmatian,
		Herze-
		govinian,
		and
		Montene-
		grin)
Breton	Little Russian	Slovak
Bulgarian	Lithuanian	Slovenian
Chinese	Magyar	Spanish
Danish	Moravian	Swedish
Dutch	Norwegian	Syrian
Finnish	Polish	Turkish
Flemish	Portuguese	Welsh
French	Rhaeto-Romanish (including including Ladin and Frilulan)	Wendish
Greek	Roumanian	Yiddish
Gypsy	Russian	
Irish	Ruthenian	

135. Do not write "Austrian," but write *German, Bohemian, Ruthenian, Roumanian, Slovenian, Slovak,* or such other term as correctly defines the language spoken.

136. Do not write "Slavic" or "Slavonian," but write *Slovak, Slovenian, Russian,* etc., as the case may be.

137. Do not write "Macedonian," but write *Bulgarian, Turkish, Greek, Servian,* or *Roumanian,* as the case may be.

138. Do not write "Czech," but write *Bohemian, Moravian,* or *Slovak,* as the case may be.

139. Write *Magyar* instead of "Hungarian."

140. Write *Croatian* instead of "Hervat."

141. Write *Little Russian* instead of "Ukrainian."

142. Write *Ruthenian* instead of "Rosniak" or "Russine."

143. Write *Roumanian* instead of "Moldavian," "Wallachian," "Tsintsar," or "Kutzo-Vlach."

OCCUPATION

144. Column 18. Trade or profession.—An entry should be made in this column for every person enumerated. The occupation, if any, followed by a child, of any age, or by a woman is just as important, for census purposes, as the occupation followed by a man. Therefore it must never be taken for granted, without inquiry, that a woman, or child, has no occupation.

145. The entry in column 18 should be either (1) the occupation pursued—that is, the word or words which most accurately indicate the particular kind of work done by which the person enumerated earns money or a money equivalent, as *physician, carpenter, dressmaker, night watchman, laborer, newsboy;* or (2) *own income;* or (3) *none* (that is, no occupation).

146. The entry *own income* should be made in the case of all persons who follow no specific occupations but have an independent income upon which they are living.

147. The entry *none* should be made in the case of all persons who follow no occupation and who do not fall within the class to be reported as *own income.*

148. Persons retired or temporarily unemployed.—Care should be taken in making the return for persons who on account of old age, permanent invalidism, or otherwise are no longer following an occupation. Such persons may desire to return the occupations formerly followed, which would be incorrect. If living on their own income the return should be *own income.* If they are supported by other persons or institutions, the return should be *none.* On the other hand, persons out of employment when visited by the enumerator may state that they have no occupation, when the fact is that they usually have an occupation but merely happen to be idle or unemployed at the time of the visit. In such cases the return should be the occupation followed when the person is employed.

149. Persons having two occupations.*If a person has two occupations, return only the more important one that is, the one from which he gets the more money. If you can not learn that, return the one at which he spends the more time. For example: Return a man*

as farmer if he gets most of his income from farming, although he may also follow the occupation of a clergyman or preacher; but return him as a *clergyman* if he gets more of his income from that occupation.

150. Column 19. Industry.—An entry should be made in this column in all cases where the entry in column 18 has been that of an occupation. But where the entry in column 18 is own income or none, leave this column blank. The entry, when made, should consist of the word or words which most accurately describe the branch of industry, kind of business or establishment, line of work, or place in which this person works, as *cotton mill, general farm, dry-goods store, insurance office, bank.*

151. The purpose of columns 18 and 19 is thus to bring out, on the one hand, in column 18, the specific occupation or work performed, if any, by each person enumerated, and on the other, in column 19, the character of the industry or place in which such work is performed.

152. Farm workers.   Return a person in charge of a farm as a *farmer*, whether he owns it or operates it as a tenant, renter, or cropper; but a person who manages a farm for some one else for wages or a salary should be reported as a farm manager or farm overseer; and a person who works on a farm for some one else, but not as a manager, tenant, or cropper, should be reported as a farm laborer.

153. Women doing housework.—In the case of a woman doing housework in her own home, without salary or wages, and having no other employment, the entry in column 18 should be none. But a woman working at *housework for wages* should be returned in column 18 as *housekeeper, servant, cook,* or *chambermaid*, as the case may be; and the entry in column 19 should state the kind of place where she works, as *private family, hotel,* or *boarding house.* Or, if a woman, in addition to doing housework in her own home, *regularly* earns money by some other occupation, whether pursued in her own home or outside, that occupation should be returned in columns 18 and 19. For instance, a woman who regularly takes in washing should be reported as *laundress* or *washerwoman*, followed in column 19 by *at home.*

154. Women doing farm work.—A woman working regularly at outdoor farm work, even though she works on the home farm for her husband, son, or other relative and does not receive money wages, should be returned in column 18 as a *farm laborer.* Distinguish, however, such women who work on the home farm from those who work away from home,

by writing in column 19 either *home farm* or *working out*, as the case may require. Of course, a woman who herself operates or runs a farm should be reported as a *farmer*, and not as a "farm laborer."

155. Children on farms.—In the case of children who work for their own parents on a farm, the entry in column 18 should be *farm laborer* and in column 19 *home farm;* but for children who work as farm laborers for others, the entry in column 19 should be *working out.*

156. Children working for parents.—Children who work for their parents at home merely on general household work, on chores, or at odd times on other work, should be reported as having no occupation. Those, however, who materially assist their parents in the performance of work other than household work should be reported as having an occupation.

157. Keeping boarders.—Keeping boarders or lodgers should be returned as an occupation if the person engaged in it relies upon it as his (or her) principal means of support or principal source of income. In that case the return should be keeper—*boarding house* or keeper—*lodging house.* If, however, a family keeps a few boarders or roomers merely as a means of supplementing or eking out the earnings or income obtained from other occupations or from other sources, no one in the family should be returned as a boarding or lodging house keeper.

158. Officers, employees, and inmates of institutions or homes.—For an *officer* or *regular employee* of an institution or home, such as an asylum, penitentiary, jail, reform school, convict camp, state farm worked by convicts, etc., return the occupation followed in the institution. For an *inmate* of such institution, if regularly employed, return the occupation pursued in the institution, whether the employment be at productive labor or at other duties, such as cooking, scrubbing, laundry work, etc.; but if an inmate is not regularly employed—that is, has not specific duties or work to perform, write *none* in column 18.

159. Avoid general or indefinite terms.—Give the occupation and industry precisely. For example, return a worker in a coal mine as a miner—*coal mine, laborer—coal mine, driver—coal mine*, etc., as the case may be.

160. The term "laborer" should be avoided if any more precise definition of the occupation can be secured. Employees in factories and mills, for example, usually have some definite designation, as *weaver, roller, puddler,* etc. Where the term "laborer" is used, be careful to define accurately the industry in column 19.

161. Avoid in all cases the use of the word "mechanic," but give the exact occupation, as *carpenter, painter, machinist*, etc.

162. Distinguish carefully the different kinds of "agents" by stating in column 19 the line of business followed.

163. Distinguish carefully between retail and wholesale merchants, as *retail merchant—dry-goods; wholesale merchant—dry-goods.*

164. Avoid the use of the word "clerk" wherever a more definite occupation can be named. Thus a person in a store, often called a clerk, who is wholly or principally engaged in selling goods should be called a *salesman. A stenographer, typewriter, accountant, bookkeeper,* or *cashier,* etc., should be reported as such, and not as a clerk.

165. Distinguish a traveling salesman from a salesman in a store; the former preferably should be reported as a *commercial traveler.*

166. If any person in answer to the occupation question says that he is "in business," you must find out what branch of business and what kind of work he does or what position he holds.

167. Illustrations of occupations.—The following examples, in addition to the occupations given in the illustrative schedule, will illustrate the method of returning some of the common occupations and industries; they will also suggest to you distinctions which you should make in other cases:

Column 18	Column 19	Column 18	Column 19
farm laborer	working out	commercial traveler	dry goods
farm laborer	home farm	salesman	department store
laborer	odd jobs	bookkeeper	department store
laborer	street work	cash girl	department store
laborer	garden	cashier	department store
laborer	nursery	cashier	bank
laborer	railroad	conductor	steam railroad
brakeman	railroad	conductor	street car
weaver	cotton mill	farmer	general farm
laborer	cotton mill	farmer	truck farm
doffer	cotton mill	gardener	private estates
engineer	locomotive	lawyer	general practice
engineer	lumber mill	manager	general farm
fireman	lumber mill	overseer	truck farm
fireman	fire department	president	life insurance co.
civil engineer	general practice	president	bank
electrical engineer	street railway	superintendent steel works	
carpenter	car factory	foreman	cotton mill
carpenter	ship yard	newsboy	street
carpenter	house	newsdealer	store
blacksmith	carriage factory	wagon driver	groceries
blacksmith	own shop	wagon driver	express
agent	real estate	chauffeur	express wagon
agent	insurance	chauffeur	private family
cook	hotel	miner	coal miner
servant	private family	laborer	coal mine
retail merchant	groceries	quarryman	marble
wholesale merchant	leather	janitor	house

EMPLOYER, EMPLOYEE, OR WORKING ON OWN ACCOUNT

168. Column 20. Whether employer, employee, or working on own account. For one employing persons, other than domestic servants, in transacting his own business, write "Emp" (for employer). For a person who works for wages or a salary, write "W" (for wage-earner). For a gainful worker who is neither an employer nor an employee, write "OA" (for own account). For all persons returned as having no occupation, leave the column blank.

169. Employer. An employer is one who employs helpers, other than domestic servants, in transacting his *own* business. The term *employer* does not include the superintendent, agent, manager, or other person *employed* to manage an establishment or business; and it does not include the foreman of a room, the boss of a gang, or the coal miner who hires his helper. All such should be returned as employees, for, while any one of these may employ persons, none of them does so in transacting his *own* business. Thus no individual working for a corporation either as an officer or otherwise should be returned as an employer.

170. A person employing domestic servants in his own home but not employing any helpers in his business *should not be* returned as an employer. But, on the other hand, a person who is the proprietor of a hotel or boarding or lodging house and employs servants in running that hotel or boarding or lodging house *should be* returned as an employer, because he employs these servants in his business.

171. Employee.—Any person who works for wages or a salary and is subject to the control and direction of an employer, is an employee, whether he be president of a large corporation or only a day laborer, whether he be paid in money or in kind, and whether he be employed by his own parent or by another. The term *employee* does not include lawyers, doctors, and others who render professional services for fees,

and who, in their work, are not subject to the control and direction of those whom they serve. It does include actors, professors, and others who are engaged to render professional services for wages or salaries. A domestic servant should always be returned as an employee even though, as previously explained, the person employing a domestic servant is not always returned as an employer.

172. Working on own account.—Persons who have a gainful occupation and are neither employers nor employees are considered to be working on their own account. They are the independent workers. They neither pay nor receive salaries or regular wages. Examples of this class are: Farmers and the owners of small establishments who do not employ helpers; professional men who work for *fees* and employ no helpers; and, generally speaking, hucksters, peddlers, newsboys, boot-blacks, etc., although it not infrequently happens that persons in these pursuits are employed by others and are working for wages, and in such case should, of course, be returned as employees.

173. Illustrative examples.—In many occupations a man may be either an employer, or an employee, or working on own account. For example, a physician is working on his *own account* if, as explained above, he works for fees solely and employs no helpers; if, however, he employs an assistant in his office he becomes an *employer;* but if he works for a salary, say in a hospital or institution, he is an *employee.* It may happen, however, that he receives a salary and also works for fees, in which case he should be classed with respect to his principal source of income.

174. A dressmaker who works out by the day for day wages should be returned as an *employee;* but a dressmaker who works at home or in her own shop should be returned as working on *own account,* unless she employs helpers, in which case she becomes an *employer.*

175. Similarly, a washerwoman or laundress who works out by the day is an *employee,* but a washerwoman or laundress who takes in washing is either working on *own account,* or, it may be, is an *employer.*

176. Case of wife working for husband or child working for parents.—When, in accordance with the preceding instructions, a wife working for her husband or a child working for its parents is returned as having an occupation, the wife or child should be returned as an *employee,* even though not receiving wages. The husband or parent in such case should be returned as an *employer,* unless, as may happen, he is working for wages, in which case he, as well as the wife or child, should be classed as an *employee.*

UNEMPLOYMENT

177. What is meant by "out of work."—The purpose of inquiries 21 and 22 is to ascertain the amount of enforced unemployment—the extent to which persons *want work and can not find it.* Do not, therefore, include with those "out of work" those who are *on a strike,* those who are *voluntarily idle,* those who are *incapacitated for any work,* or those who are *on sick leave or on a vacation.* School-teachers, artists, and music teachers are often unemployed during a portion of the year, but should not be considered as "out of work," in the sense in which the term is used for the purposes of the census.

178. Column 21. If an employee, whether out of work on April 15, 1910.—If a person reported as an employee (W) in column 20 was out of work on April 15, 1910, write "*Yes;*" but if such person had work on that date, write "*No.*" For persons other than employees, leave the column blank.

179. Column 22. If an employee, number of weeks out of work during year 1909.—If a person reported as an employee (W) in column 20 was out of work during any part of the year 1909, enter the number of weeks out of work; but if such person was not out of work at all during the year, *do not leave the column blank,* but write "0." For persons other than employees, leave the column blank.

180. Person not employed at his principal or usual occupation but engaged in some side or temporary work is not to be considered as unemployed, the intent of this question being to find out the number of weeks during which the person was *unable to secure any employment.*

EDUCATION

181. Column 23. Whether able to read.—Write "*Yes*" for all persons 10 years of age and over who can *read any* language, whether English or some other, and "*No*" for all such persons who can not read *any* language. For persons under 10 years of age, leave the column blank.

182. For a person reported as "blind" (column 31), write "*Yes*" if he could read any language before becoming blind or, if born blind, if he has been taught to read any language.

183. Column 24. Whether able to write.—Write "*Yes*" for all persons 10 years of age and over who can write any language, whether English or some other, and "*No*" for all such persons who can not write *any* language. For persons under 10 years of age, leave the column blank.

184. For a person reported as "blind" (column 31), write "*Yes*" if he could write any language before becoming blind or, if born blind, if he has been taught to write any language.

185. Column 25. Attended school any time since September 1, 1909.—Write "*Yes*" for any person who attended school, college, or any educational institution at any time since September 1, 1909, and "*No*" for any person of school age—5 to 21 years—who has not attended school since that date. For persons below or above school age, leave the column blank, unless they actually attended school.

OWNERSHIP OF HOME

186. Column 26. Home owned or rented.—This question is to be answered only opposite the name of the head of each family. If a dwelling is occupied by more than one family it is the home of each of them, and the question should be answered with reference to each family in the dwelling. If the home is *owned,* write opposite the name of the head of the family "O." If the home is *rented,* write "R." Make no entries in this column for the other members of the family.

187. Owned homes.—A home is to be classed as *owned* if it is owned wholly or in part by the head of the family living in the home, or by the wife of the head, or by a son, or a daughter, or other *relative* living in the same house with the head of the family. It is not necessary that full payment for the property should have been made or that the family should be the sole owner.

188. Rented homes.—Every home not owned, either wholly or in part, by the family living in it should be classed as *rented,* whether rent is actually paid or not.

189. Column 27. Home owned free or mortgaged.—This question applies only to those homes classed in column 26 as owned homes and not to rented homes. Write "M" for mortgaged and "F" for owned free. These entries should be made opposite the name of the head of the family. All owned homes which are not fully paid for, or upon which there is any encumbrance in the form either of a mortgage or of a lien upon which judgment has been had in a court, are to be reported as mortgaged.

190. Column 28. Farm or house.— This column is intended merely to distinguish farm homes from other homes. If the home is a farm home, write "F" (for farm) opposite the name of the head of the family. If it is not a farm home, write "H" (for house). A farm home is a home located on a farm, for which a farm schedule should be secured. Any other home is to be reported simply as a house.

191. Column 29. Number of farm schedule.—This question applies only to farm homes. If the home is a farm home, enter in this column simply the number of the agricultural schedule filled out for this farm. Make this entry opposite the name of the member of the family operating the farm. Usually this will be the head of the family.

SURVIVORS OF THE CIVIL WAR

192. Column 30. Whether a survivor of the Union or Confederate Army or Navy.—This question should be asked as to all males over 50 years of age who were born in the United States and all foreign born males who immigrated to this country before 1865. Write "UA" if a survivor of the Union Army; "UN" if a survivor of the Union Navy; "CA" if a survivor of the Confederate Army; and "CN" if a survivor of the Confederate Navy. For all other persons leave the column blank.

BLIND AND DEAF AND DUMB PERSONS

193. Column 31. Whether blind (both eyes).—If a person is either totally or partially blind, in both eyes, so as not to be able to read even with the help of glasses, write "Bl." For all other persons leave the column blank.

194. Columns 32. Whether deaf and dumb.—If a person is *both* deaf and dumb, write "DD." For all other persons leave the column blank. Persons who are deaf but not dumb, or persons who are dumb but not deaf, are not to be reported.

SPECIAL INDIAN SCHEDULE

195. When to be used.—This schedule (Form 8 1857) is a modified form of the general population schedule; it is to be used principally for the enumeration of Indians living on reservations or in tribal relations, and also by the enumerators in certain counties containing a considerable number of Indians.

196. If any copies of this schedule are enclosed in the portfolio for your district, you are required to enumerate thereon all Indian families living in your district, in accordance with the instructions printed upon the schedule itself.

1910 QUESTIONNAIRE—INDIAN POPULATION

(23" X 16", printed on two sides, space for 20 entries on each side, reverse side contained continuation of instructions. The top of the questionnaire contained questions 1-28 which were identical with those on the general schedule.)

INSTRUCTION FOR ENUMERATORS
INSTRUCTIONS FOR FILING THIS SCHEDULE

This modified form of the general schedule for population is to be used in making the enumeration of Indians, both those on reservations and those living in family groups outside of reservations.

Detached Indians living either in white or negro families outside of reservations should be enumerated on the general population schedule (Form 8-1589) as members of the families in which they are found; but detached whites or negroes living in Indian families should be enumerated on this special Indian schedule as members of the Indian families in which they are found. In other words, every family composed mainly of Indians should be reported *entirely* on this special schedule, and every family composed mainly of persons not Indians should be reported *entirely* on the general population schedule.

Spaces are provided for entries for 20 persons on each side (A and B) of the sheet, the entries for each person running twice to the page. Columns 1 to 46 are to be filled for each individual case, if applicable, according to the instructions.

Columns 1 to 32.—These columns are identical with those on the general population schedule. Fill each column, so far as the inquiry applies, in accordance with the instructions for filling the corresponding column in the general population schedule, but note the following additional instructions in relation to filling columns 1 and 2, column 7, and columns 18 and 19.

Columns 1 and 2. Visitation numbers.—If, in canvassing a given territory, you are using both the general population schedule (Form 8-1589) and this schedule for Indian population, make two independent series of numbers for these columns, one series in each kind of schedule, so that the last number in column 1 on this schedule added to the last number in column 1 on the general population schedule will give the whole number of dwellings visited, and, likewise, the last number in column 2 on this schedule added to the last number in column 2 on the general population schedule will give the whole number of families visited and enumerated in your district.

Column 7. Age at last birthday.—Some difficulty may be met in ascertaining the exact ages of Indians, as they frequently reckon their ages from notable events occurring in the history of the respective tribes. Endeavor to ascertain the years in which these notable events occurred, and with a little calculation on your part you should be able to ascertain the exact age of each Indian.

Columns 18 and 19. Occupation. If the Indian is wholly self-supporting, enter his or her occupation in columns 18 and 19 in accordance with the general instructions for returning occupations. If the Indian—man, woman, or child—has no occupation and is wholly dependent on the Government for support, write "Ration Indian" in column

18. If the Indian is partly self-supporting and partly dependent up the Government, write the occupation in columns 18 and 19, and then the letter "R" (for ration).

INSTRUCTIONS CONTINUED ON "B" SIDE OF SHEET INSTRUCTIONS FOR FILLING THIS SCHEDULE CONTINUED FROM "A" SIDE OF SHEET

The following instructions apply to columns 33 to 46:

Columns 33, 34, and 35. Tribal relations. If the Indian was born in this country answers should be obtained, if possible, to inquiries 12, 13, and 14, relating to the state or territory of birth of the person and of his or her parents. In any event, take particular pains to secure the name of the tribe with which the person is connected and the name of the tribe of each of his or her parents, and enter the same in columns 33, 34, and 35.

Columns 36, 37, and 38. Proportions of Indian and other blood.—If the Indian is a full-blood, write "full" in column 36, and leave columns 37 and 38 blank. If the Indian is of mixed blood, write in column 36, 37, and 38 the fractions which show the proportions of Indian and other blood, as (column 36, Indian) 3/4, (column 37, white) 1/4, and (column 38, negro) 0. For Indians of mixed blood all three columns should be filled, and the sum, in each case, should equal 1, as 1/2, 0, 1/2; 3/4, 1/4, 0; 3/4, 1/8, 1/8; etc. Wherever possible, the statement that an Indian is of full blood should be verified by inquiry of the older men of the tribe, as an Indian is sometimes of mixed blood without knowing it.

Column 39. Number of times married.—If the Indian is married, enter in this column the number of times he or she has been married.

Column 40. Whether now living in polygamy.—If the Indian man is living with more than one wife, write "Yes" in this column; otherwise, write "No."

Column 41. If living in polygamy, whether the wives are sisters.—If the Indian man is living with more than one wife, and if his wives are sisters, write "Yes" in this column. If his wives are not sisters, write "No."

Column 42. Graduated from what educational institution.—If the Indian is a graduate of any educational institution, give the name and location of such institution.

Column 43. Is this Indian taxed?—An Indian is to be considered "taxed" if he or she is detached from his or her tribe and is living among white people as an individual, and as such is subject to taxation (whether he or she actually pays taxes or not); or if he or she is living with his or her tribe but has received an allotment of land, and thereby has acquired citizenship. In either of these two cases write "Yes" in this column.

An Indian on a reservation, without an allotment, or roaming over unsettled territory, is considered "not taxed," and for such Indians the answer to this inquiry is "No."

Column 44. If Indian has received allotment, give year of allotment.—If the Indian has received an allotment of land, enter, in column 44, the year in which the allotment was made.

Column 45. Residing on his own lands.—If the Indian lives on his or her own land, write "Yes" in this column; if the Indian lives elsewhere, write "No."

Column 46. Living in civilized or aboriginal dwelling.—If the Indian is living in a house of civilized designs, as a log, frame, brick, or stone house, write "Civ." (for civilized) in this column; but if the Indian is living in a dwelling of aboriginal design, as a tent, tepee, cliff dwelling, etc., write "Abor." (for aboriginal).

U.S. Census Bureau

1920 QUESTIONNAIRE

(23″ X 16″, printed on two sides, space for 50 entries on each side; reverse side was identical except that lines were numbered 50 to 100). Similar schedules were printed for use in Alaska, Hawaii, and Puerto Rico (in Spanish), but had space for only 25 entries on each side (23″X10 1/2″).

A population schedule for "Military and Naval Population, Etc., Abroad" was identical in size and content with the principal schedule except for a simplified occupation inquiry and the additional requests for rank and for the U.S. address of each person enumerated. There was no Indian schedule for 1920.

PLACE OF ABODE.				NAME	RELATION.	TENURE.		PERSONAL DESCRIPTION.				CITIZENSHIP.			EDUCATION.		
Street, avenue, road, etc.	House number or farm, etc. (See Instructions.)	Number of dwelling house in order of visitation.	Number of family in order of visitation.	of each person whose place of abode on January 1, 1920, was in this family. Enter surname first, then the given name and middle initial, if any. Include every person living on January 1, 1920. Omit children born since January 1, 1920.	Relationship of this person to the head of the family.	Home owned or rented.	If owned, free or mortgaged.	Sex.	Color or race.	Age at last birthday.	Single, married, widowed, or divorced.	Year of immigration to the United States.	Naturalized or alien.	If naturalized, year of naturalization.	Attended school any time since Sept. 1, 1919.	Whether able to read.	Whether able to write.
1	2	3	4	5	6	7	8	9	10	11	12	13	14	15	16	17	18
1																	
2																	
3																	

NATIVITY AND MOTHER TONGUE.						Whether able to speak English.	OCCUPATION.			
PERSON.		FATHER.		MOTHER.			Trade, profession, or particular kind of work done, as spinner, salesman, laborer, etc.	Industry, business, or establishment in which at work, as cotton mill, dry goods store, farm, etc.	Employer, salary or wage worker, or working on own account.	Number of farm schedule.
Place of birth.	Mother tongue.	Place of birth.	Mother tongue.	Place of birth.	Mother tongue.					
19	20	21	22	23	24	25	26	27	28	29
										1
										2
										3

Instructions to Enumerators

Except for detailed rules for house-to-house canvassing and for applying the "usual place of abode" criterion ("the place persons may be said to live or belong, or the place which is their home. . .where a person regularly sleeps") in determining whether or not to list someone, the enumerators' instructions for 1920 were substantially the same as for 1910. Age for children under 5 years was to be reported in complete years and months.

1930 QUESTIONNAIRE—POPULATION

(23 3/4" x 16 1/2", printed on both sides, space for 50 entries on each side; reverse side was identical except that lines were numbered 50 to 100

PLACE OF ABODE				NAME	RELATION	HOME DATA				PERSONAL DESCRIPTION				
Street, avenue, road, etc.	House number (in cities or towns)	Number of dwelling house in order of visitation	Number of family in order of visitation	of each person whose *place of abode* on April 1, 1930, was in this family — Enter surname first, then the given name and middle initial, if any — Include every person living on April 1, 1930. Omit children born since April 1, 1930	Relationship of this person to the head of the family	Home owned or rented	Value of home, if owned, or monthly rental, if rented	Radio set	Does this family live on a farm?	Sex	Color or race	Age at last birthday	Marital condition	Age at first marriage
1	2	3	4	5	6	7	8	9	10	11	12	13	14	15
1														
2														
3														

EDUCATION		PLACE OF BIRTH			MOTHER TONGUE (OR NATIVE LANGUAGE) OF FOREIGN BORN				CITIZENSHIP, ETC.			OCCUPATION AND INDUSTRY	
Attended school or college anytime since Sept. 1, 1929	Whether able to read and write	Place of birth of each person enumerated and of his or her parents. If born in the United States, give State or Territory. If of foreign birth, give country in which birthplace is now situated. (See Instructions.) Distinguish Canada-French from Canada-English, and Irish Free State from Northern Ireland			Language spoken in home before coming to the United States	CODE (For office use only. Do not write in these columns)			Year of immigration to the United States	Naturalization	Whether able to speak English	OCCUPATION — Trade, profession, or particular kind of work, as spinner, salesman, riveter, teacher, etc.	INDUSTRY — Industry or business, as cotton mill, dry-goods store, shipyard, public school, etc.
		PERSON	FATHER	MOTHER		State or M. T.	Country	Nativity					
16	17	18	19	20	21	A	B	C	22	23	24	25	26

Instructions to Enumerators

These generally followed the directions given in 1910 and 1920. College students, except cadets at Annapolis and West Point, were to be enumerated at their homes, but student nurses were to be counted where they were being trained. Veteran status (items 30 and 31) excluded persons who served only during peacetime. The war or expedition was to be entered by an abbreviation: World War, WW; Spanish-American War, Sp; Civil War, Civ; Philippine insurrection, Phil; Boxer rebellion, Box; or Mexican expedition, Mex.

There were specific instructions for reporting race. A person of mixed White and Negro blood was to be returned as Negro, no matter how small the percentage of Negro blood; someone part Indian and part Negro also was to be listed as Negro unless the Indian blood predominated and the person was generally accepted as an Indian in the community.

A person of mixed White and Indian blood was to be returned as an Indian, except where the percentage of Indian blood was very small or where he or she was regarded as White in the community. For persons reported as American Indian in column 12 (color or race), columns 19 and 20 were to be used to indicate the degree of Indian blood and the tribe, instead of the birthplace of father and mother.

In order to obtain separate figures for Mexicans, it was decided that all persons born in Mexico, or having parents born in Mexico, who were not definitely White, Negro, Indian, Chinese, or Japanese, would be returned as Mexicans (Mex).

Any mixture of White and some other race was to be reported according to the race of the parent who was not White; mixtures of colored races were to be listed according to the father's race, except Negro-Indian (discussed above).

1930 QUESTIONNAIRE—CENSUS OF UNEMPLOYMENT

(18″ X 11 1/2″, printed on two sides, space for 30 entries on each side, reverse side identical except that lines were numbered 31 to 60, yellow stock.)

	Date of enumeration	POPULATION SCHEDULE		NAME	Does this person usually work at a gainful occupation?	Does this person have a job of any kind?	IF THIS PERSON HAS A JOB—					
		Sheet No.	Line No.	Of each person who *usually* works at a gainful occupation but did not work yesterday (or on the last regular working day)			How many weeks since he has worked on that job?	Why was he not at work yesterday? (Or in case yesterday was not a regular working day, why did he not work on the last regular working day?) For example, *sickness, was laid off, voluntary lay-off, bad weather, lack of materials, strike, etc.*	CODE (For office use only)	Does he lose a day's pay by not being at work?	How many days did he work last week?	How many days in a full-time week?
					Yes or No	*Yes or No*				*Yes or No*		
	1	2	3	4	5	6	7	8	A	9	10	11
1												
2												
3												

IF THIS PERSON HAS NO JOB OF ANY KIND—					FOR OFFICE USE ONLY NOT TO BE FILLED OUT BY ENUMERATOR											
Is he able to work?	Is he looking for a job?	For how many weeks has he been without a job?	Reason for being out of a job (or for losing his last job), as *plant closed down, sickness, off season, job completed, machines introduced, strike, etc.*	CODE (For office use only)	Classification	Relationship	Sex	Color and nativity	Age	Marital condition	Occupation	Class of worker	Persons in family	Other employed persons	Others unemployed	
Yes or No	*Yes or No*															
12	13	14	15	B	C	D	E	F	G	H	I	K	L	M	N	
																1
																2
																3

1930 QUESTIONNAIRE—"SUPPLEMENTAL SCHEDULE FOR INDIAN POPULATION"

(10 1/2" X 8", printed on two sides, green stock.)

Form 15-269

DEPARTMENT OF COMMERCE—BUREAU OF THE CENSUS

FIFTEENTH CENSUS OF THE UNITED STATES: 1930

SUPPLEMENTAL SCHEDULE FOR INDIAN POPULATION

For instructions and illustrative example see other side of this sheet

State_____ County_____ Supervisor's District No._____ Enumeration District No._____

Township or other division of county_____ Name of city, town, or village_____

Institution (if any)_____ Enumerator_____
(Signature)

Population Schedule		Name	Sex	Age	Full Blood or Mixed Blood	Tribe	Post-Office Address	Agency Where Enrolled
Sheet No.	Line No.							
1	2	3	4	5	6	7	8	9
1								
2								
3								

(23 3/4″ X 18 1/2″, printed on two sides, space for 40 entries on each side plus two additional lines for the 5-percent sample questions; reverse side was identical except that lines were numbered 41 to 80, and the sample-line numbers were different.) Similar, but less detailed forms were used outside the continental United States.

	LOCATION		HOUSEHOLD DATA				NAME	RELATION		PERSONAL DESCRIPTION				EDUCATION		
Line No.	Street, avenue, road, etc.	House number (in cities and towns)	Number of household in order of visitation	Home owned (O) or rented (R)	Value of home, if owned, or monthly rental, if rented	Does this household live on a farm? (Yes or No)	Name of each person whose *usual place of residence* on April 1, 1940, was in this household. BE SURE TO INCLUDE: 1. Persons temporarily absent from household. Write "Ab" after names of such persons. 2. Children under 1 year of age. Write "Infant" if child has not been given a first name. Enter Ⓧ after name of person furnishing information.	Relationship of this person to the head of the household, as wife, daughter, father, mother-in-law, grandson, lodger, lodger's wife, servant, hired hand, etc.	CODE (Leave blank)	Sex—Male (M), Female (F)	Color or race	Age at last birthday	Marital status—Single (S), Married (M), Widowed (Wd), Divorced (D)	Attended school or college any time since March 1, 1940? (Yes or No)	Highest grade of school completed	CODE (Leave blank)
	1	2	3	4	5	6	7	8	A	9	10	11	12	13	14	B

PLACE OF BIRTH		CITI-ZEN-SHIP	RESIDENCE, APRIL 1, 1935				
If born in the United States, give State, Territory, or possession. If foreign born, give country in which birthplace was situated on January 1, 1937. Distinguish Canada-French from Canada-English and Irish Free State (Eire) from Northern Ireland.	CODE (Leave blank)	Citizenship of the foreign born	IN WHAT PLACE DID THIS PERSON LIVE ON APRIL 1, 1935? For a person who, on April 1, 1935, was living in the same house as at present, enter in Col. 17 "Same house," and for one living in a different house but in the same city or town, enter, "Same place," leaving Cols. 18, 19, and 20 blank, in both instances. For a person who lived in a different place, enter city or town, county, and State, as directed in the Instructions. (Enter actual place of residence, which may differ from mail address.)				
			City, town, or village having 2,500 or more inhabitants. Enter "R" for all other places.	COUNTY	STATE (or Territory or foreign country)	On a farm? (Yes or No)	CODE (Leave blank)
15	C	16	17	18	19	20	D

PERSONS 14 YEARS OLD AND OVER—EMPLOYMENT STATUS

Was this person AT WORK for pay or profit in private or nonemergency Govt. work during week of March 24-30? (Yes or No)	If not, was he at work on, or assigned to, public EMERGENCY WORK (WPA, NYA, CCC, etc.) during week of March 24-30? (Yes or No)	Was this person SEEKING WORK? (Yes or No)	If not seeking work, did he HAVE A JOB, business, etc.? (Yes or No)	For persons answering "No" to quest. 21, 22, 23, and 24 Indicate whether engaged in home housework (H), in school (S), unable to work (U), or other (Ot)	CODE	If at private or nonemergency Government work. ("Yes" in Col. 21) Number of hours worked during week of March 24-30, 1940	If seeking work or assigned to public emergency work. ("Yes" in Col. 22 or 23) Duration of unemployment up to March 30, 1940—in weeks	OCCUPATION Trade, profession, or particular kind of work, as— frame spinner salesman laborer rivet heater music teacher	INDUSTRY Industry or business, as— cotton mill retail grocery farm shipyard public school	Class of worker	CODE (Leave blank)	Number of weeks worked in 1939 (Equivalent full-time weeks)	Amount of money wages or salary received (including commissions)	Did this person receive income of $50 or more from sources other than money wages or salary? (Yes or No)	Number of Farm Schedule	Line No.
								OCCUPATION, INDUSTRY, AND CLASS OF WORKER					INCOME IN 1939 (12 months ending December 31, 1939)				
21	22	23	24	25	E	26	27	28	29	30	F	31	32	33	34	

For a person at work, assigned to public emergency work, or with a job ("Yes" in Col. 21, 22, or 24), enter present occupation, industry, and class of worker.
For a person seeking work ("Yes" in Col. 23): (a) If he has previous work experience, enter last occupation, industry, and class of worker; or (b) if he does not have previous work experience, enter "New worker" in Col. 28, and leave Cols. 29 and 30 blank.

SUPPLEMENTARY QUESTIONS
For Persons Enumerated on Lines 14 and 29

FOR PERSONS OF ALL AGES

Line No.	NAME	PLACE OF BIRTH OF FATHER AND MOTHER		CODE (Leave blank)	MOTHER TONGUE (OR NATIVE LANGUAGE) Language spoken in home in earliest childhood	CODE (Leave blank)	VETERANS			CODE (Leave blank)
		If born in the United States, give State, Territory, or possession. If foreign born, give country in which birthplace was situated on January 1, 1937. Distinguish Canada-French from Canada-English and Irish Free State (Eire) from Northern Ireland					Is this person a veteran of the United States military forces; or the wife, widow, or under-18-year-old child of a veteran?			
		FATHER	MOTHER				If so, enter "Yes"	If child, is veteran-father dead? (Yes or No)	War or military service	
	35	36	37	G	38	H	39	40	41	I
14										
29										

FOR PERSONS 14 YEARS OLD AND OVER

SOCIAL SECURITY			USUAL OCCUPATION, INDUSTRY, AND CLASS OF WORKER				FOR ALL WOMEN WHO ARE OR HAVE BEEN MARRIED			FOR OFFICE USE ONLY—DO NOT WRITE IN THESE COLUMNS														
Does this person have a Federal Social Security number? (Yes or No)	Were deductions for Federal Old-Age Insurance or Railroad Retirement made from wages or salary in 1939? (Yes or No)	If so, were deductions made from (1) all, (2) one-half or more, (3) part, but less than half of wages or salary?	USUAL OCCUPATION	USUAL INDUSTRY	Usual class of worker	CODE (Leave blank)	Has this woman been married more than once? (Yes or No)	Age at first marriage	Number of children ever born (Do not include stillbirths)	Tnt. (4)	V-B (5)	Fm. res. and nat. sex (9, 13, 14, 26, 27)	Color and nat. sex (9,13,14, 26, 27)	Age (11)	Mar. st. (12)	Sr. com. (3)	Cit. (16)	Wrk. st. (5)	Hrs. wkd. or Dur. un. (26 or 27)	Occupation, industry, and class of worker (7)	Wks. wkd. (31)	Wages (32)	Ot. inc. (33)	Line No.
42	43	44	45	46	47	J	48	49	50	K	L	M	N	O	P	Q	R	S	T	U	V	W	X	Y	Z
																									14
																									29

Instructions to Enumerators

In order to make the census as complete as possible, enumerators were provided with several kinds of schedules (not reproduced here) for use in obtaining information about nonresidents who might not be reported at their homes, transients, new occupants of then vacant living quarters, absent households, etc. A "household" was defined in terms of "one set of cooking facilities or housekeeping arrangements."

With regard to race, the only change from 1930 was that Mexicans were to be listed as White unless they were definitely Indian or some race other than White.

There were detailed rules for completing the employment portion of the schedule (cols. 21-31) and for coding column 30 on the basis of the occupation entered in column 28.

Veteran status (col. 39) was extended to peacetime service as well as during wars and expeditions.

Enumerators carried a supply of a separate report form, P-16, which persons unwilling to give income information verbally could use. The completed form was to be inserted in an accompanying envelope, sealed, and given to the census taker for mailing.

It should be noted that questions 35 through 50 were asked only of a 5-percent sample of the population.

1940 QUESTIONNAIRE—CENSUS OF OCCUPIED DWELLINGS

(23 1/2" X 19," printed on two sides, space for 15 entries on each side, reverse side identical except that the lines were numbered 16 to 30; yellow stock)

SECTION	I. LOCATION AND HOUSEHOLD DATA							II. CHARACTERISTICS OF STRUCTURE				
	1	2	3	4	5	6	7	8	9	10	11	12
	No. of structure in order of visitation	Population Line No. ___ Block No. ___	Color or race of head	Number of persons in household	Live on a farm?	Home tenure	Value of home or monthly rental	Type of structure in which this dwelling unit is located	Originally built as:	Exterior material	Structure in need of major repairs?	Year originally built
1	Dwelling unit No. within structure	Name of head ___ Street and No. ___ Apt. No. or location ___	White ☐1 Negro ☐2 All other ☐3		Yes ☐1 No ☐0	Owned ☐0 Rented ☐1	$___ Est. rent of owned nonfarm home $___	Structure without business 1-family detached ☐V 1-family attached ☐0 2-family side-by-side ☐1 2-family other ☐2	No. of units 3-or-more fam. struct. without bus. ___ Struct. with business ___ Other dwelling place ___	Resid. struct. same no. dwlg. units ☐1 Resid. struct. differ. no. dwlg. units ☐2 Nonresid. struct. ☐3	Wood ☐1 Brick ☐2 Stucco ☐3 Other ☐4	Yes ☐1 No ☐0 A

13	14	15	16	17	18	19	20	21	22
Number of rooms	Water supply	Toilet facilities	Bathtub or shower with running water in structure	Principal lighting equip't	Principal refrigeration equip't	Radio in dwelling unit?	Heating equipment	Principal fuel used for heating	Principal fuel used for cooking
B	Running water in dwelling unit ☐1 Hand pump in dwelling unit ☐2 Running water within 50 ft ☐3 Other supply within 50 ft ☐4 No water supply within 50 ft ☐5	Flush toilet in str., excl. use ☐1 Flush toilet in str., shared ☐2 Nonflush toilet in structure ☐3 Outside toilet or privy ☐4 No toilet or privy ☐5	Exclusive use ☐1 Shared ☐2 None ☐3	Electric ☐1 Gas ☐2 Ker. gasol. ☐3 Other ☐4	Mechanical ☐1 Ice ☐2 Other ☐3 None ☐4	Yes ☐1 No ☐0	Steam or hot water system ☐1 Piped warm air system ☐2 Pipeless warm air furnace ☐3 Heating stove ☐4 Other or none ☐5	Coal or coke ☐1 Wood ☐2 Gas ☐3 Elec-tric ☐4 Fuel oil ☐5 Ker. or gasol. ☐6 Other ☐7 None ☐8	Coal or coke ☐1 Wood ☐2 Gas ☐3 Electric ☐4 Ker. or gasol. ☐6 Other ☐7 None ☐8 C

23	24	25	26	27	28	29	30	31
Furniture incl. in rent?	Average monthly cost of—	Value of property	Mortgage on property	Regular payments required	Do payments include an amount for reduction of principal?	Do payments include real estate taxes?	Interest rate now chg'd	Holder of first mortgage (or land contract)
Yes ☐1 No ☐0 Est. rent without furniture $___	Elec. $___ Gas $___ Other fuel $___ Water $___	$___ No. of dwlg. units ___ D	Yes ☐1 No ☐0 Present debt On 1st mtg. $___ On 2d mtg. $___	Monthly ☐1 Quarterly ☐2 Semi-annual ☐3 Annual ☐4 Other reg. pmt. plan ☐5 No reg. pmt. required ☐6 Amount of each pmt. $___	Yes ☐1 No ☐0	Yes ☐1 No ☐0	___% E	Bldg. & Loan ☐1 Com. Bank ☐2 Savings Bank ☐3 Life Insur. Co. ☐4 Mtg. Co. ☐5 HOLC ☐6 Individual ☐7 Other ☐8

1940 QUESTIONNAIRE—CENSUS OF VACANT DWELLINGS

(16″ X 19,″ printed on two sides, space for 15 entries on each side, reverse side identical excerpt that lines were numbered 16 to 30, yellow stock.) "Color or race of head" and "Number of persons in household" (items 3 and 4 on "Occupied-Dwelling Schedule") did not appear on the "Vacant-Dwelling Schedule;" items 8-17 were the same as items 8-17 on the "Occupied Dwelling Schedule;" items 18-31 which appeared on the "Occupied Dwelling Schedule" were omitted from the "Vacant-Dwelling Schedule."

Instructions to Enumerators

The term "structure" was roughly comparable with "dwelling house" used in previous censuses, and 1940 "occupied dwelling units" could be equated with "homes" in 1930. The 1940 housing census, however, included vacant, habitable dwelling units and structures. It excluded units occupied by quasi households (defined as 10 or more lodgers) and various types of institutional and other places (later called "group quarters") not generally considered as part of the U.S. housing market. The dwelling unit itself was defined as "the living quarters occupied by, or intended for occupancy by, one household."

The instructions for answering the questions on the occupied and vacant dwelling schedules were fairly simple, and in many cases were spelled out on the forms themselves. Item 11 (state of repair) required the enumerator to report the structure as "needing major repairs" when parts of it, such as floors, roof, walls, or foundations required repair or replacement, "the continued neglect of which would impair the soundness of the structure and create a hazard to its safety as a place of residence."

1950 QUESTIONNAIRE—POPULATION

The basic schedule, form P1, was a white 19″ X 22″ sheet, printed in green ink on both sides. The front included space for population information for 30 persons, with a separate line for each person enumerated. (The reverse side, the housing schedule, contained spaces for information for 12 dwelling units that housed the persons enumerated on the population side of the form.) Questions 15 through 20 were asked only for persons 14 years of age and over.

Questions at the bottom of the schedule (21-33c) were asked for the one person in five whose name fell on a sample line that was indicated in black. (There were five printings to vary the sample lines.) The person whose name fell on the last sample line was also asked the additional questions from 34 on. Of the sample items, Nos. 29 on applied only to persons 14 years of age and over.

1950 Questionnaire—Population

FOR PERSONS 14 YEARS OF AGE AND OVER

1. If employed (Wk in item 15, or Yes in item 16 or item 18), describe job or business held last week
2. If looking for work (Yes in item 17), describe last job or business
3. For all other persons, leave blank

What was this person doing most of last week—working, keeping house, or something else? (Wk, H, Ot, or U for unable to work)	If H or Ot in item 15— Did this person do any work at all last week, not counting work around the house? (Include work for pay, in own business, profession, on farm, or unpaid family work) (Yes or No)	If No in item 16— Was this person looking for work? (See Special Cases below) (Yes or No)	If No in item 17— Even though he didn't work last week, does he have a job or business? (Yes or No)	If Wk in item 15 or Yes in item 16— How many hours did he work last week? (Include unpaid work on family farm or business) (Number of hours)	What kind of work was he doing? For example: Nails heels on shoes Chemistry professor Farmer Farm helper Armed forces Never worked (Occupation)	What kind of business or industry was he working in? For example: Shoe factory State university Farm Farm (Industry)	Class of worker For PRIVATE employer (P) For GOVERNMENT (G) In OWN business (O) WITHOUT PAY on family farm or business (NP) (P, G, O, or NP)	LEAVE BLANK	LINE NUMBER
15	16	17	18	19	20a	20b	20c	C	
									1
									2
									③ ASK QUES. BELOW
									4
									5
									6
									7
									⑧ ASK QUES. BELOW

FOR ALL AGES

SAMPLE LINE	Was he living in this same house a year ago?	If No in item 21— Was he living on a farm a year ago?	Was he living in this same county a year ago?	If No in item 23— What county and State was he living in a year ago? County (If county unknown, enter name of place or nearest place)	State or foreign country	LEAVE BLANK	What country were his father and mother born in? (Enter US or name of Territory, possession, or foreign country)	LEAVE BLANK	What is the highest grade of school that he has attended? (Enter one grade—see codes below)	Did he finish this grade?	Has he attended school at any time since February 1st? (For those under 30 years of age check Yes or No For those 30 years old or over, check 30 or over)
	21	22	23	24a	24b	D	25	E	26	27	28
③	☐ Yes ☐ No	☐ Yes ☐ No	☐ Yes ☐ No	County: _____ or nearest place:			Father: _____ Mother:			☐ Yes ☐ No	1 ☐ Yes 2 ☐ No V ☐ 30 or over
⑧	☐ Yes ☐ No	☐ Yes ☐ No	☐ Yes ☐ No	County: _____ or nearest place:			Father: _____ Mother:			☐ Yes ☐ No	1 ☐ Yes 2 ☐ No V ☐ 30 or over
⑬	☐ Yes ☐ No	☐ Yes ☐ No	☐ Yes ☐ No	County: _____ or nearest place:			Father: _____ Mother:			☐ Yes ☐ No	1 ☐ Yes 2 ☐ No V ☐ 30 or over
⑱	☐ Yes ☐ No	☐ Yes ☐ No	☐ Yes ☐ No	County: _____ or nearest place:			Father: _____ Mother:			☐ Yes ☐ No	1 ☐ Yes 2 ☐ No V ☐ 30 or over
㉓	☐ Yes ☐ No	☐ Yes ☐ No	☐ Yes ☐ No	County: _____ or nearest place:			Father: _____ Mother:			☐ Yes ☐ No	1 ☐ Yes 2 ☐ No V ☐ 30 or over
㉘	☐ Yes ☐ No	☐ Yes ☐ No	☐ Yes ☐ No	County: _____ or nearest place:			Father: _____ Mother:			☐ Yes ☐ No	1 ☐ Yes 2 ☐ No V ☐ 30 or over

Item 17: SPECIAL CASES—Enter Yes also for persons who would have been looking for work except for—

(a) own temporary illness;
(b) indefinite or more than 30-day layoff;
(c) belief that no work was available.

Item 26: CODES for GRADE ATTENDED	Code
None	0
Kindergarten	K
ELEMENTARY, HIGH	
Elementary (8 grades)	S1 to S8
High (4 years)	S9, S10, S11, S12
ELEMENTARY, JUNIOR-SENIOR HIGH	
Elementary (6 grades)	S1 to S6
Junior high (3 years)	S7, S8, S9
Senior high (3 years)	S10, S11, S12
COLLEGE OR UNIVERSITY	
Undergraduate (4 years)	C1, C2, C3, C4
Graduate or professional school (1 year or more)	C5

Items 27a, 27b, and 27c: DEFINITION OF FAMILY HEAD

A family head is—

Either (a) head of household with related persons present in household

or (b) person unrelated to household head but with persons related to him listed below him on the schedule—for example: Lodger with wife present in household

FOR DISTRICT OFFICE USE ONLY

Number of lines on this sheet	Number of cancelled lines on this sheet	Number of persons enumerated on this sheet
30	—	=

㉘ CONT.

FOR PERSONS 14 YEARS OF AGE AND OVER

If looking for work (Yes in item 17)— How many weeks has he been looking for work? (Number of weeks)	Last year, in how many weeks did this person do any work at all, not counting work around the house? (Number of weeks in 1949)	Income received by this person in 1949				If this person is a family head (see definition below)— Income received by his relatives in this household				If Male— (Ask each question) Did he ever serve in the U. S. Armed Forces during—				
		Last year (1949), how much money did he earn working as an employee for wages or salary? (Enter amount before deductions for taxes, etc.)	Last year, how much money did he earn working in his own business, professional practice, or farm? (Enter net income)	Last year, how much money did he receive from interest, dividends, veteran's allowances, pensions, rents, or other income (aside from earnings)?	LEAVE BLANK	Last year (1949), how much money did his relatives in this household earn working for wages or salary? (Amount before deductions for taxes, etc.)	Last year, how much money did his relatives in this household earn in own business, professional practice, or farm? (Net income)	Last year, how much money did his relatives in this household receive from interest, dividends, veteran's allowances, pensions, rents, or other income (aside from earnings)?	LEAVE BLANK	World War II	World War I	Any other time, including present service	LEAVE BLANK	SAMPLE LINE
29	30	31a	31b	31c	F	32a	32b	32c	G	33a	33b	33c	H	
☐ None ___ (Weeks)	☐ None ___ (Weeks)	☐ None $___	☐ None $___	☐ None $___		☐ None $___	☐ None $___	☐ None $___		☐ Yes ☐ No	☐ Yes ☐ No	☐ Yes ☐ No		③
☐ None ___ (Weeks)	☐ None ___ (Weeks)	☐ None $___	☐ None $___	☐ None $___		☐ None $___	☐ None $___	☐ None $___		☐ Yes ☐ No	☐ Yes ☐ No	☐ Yes ☐ No		⑧
☐ None ___ (Weeks)	☐ None ___ (Weeks)	☐ None $___	☐ None $___	☐ None $___		☐ None $___	☐ None $___	☐ None $___		☐ Yes ☐ No	☐ Yes ☐ No	☐ Yes ☐ No		⑬
☐ None ___ (Weeks)	☐ None ___ (Weeks)	☐ None $___	☐ None $___	☐ None $___		☐ None $___	☐ None $___	☐ None $___		☐ Yes ☐ No	☐ Yes ☐ No	☐ Yes ☐ No		⑱
☐ None ___ (Weeks)	☐ None ___ (Weeks)	☐ None $___	☐ None $___	☐ None $___		☐ None $___	☐ None $___	☐ None $___		☐ Yes ☐ No	☐ Yes ☐ No	☐ Yes ☐ No		㉓
☐ None ___ (Weeks)	☐ None ___ (Weeks)	☐ None $___	☐ None $___	☐ None $___		☐ None $___	☐ None $___	☐ None $___		☐ Yes ☐ No	☐ Yes ☐ No	☐ Yes ☐ No		

34. To enumerator: If worked last year (1 or more weeks in item 30): Is there any entry in items 20a, 20b, and 20c?
☐ Yes—Skip to item 36
☐ No—Make entries in items 35a, 35b, and 35c

35a. What kind of work did this person do in his last job?

35b. What kind of business or industry did he work in?

35c. Class of worker (P, G, O, or NP, as in item 20c)

㉖

36. If ever married (Mar, Wd, D, or Sep in item 12)—
Has this person been married more than once?
☐ Yes ☐ No

37. If Mar—How many years since this person was (last) married?
If Wd —How many years since this person was widowed?
If D   —How many years since this person was divorced?
If Sep —How many years since this person was separated?
_____ years, or ☐ Less than 1 year

38. If female and ever married (Mar, Wd, D, or Sep in item 12)—
How many children has she ever borne, not counting stillbirths?
_____ children, or ☐ None

Instructions to Enumerators

Changes from 1940 were few. Special pains were taken in the 1950 census, however, to distinguish among institutions, households, and quasi households (five or more nonrelatives of the head, other than employees).

College students were to be enumerated where they lived while attending school, rather than where their homes were located. Members of the Armed Forces who slept off post would be counted where they slept rather than where they were stationed.

The instructions continued to allow anyone to be designated as head of the household for relationship purposes, but if a woman was listed as head and her husband was present, he was reclassified as the head when the completed schedule was reviewed in the office. (At the time, the number of such cases was relatively small.)

A "family" was distinguished from a "household" in that the family represented a group of two or more persons related by blood, marriage, or adoption. A household could contain one or more families, or none, but would occupy only one dwelling unit (quarters with separate cooking equipment or (new for 1950) a separate entrance.)

As in 1940, there was a separate form a respondent could use to report income. However, this was now a self-mailing piece (form P6) which the householder was asked to complete and post (rather than hand it to the enumerator).

A supplemental schedule (form P8) was used to obtain additional information on Indian reservations. In addition to entering each person's name as it appeared on the regular schedule, the enumerator wrote in any other name(s) by which that person was known.

1950 QUESTIONNAIRE—HOUSING

SHEET NO.		FOR ALL DWELLING UNITS										
1	2	3	4	5	6	7	8	9	10	11	12	13
Serial number of dwelling unit	Block number	TYPE OF LIVING QUARTERS 1 ☐ House, apartment, flat 2 ☐ Trailer 3 ☐ Tent, boat, railroad car X ☐ Nondwelling-unit quarters in large rooming house, institution, hotel, tourist court, etc. (If nondwelling unit, do not ask remaining items)	TYPE OF STRUCTURE 1 ☐ Detached 2 ☐ Semi-detached 3 ☐ Attached	NUMBER OF DWELLING UNITS IN STRUCTURE (Number)	BUSINESS UNIT IN STRUCTURE 1 ☐ Yes 2 ☐ No	CONDITION OF UNIT 1 ☐ Not dilapidated 2 ☐ Dilapidated	We have listed (number) persons who live here. Have we missed anyone away traveling? Babies? Lodgers? Other persons staying here who have no home anywhere else? (Add names on other side if necessary) Enter correct number of persons: _____ (Final count) X ☐ Occupied entirely by nonresidents V ☐ Vacant	How many rooms are in this unit, not counting bathrooms? (Number)	PIPED WATER SUPPLY 1 ☐ Hot and cold piped running water inside this structure 2 ☐ Only cold piped running water inside this structure 3 ☐ Piped running water outside this structure 4 ☐ No piped running water (hand pump, well, etc.)	TYPE OF TOILET 1 ☐ Flush toilet inside this structure 2 ☐ Flush toilet outside this structure 3 ☐ Privy, outhouse, or chemical toilet 4 ☐ No toilet for this unit	TOILET—EXCLUSIVE USE 1 ☐ For this unit's exclusive use 2 ☐ Shared with another unit 3 ☐ No toilet for this unit	INSTALLED BATHTUB OR SHOWER 1 ☐ For this unit's exclusive use 2 ☐ Shared with another unit 3 ☐ No bathtub or shower for this unit

14	15	16	FOR ALL VACANT UNITS	FOR NONFARM VACANT UNITS ONLY		FOR NONFARM UNITS OCCUPIED BY OWNER			FOR NONFARM UNITS OCCUPIED BY RENTER			
			17	18	19	20	21	22	23	24	25	26
c. ③ Is there a radio in this unit? 1 ☐ Yes 2 ☐ No V ☐ Vacant	c. Is there a television set in this unit? 1 ☐ Yes 2 ☐ No V ☐ Vacant	OCCUPANCY Occupied— 1 ☐ By owner 2 ☐ By renter 3 ☐ Rent free Vacant— 4 ☐ For rent 5 ☐ For sale only 6 ☐ Not for rent or sale	1 ☐ Nonseasonal 2 ☐ Seasonal	If "For rent"—Monthly rent for this unit— $_____	If "For sale only"—Sale price asked— $_____	How much would this property sell for? $_____	How many dwelling units are included in this property? (Number)	Is there any mortgage (trust) on this property? 1 ☐ Yes 2 ☐ No	What is the monthly rent for this unit? $_____	In addition to rent, how much do you pay for— Enter amount in dollars / Nothing paid Electricity? $_____ (Monthly average) ☐ Gas? $_____ (Monthly average) ☐ Water? $_____ (Monthly average) ☐ Wood? Coal? Oil? $_____ (12 months total)	Is this unit rented— 1 ☐ Unfurnished or 2 ☐ Furnished	If rented furnished—What would it rent for monthly if unfurnished? $_____

Instructions to Enumerators—Housing

The census takers continued to define "nondwelling-unit quarters" (item 3) as they had in 1940, including as dwelling units those places with fewer than 10 lodgers. However, in subsequent office coding, any residence with 5 to 9 lodgers was reclassified as a nondwelling unit and excluded from the housing inventory. Vacant trailers, tents, boats, etc., were not enumerated.

There were detailed instructions for classifying various facilities (such as plumbing), equipment, and rooms for inclusion in the census.

In item 7 (condition of unit), the enumerator had to decide whether or not the place was "dilapidated," which, in conjunction with the information on plumbing facilities (items 10-13) would provide an indicator of housing quality. The reference manual had a special illustrated section devoted to item 7 and training was augmented with a filmstrip. With this background, "dilapidated" or "not dilapidated" was to be checked without asking the householder about the condition of the unit. The decision was to be made on the basis of observation, looking for critical and minor housing deficiencies or for the adequacy of the original construction. A dilapidated unit, the census taker was told, was "below the generally accepted minimum standard for housing." It failed to protect the occupants from the elements or endangered their health or safety. It could be dilapidated because it had been neglected or because the original construction had been inadequate in the first place. A unit was not to be reported as "dilapidated" simply because it was old or dingy, nor was it "not dilapidated" because it happened to be freshly painted or shingled over.

Items 14 and 15 were five different sets of questions, and each household answered the set found on the line on which it was enumerated (thus constituting a 20-percent sample for these items).

1960 QUESTIONNAIRE

The responses supplied by householders to the inquiries shown below were transcribed by enumerators to machine-readable forms, 14 1/8" X 17 1/4," which were the official 1960 schedules.

Instructions

For the population inquiries, questions P3-P7 were asked for all persons, but the other items (P8ff.) were collected on a 25-percent basis. In 1960, the housing unit or the group quarters (the dwelling or nondwelling units in 1950) was the sampling unit, so that everyone living in that unit fell in the sample. There were special procedures for sampling persons in institutions and similar facilities, however. A unit with five or more lodgers or six unrelated individuals (one of whom was designated as head) was classified as "group quarters."

The month of birth (P6) was collected for everyone, but only the quarter was transcribed to the official schedule.

The instructions for completing P5 (race or color) by observation directed that Puerto Ricans, Mexicans, or other persons of Latin descent would be classified as "White" unless they were definitely Negro, Indian, or some other race. Southern European and Near Eastern nationalities also were to be considered White. Asian Indians were to be classified as "Other," and "Hindu" written in.

The husband of a married couple was always to be listed as the head of the household if he was present.

Housing questions H3-H16 were asked for all housing units, and the others (H17H46) on either a 25-, 20-, or 5-percent sample basis. (The 20- and 5-percent samples were subdivisions of the 25-percent selection.)

Questions on the presence of a kitchen sink and electric lighting, and the type of refrigerator asked in 1950 were omitted. A number of new sample items were added, however, mainly on facilities and equipment, and detailed instructions were supplied.

In question H6 (condition), the category "Not dilapidated" was subdivided into "sound" (in good repair) and "deteriorating" (in need of repair), and the enumerator was given a list of "slight," "intermediate," and "critical" defects by which a determination could be made.

As before, vacant trailers, boats, etc., were not enumerated.

P2. Name of this person .... (Enter last name first)

P3. What is the relationship of this person to the head of this household?

Head _ _ _ _ _ _ _ _ _ _ _ _ _ _ ☐

Wife of head _ _ _ _ _ _ _ _ _ _ _ ☐

Son or daughter of head _ _ _ _ ☐

Other—Write in: ·················

(For example: Son-in-law, mother, uncle, cousin, etc.)

P8. Where was this person born?

(If born in hospital, give residence of mother, not location of hospital)

If born in the United States, write name of State.

If born outside the United States, write name of country, U.S. possession, etc. Use international boundaries as now recognized by the U.S. Distinguish Northern Ireland from Ireland (Eire).

···

(State, foreign country, U.S. possession, etc.)

P9. If this person was born outside the U.S.—
What language was spoken in his home before he came to the United States?

···

P10. What country was his father born in?

United States _ ☐ **OR** ································

(Name of foreign country; or Puerto Rico, Guam, etc.)

P11. What country was his mother born in?

United States _ ☐ **OR** ································

(Name of foreign country; or Puerto Rico, Guam, etc.)

P12. When did this person move into this house (or apartment)?
(Check date of last move)

In 1959 or 1960 _ _ _ ☐   Jan. 1954 to March 1955 _ _ _ ☐

In 1958 _ _ _ _ _ _ _ _ _ ☐   1950 to 1953 _ _ _ ☐

In 1957 _ _ _ _ _ _ _ _ _ ☐   1940 to 1949 _ _ _ _ ☐

April 1955 to Dec. 1956 _ _ _ _ _ ☐   1939 or earlier _ _ _ ☐

                          Always lived here _ ☐

P13. Did he live in this house on April 1, 1955?
(Answer 1, 2, or 3)

1. Born April 1955 or later _ _ _ _ _ ☐

OR

2. Yes, this house _ _ _ _ _ _ _ _ _ _ ☐

OR

3. No, different house _ _ _ ☐

Where did he live on April 1, 1955?

a. City or town ································

b. If city or town—Did he live inside the city limits? - - - { Yes _ _ _ ☐   No _ _ _ ☐ }

c. County ································
AND State, foreign country, U.S. possession, etc. ················

P14. What is the highest grade (or year) of regular school this person has ever attended? (Check one box)

If now attending a regular school or college, check the grade (or year) he is in. If it is in junior high school, check the box that stands for that grade (or year).

Never attended school _ _ ☐

Kindergarten _ _ _ _ _ _ _ _ ☐

Elementary school (Grade) _ _ _ _ _ _ _ _   1 ☐ 2 ☐ 3 ☐ 4 ☐ 5 ☐ 6 ☐ 7 ☐ 8 ☐

High school (Year) _ _ _ _ _   1 ☐ 2 ☐ 3 ☐ 4 ☐

College (Year) _ _ _ _ _ _ _ _ _   1 ☐ 2 ☐ 3 ☐ 4 ☐ 5 ☐ 6 or more ☐

P15. Did he finish the highest grade (or year) he attended?

Finished this grade _ _ ☐   Did not finish this grade _ _ _ ☐   Never attended school _ _ _ ☐

P16. Has he attended regular school or college at any time since February 1, 1960?

If he has attended only nursery school, business or trade school, or adult education classes, check "No".

Yes _ _ _ ☐   No _ _ _ _ ☐

↓

P17. Is it a public school or a private school?

Public school _ _ _ _ _ _ _ ☐

Private or parochial school _ _ _ _ ☐

P18. If this person has ever been married—
Has this person been married more than once?

    Once   More than once

    ↓   ↓

P19. When did he get married?   When did he get married for the first time?

Month . . . .   Month . . . .

Year . . . .   Year . . . .

P20. If this is a woman who has ever been married—
How many babies has she ever had, not counting stillbirths?

Do **not** count her stepchildren or adopted children.

. . . .   **OR**   None _ _ ☐
(Number)

P21. When was this person born?

Born before April 1946   Born April 1946 or later

☐   ☐

↓   ↓

Please go on with questions P22 to P35. Answer the questions regardless of whether the person is a housewife, student, or retired person, or a part-time or full-time worker.   *Please omit questions P22 to P35 and turn the page to the next person.*

Space for any notes about the entries for this person

································

································

P22. Did this person work at any time last week?

Include part-time work such as a Saturday job, delivering papers, or helping without pay in a family business or farm.   Do **not** count own housework.

Yes _ _ _ _ _ ☐   No _ _ _ _ _ ☐

P23. How many hours did he work last week (at all jobs)?
(If exact figure not known, give best estimate)

1 to 14 hours _ _ _ _ ☐	40 hours _ _ _ _ _ _ _ _ _ ☐
15 to 29 hours _ _ _ _ ☐	41 to 48 hours _ _ _ _ _ ☐
30 to 34 hours _ _ _ _ ☐	49 to 59 hours _ _ _ _ _ ☐
35 to 39 hours _ _ _ _ ☐	60 hours or more _ _ _ ☐

P24. Was this person looking for work, or on layoff from a job?

Yes _ _ _ _ ☐   No _ _ _ _ ☐

P25. Does he have a job or business from which he was temporarily absent all last week because of illness, vacation, or other reasons?

Yes _ _ _ _ ☐   No _ _ _ _ ☐

P26. When did he last work at all, even for a few days?
(Check one box)

Working now _ _ ☐	1949 or earlier _ _ _ ☐
In 1960 _ _ _ _ _ _ ☐	
In 1959 _ _ _ _ _ _ _ ☐	Never worked _ _ _ _ _ ☐
1955 to 1958 _ _ ☐	
1950 to 1954 _ _ ☐	

P27. Occupation (Answer 1, 2, or 3)

1. This person **last** worked in 1949 or earlier _ _ _ } ☐
This person has never worked _ _ _ _ _ _ _ _ _ _ _ _

OR

2. On active duty in the Armed Forces now _ _ _ _ _ _ _ _ ☐

OR

3. Worked in 1950 or later _ _ ☐   Answer a to e, below.

Describe this person's job or business last week, if any, and write in name of employer.   If this person had no job or business last week, give information for last job or business since 1950.

a. For whom did he work?

. . . .
(Name of company, business, organization, or other employer)

b. What kind of business or industry was this?
Describe activity at location where employed.

. . . .
(For example: County junior high school, auto assembly plant, TV and radio service, retail supermarket, road construction, farm)

c. Is this primarily: (Check one box)

Manufacturing _ _ _ _ _ _ _ _ _ _ _ _ _ _ _ _ ☐

Wholesale trade _ _ _ _ _ _ _ _ _ _ _ _ _ _ _ ☐

Retail trade _ _ _ _ _ _ _ _ _ _ _ _ _ _ _ _ _ ☐

Other (services, agriculture, government, construction, etc.) _ _ _ ☐

d. What kind of work was he doing?

. . . .
(For example: 8th grade English teacher, paint sprayer, repairs TV sets, grocery checker, civil engineer, farmer, farm hand)

e. Was this person: (Check one box)

Employee of **private** company, business, or individual, for wages, salary, or commissions _ _ _ _ _ _ ☐

Government employee (Federal, State, county, or local) _ _ _ _ _ _ _ _ _ _ _ _ _ _ ☐

Self-employed in **own** business, professional practice, or farm _ _ _ _ _ _ _ _ _ _ _ ☐

Working **without pay** in a family business or farm _ _ _ _ _ _ _ _ _ _ _ _ ☐

If this person worked last week, answer questions P28 and P29.

P28. What city and county did he work in last week?
If he worked in more than one city or county, give place where he worked most last week.

a. City or town . . . .

b. If city or town—Did he work inside the city limits? _ _ _ _ _ _ _ _ _ { Yes _ _ ☐   No _ _ ☐

c. County . . . . State . . . .

P29. How did he get to work last week?
(Check one box for principal means used last week)

Railroad _ _ _ _ ☐	Taxicab _ _ _ _ _ _ ☐	Walk only _ _ _ _ ☐
Subway or elevated _ _ _ _ ☐	Private auto or car pool _ _ ☐	Worked at home _ _ _ _ _ _ _ _ ☐
Bus or streetcar _ _ _ ☐	Other means—Write in:	

. . . .

P30. Last year (1959), did this person work at all, even for a few days?

Yes _ _ ☐   No _ _ ☐

P31. How many weeks did he work in 1959, either full-time or part-time? Count paid vacation, paid sick leave, and military service as weeks worked.

(If exact figure not known, give best estimate)

13 weeks or less _ ☐	40 to 47 weeks _ _ _ ☐
14 to 26 weeks _ _ ☐	48 to 49 weeks _ _ _ ☐
27 to 39 weeks _ _ ☐	50 to 52 weeks _ _ _ ☐

P32. How much did this person earn in 1959 in wages, salary, commissions, or tips from all jobs?

Before deductions for taxes, bonds, dues, or other items. (Enter amount or check "None."   If exact figure not known, give best estimate.)

$ _ _ _ _ _ _ _ _ _ _ .00   **OR**   None _ _ ☐
(Dollars only)

P33. How much did he earn in 1959 in profits or fees from working in his own business, professional practice, partnership, or farm?

Net income after business expenses.   (Enter amount or check "None."   If exact figure not known, give best estimate.   If business or farm lost money, write "Loss" after amount.)

$ _ _ _ _ _ _ _ _ _ _ .00   **OR**   None _ _ ☐
(Dollars only)

P34. Last year (1959), did this person receive any income from:
Social security
Pensions
Veteran's payments
Rent (minus expenses)
Interest or dividends
Unemployment insurance
Welfare payments
Any other source not already entered

Yes _ _ ☐   No _ _ ☐

What is the amount he received from these sources in 1959? (If exact figure not known, give best estimate)

$ _ _ _ _ _ _ _ _ _ _ .00
(Dollars only)

P35. *If this is a man—*

Has he ever served in the Army, Navy, or other Armed Forces of the United States?

Yes _ _ _ ☐   No _ _ _ ☐   (Check one box on each line)

Was it during:	Yes	No
Korean War (June 1950 to Jan. 1955) _ _ _ _ _	☐	☐
World War II (Sept. 1940 to July 1947) _ _ _ _	☐	☐
World War I (April 1917 to Nov. 1918) _ _ _ _ _	☐	☐
Any other time, including present service _ _ _	☐	☐

3

QUESTIONS FOR NEXT PERSON ARE ON FOLLOWING PAGE ➡

PLEASE NOTE: These housing questions begin with number H19 because the Census Taker has already obtained the answers to the earlier questions.

The term "house" or "apartment" covers your **house** or **part of the house** you occupy, or the **apartment, flat,** or **rooms** in which you live. Most of these questions refer to your own house or apartment **but note** that questions H20, H33, and H34 are about the **whole building** in which you live.

H19. How many bedrooms are in your house or apartment?

Count rooms whose main use is as bedrooms even if they are occasionally used for other purposes.

If you live in a one-room apartment without a separate bedroom, check "No bedroom."

No bedroom _____ ☐
1 bedroom _____ ☐
2 bedrooms _____ ☐
3 bedrooms _____ ☐
4 bedrooms or more __ ☐

H20. About when was this house originally built?

In 1959 or 1960 ____ ☐
1955 to 1958 _____ ☐
1950 to 1954 _____ ☐
1940 to 1949 _____ ☐
1930 to 1939 _____ ☐
1929 or earlier _____ ☐

H21. How is your house or apartment heated?
Check ONLY the kind of heat you use the most.

Heated by:
Steam or hot water _____ ☐
Warm air furnace with individual room registers __ ☐
Floor, wall, or pipeless furnace _____ ☐
Built-in electric units _____ ☐
Room heater(s) connected to chimney or flue _____ ☐
Room heater(s) **not** connected to chimney or flue __ ☐

Other method — *Write in:*

. . . .

. . . .

Not heated _____ ☐

H22. Here is a list of fuels. In the first column, check which one is used most for **heating**. In the second column, check the one used most for **cooking**. In the third column, check the fuel used most for **heating water.**

(Check one in each column)

List of fuels	A House heating fuel	B Cooking fuel	C Water heating fuel
Coal or coke _____	☐	☐	☐
Wood _____	☐	☐	☐
Utility gas from underground pipes serving the neighborhood ____	☐	☐	☐
Bottled, tank, or LP gas ____	☐	☐	☐
Electricity _____	☐	☐	☐
Fuel oil, kerosene, etc ____	☐	☐	☐
Other fuel _____	☐	☐	☐
No fuel used _____	☐	☐	☐

H23. Do you have a clothes washing machine?
Do **not** count machines shared with any other household in this building.

Machine with wringer or separate spinner _____ ☐
Automatic or semi-automatic machine _____ ☐
Washer-dryer combination (single unit) _____ ☐
No washing machine _____ ☐

H24. Do you have an electric or gas clothes dryer?
Do **not** count dryers shared with any other household in this building.

Electrically heated dryer ____ ☐
Gas heated dryer _____ ☐
No dryer _____ ☐

H25. Do you have any television sets?
Count only sets in working order. Count floor, table, and portable television sets as well as combinations.

1 set _____ ☐
2 sets or more _____ ☐
No television sets ___ ☐

H26. Do you have any radios?
Count only sets in working order. Count floor, table, and portable radios as well as radio combinations. Do **not** count automobile radios.

1 radio _____ ☐
2 radios or more ___ ☐
No radios _____ ☐

H27. Do you have any air conditioning?
Count only equipment which cools the air by refrigeration.

Room unit — 1 only _____ ☐
Room units — 2 or more _____ ☐
Central air conditioning system ___ ☐
No air conditioning _____ ☐

H28. Do you have a home food freezer which is separate from your refrigerator?

Yes ___ ☐
No ___ ☐

H30. How many bathrooms are in your house or apartment?
A **complete** bathroom has **both** flush toilet and bathing facilities (bathtub or shower).
A **partial** bathroom has a flush toilet **or** bathing facilities, but not both.

No bathroom, or only a partial bathroom _____ ☐
1 complete bathroom _____ ☐
1 complete bathroom, plus partial bathroom(s) ___ ☐
2 or more complete bathrooms _____ ☐

H33. Is this house built:
with a basement? _____ ☐
on a concrete slab? ___ ☐
in another way? _____ ☐

H34. Does this building have:
3 stories or less? _____ ☐
4 stories or more —
   with elevator? ☐
   walk-up? _____ ☐

H35. Is there a telephone on which people who live here can be called?

Yes _____ ☐ ➞ What is the
telephone number?...................

No _____ ☐

H36. How many passenger automobiles are owned or regularly used by people who live here?

Count company cars kept at home.

No automobile _____ ☐

1 automobile _____ ☐

2 automobiles _____ ☐

3 automobiles or more _____ ☐

H37. If you live in a trailer, is it:

mobile (on wheels, or can easily be put on wheels)? _____ ☐

on a permanent foundation? __ ☐

ANSWER QUESTIONS H43 TO H46 IF YOU PAY RENT FOR YOUR HOUSE, APARTMENT, OR FLAT

H43 and H44. In addition to rent, do you also pay for:

Electricity? *(Check one box)*

Yes ☐ ➞ What is the average monthly cost for electricity? $..........00
(See instructions below)

No ☐

Gas? *(Check one box)*

Yes ☐ ➞ What is the average monthly cost for gas? $..........00
(See instructions below)

No ☐

Water? *(Check one box)*

Yes ☐ ➞ What is the average monthly cost for water? $..........00
(See instructions below)

No ☐

H45 and H46. In addition to rent, do you also pay for oil, coal, kerosene, or wood?

Yes ☐ ➞ About how much do you pay for such fuel per year? $..........00
(See instructions below)

No ☐

HOW TO FIGURE COST OF UTILITIES AND FUEL

Enter the cost to the nearest dollar

Utilities

If you don't know exactly how much you have spent and if you don't have records, put down the approximate costs.

Fuels

If you don't know how much fuels cost per year, one of the following methods may help you figure the approximate costs:

Fuel used	Method
Coal	Multiply number of tons used per year by the cost per ton.
Oil or kerosene	Multiply number of gallons used per year by the cost per gallon; OR multiply number of deliveries by average cost per delivery.
Wood	Multiply number of cords (or loads) used per year by cost per cord (or load).

NOTE: If you buy fuel in small quantities (such as kerosene by the can or coal by the bag), it may be easier to figure about how much you spend for fuel per week, and multiply by the number of weeks during which it is used.

Space for any notes about the housing entries:

....

....

....

....

....

....

....

....

....

....

....

....

....

....

....

....

....

....

....

....

....

....

AFTER YOU FINISH THE HOUSING QUESTIONS—

- *FILL THE FOLLOWING PAGES FOR PERSONS WHOSE NAMES HAVE BEEN WRITTEN IN BY THE CENSUS TAKER.*

- *MAKE SURE THAT EACH "EXTRA PERSON" QUESTIONNAIRE LEFT BY THE CENSUS TAKER IS FILLED.*

- *INCLUDE THE COMPLETED "EXTRA PERSON" QUESTIONNAIRES IN THE FAMILY'S ENVELOPE WHEN THIS FORM IS MAILED TO THE CENSUS OFFICE. Sheets filled by household members not related to the head may first be enclosed in the special smaller envelopes left for these persons.*

2

1970 Questionnaire

The 1970 census was taken principally by means of a separate questionnaire (a 9 1/2" X 10 7/8" booklet) for each household, completed by the respondent.

Instructions

Population inquiries 2-8 were asked for all persons. The remaining questions were asked on a sample basis: some at every fifth household (15 percent), others at every twentieth household (5 percent), and some at both (20 percent).

Except for questions on Spanish origin or descent, citizenship, year of immigration, vocational training completed, presence and duration of disability, and activity 5 years ago, the 1970 population items were comparable to those in 1960.

All answers were designed for self-identification on the part of the respondent, but the enumerator was allowed to fill in blanks by observation when this was possible. For item 4 (color or race), it was assumed that the respondent's relatives living in the unit were also of the same race unless the census taker learned otherwise. The enumerator's manual included a long list of possible written-in entries and how they were to be classified: For example, "Chicano," "LaRaza," "Mexican American," "Moslem," or "Brown" were to be changed to White, while "Brown (Negro)" would be considered as Negro or Black for census purposes.

Although not specified on the questionnaire, the enumerator was instructed to limit question 25 (children ever born) to mothers who were or had been married unless a son or daughter had been listed.

The housing items were part of the household questionnaire. Except for the elimination of the inquiries on condition and land used for farming, and the addition of items on dishwashers and second homes, the 1970 housing items were much the same as those used in 1960.

The 1970 definition of a housing unit specified "complete kitchen facilities" rather than just cooking equipment as in 1960.

Question A and H1 through H12 were asked for all housing units, and H13 through H30 on a sample basis only. At vacant units, the enumerator completed only those items marked with a double underscore.

The 15-percent and 5-percent forms contain a pair of facing pages for each person in the household (as listed on page 2). Shown on each pair of pages in the 15-percent form are the questions designated as 15-percent here on pages 6, 7, and 8. Shown on each pair of pages in the 5-percent form are the questions designated as 5-percent here on pages 6, 7, and 8.

Name of person on line ① of page 2

Last name	First name	Initial

15 and 5 percent

13a. **Where was this person born?** *If born in hospital, give State or country where mother lived. If born outside U.S., see instruction sheet; distinguish Northern Ireland from Ireland (Eire).*

- ○ This State

OR

_____
(Name of State or foreign country; or Puerto Rico, Guam, etc.)

5 percent

b. **Is this person's origin or descent—** *(Fill one circle)*

- ○ Mexican   ○ Central or South American
- ○ Puerto Rican ○ Other Spanish
- ○ Cuban   ○ No, none of these

15 percent

14. **What country was his father born in?**

- ○ United States

OR

_____
(Name of foreign country; or Puerto Rico, Guam, etc.)

15. **What country was his mother born in?**

- ○ United States

OR

_____
(Name of foreign country; or Puerto Rico, Guam, etc.)

16. *For persons born in a foreign country—*
a. **Is this person naturalized?**

- ○ Yes, naturalized
- ○ No, alien
- ○ Born abroad of American parents

5 percent

b. **When did he come to the United States to stay?**

- ○ 1965 to 70 ○ 1950 to 54 ○ 1925 to 34
- ○ 1960 to 64 ○ 1945 to 49 ○ 1915 to 24
- ○ 1955 to 59 ○ 1935 to 44 ○ Before 1915

17. **What language, other than English, was spoken in this person's home when he was a child?** *Fill one circle.*

- ○ Spanish   ○ Other—
- ○ French   *Specify* _____
- ○ German   ○ None, English only

18. **When did this person move into this house (or apartment)?** *Fill circle for date of last move.*

- ○ 1969 or 70 ○ 1965 or 66 ○ 1949 or earlier
- ○ 1968   ○ 1960 to 64 ○ Always lived in
- ○ 1967   ○ 1950 to 59   this house or apartment

15 percent

19a. **Did he live in this house on April 1, 1965?** *If in college or Armed Forces in April 1965, report place of residence there.*

- ○ Born April 1965 or later ⎤ *Skip to 20*
- ○ Yes, this house .... ⎦
- ○ No, different house

b. **Where did he live on April 1, 1965?**

(1) State, foreign country, U.S. possession, etc. _____

(2) County _____

(3) Inside the limits of a city, town, village, etc.?

- ○ Yes ○ No

(4) If "Yes," name of city, town, village, etc. _____

15 percent

20. **Since February 1, 1970,** has this person attended regular school or college at any time? *Count nursery school, kindergarten, and schooling which leads to an elementary school certificate, high school diploma, or college degree.*

- ○ No
- ○ Yes, public
- ○ Yes, parochial
- ○ Yes, other private

21. **What is the highest grade (or year) of regular school he has ever attended?**
Fill one circle. If now attending, mark grade he is in.

- ○ Never attended school— *Skip to 23*
- ○ Nursery school
- ○ Kindergarten

Elementary through high school (grade or year)

1 2 3 4 5 6   7 8   9 10 11 12
○ ○ ○ ○ ○ ○   ○ ○   ○ ○ ○ ○

College (academic year)

1 2 3 4 5 6 or more
○ ○ ○ ○ ○ ○

15 and 5 percent

22. **Did he finish the highest grade (or year) he attended?**

- ○ Now attending this grade (or year)
- ○ Finished this grade (or year)
- ○ Did not finish this grade (or year)

23. **When was this person born?**

- ○ Born before April 1956— *Please go on with questions 24 through 41.*

- ○ Born April 1956 or later— *Please omit questions 24 through 41 and go to the next page for the next person.*

24. *If this person has ever been married—*
a. **Has this person been married more than once?**

- ○ Once   ○ More than once

b. **When did he get married?**   **When did he get married for the first time?**

_____   _____
Month   Year   *Month   Year*

c. *If married more than once—* **Did the first marriage end because of the death of the husband (or wife)?**

- ○ Yes ○ No

5 percent

25. *If this is a girl or a woman—*
How many babies has she ever had, not counting stillbirths?
Do not count her stepchildren or children she has adopted.

1 2 3   4 5 6 7 8
○ ○ ○   ○ ○ ○ ○ ○

9 10 11 12 or   None
       more
○ ○ ○ ○   ○

15 and 5 percent

26. *If this is a man—*
a. **Has he ever served in the Army, Navy, or other Armed Forces of the United States?**

- ○ Yes
- ○ No

15 percent

b. **Was it during—** *(Fill the circle for each period of service.)*

Vietnam Conflict *(Since Aug. 1964)* .... ○
Korean War *(June 1950 to Jan. 1955)* .... ○
World War II *(Sept. 1940 to July 1947)* .... ○
World War I *(April 1917 to Nov. 1918)* .... ○
Any other time ·························· ○

27a. Has this person ever completed a vocational training program?
For example, in high school; as apprentice; in school of business, nursing, or trades; technical institute; or Armed Forces schools.

　○ Yes　　　　　　　○ No— *Skip to 28*

b. What was his main field of vocational training? *Fill one circle.*

○ Business, office work
○ Nursing, other health fields
○ Trades and crafts *(mechanic, electrician, beautician, etc.)*
○ Engineering or science technician; draftsman
○ Agriculture or home economics
○ Other field— *Specify*

_____

5 percent

28a. Does this person have a health or physical condition which limits the kind or amount of work he can do at a job?
If 65 years old or over, skip to question 29.

○ Yes
○ No

b. Does his health or physical condition keep him from holding any job at all?

○ Yes
○ No

c. If "Yes" in a or b— How long has he been limited in his ability to work?

○ Less than 6 months　　　○ 3 to 4 years
○ 6 to 11 months　　　　　○ 5 to 9 years
○ 1 to 2 years　　　　　　○ 10 years or more

QUESTIONS 29 THROUGH 41 ARE FOR ALL PERSONS BORN BEFORE APRIL 1956 INCLUDING HOUSEWIVES, STUDENTS, OR DISABLED PERSONS AS WELL AS PART-TIME OR FULL-TIME WORKERS

29a. Did this person work at any time last week?

○ Yes— *Fill this circle if this person did full- or part-time work. (Count part-time work such as a Saturday job, delivering papers, or helping without pay in a family business or farm; and active duty in the Armed Forces)*

○ No— *Fill this circle if this person did not work, or did only own housework, school work, or volunteer work.*

　　　　　　　　　　Skip to 30

15 and 5 percent

b. How many hours did he work last week (at all jobs)?
Subtract any time off and add overtime or extra hours worked.

○ 1 to 14 hours　　　○ 40 hours
○ 15 to 29 hours　　○ 41 to 48 hours
○ 30 to 34 hours　　○ 49 to 59 hours
○ 35 to 39 hours　　○ 60 hours or more

c. Where did he work last week?
If he worked in more than one place, print where he worked most last week.
If he travels about in his work or if the place does not have a numbered address, see instruction sheet.

(1) Address *(Number and street name)* _____

(2) Name of city, town, village, etc._____

(3) Inside the limits of this city, town, village, etc.?
○ Yes
○ No

(4) County _____

(5) State　　　　　　　　(6) ZIP Code

15 percent

d. How did he get to work last week? *Fill one circle for chief means used on the last day he worked at the address given in 29c.*

○ Driver, private auto　　　│　○ Taxicab
○ Passenger, private auto　│　○ Walked only
○ Bus or streetcar　　　　 │　○ Worked at home
○ Subway or elevated　　　│　○ Other means—*Specify*
○ Railroad　　　　　　　　│

_____

After completing question 29d, skip to question 33.

30. Does this person have a job or business from which he was temporarily absent or on layoff last week?

○ Yes, on layoff
○ Yes, on vacation, temporary illness, labor dispute, etc.
○ No

31a. Has he been looking for work during the past 4 weeks?

　○ Yes　　　　○ No— *Skip to 32*

b. Was there any reason why he could not take a job last week?

○ Yes, already has a job
○ Yes, because of this person's temporary illness
○ Yes, for other reasons (in school, etc.)
○ No, could have taken a job

15 and 5 percent

32. When did he last work at all, even for a few days?

○ In 1970　│　○ 1964 to 1967　│　○ 1959 or earlier　│ *Skip*
○ In 1969　│　○ 1960 to 1963　│　○ Never worked　　│ *to 36*
○ In 1968　│

— continued —

33–35. Current or most recent job activity

Describe clearly this person's chief job activity or business last week, if any. If he had more than one job, describe the one at which he worked the most hours.

If this person had no job or business last week, give information for last job or business since 1960.

33. Industry

a. For whom did he work? *If now on active duty in the Armed Forces, print "AF" and skip to question 36.*

(Name of company, business, organization, or other employer)

b. What kind of business or industry was this?
Describe activity at location where employed.

(For example: Junior high school, retail supermarket, dairy farm, TV and radio service, auto assembly plant, road construction)

c. Is this mainly— *(Fill one circle)*

○ Manufacturing   ○ Retail trade
○ Wholesale trade   ○ Other *(agriculture, construction, service, government, etc.)*

34. Occupation

a. What kind of work was he doing?

(For example: TV repairman, sewing machine operator, spray painter, civil engineer, farm operator, farm hand, junior high English teacher)

b. What were his most important activities or duties?

(For example: Types, keeps account books, files, sells cars, operates printing press, cleans buildings, finishes concrete)

c. What was his job title?

----

35. Was this person— *(Fill one circle)*

Employee of private company, business, or individual, for wages, salary, or commissions... ○

Federal government employee .... ○
State government employee................. ○
Local government employee *(city, county, etc.)*... ○

Self-employed in own business, professional practice, or farm—
Own business not incorporated .... ○
Own business incorporated .... ○

Working without pay in family business or farm ○

36. In April 1965, what State did this person live in?

○ This State

OR

(Name of State or foreign country; or Puerto Rico, etc.)

15 and 5 percent

5 percent

GPO 902-842

---

37. In April 1965, was this person— *(Fill three circles)*

a. Working at a job or business *(full or part-time)?*
○ Yes   ○ No

b. In the Armed Forces?
○ Yes   ○ No

c. Attending college?
○ Yes   ○ No

38. If "Yes" for "Working at a job or business" in question 37—
Describe this person's chief activity or business in April 1965.

a. What kind of business or industry was this?

----

b. What kind of work was he doing (occupation)?

----

c. Was he—
An employee of a private company or government agency... ○
Self-employed or an unpaid family worker .... ○

5 percent

39a. Last year (1969), did this person work at all, even for a few days?

○ Yes   ○ No— *Skip to 41*

b. How many weeks did he work in 1969, either full-time or part-time?
Count paid vacation, paid sick leave, and military service.

○ 13 weeks or less   ○ 40 to 47 weeks
○ 14 to 26 weeks   ○ 48 to 49 weeks
○ 27 to 39 weeks   ○ 50 to 52 weeks

40. Earnings in 1969— *Fill parts a, b, and c for everyone who worked any time in 1969 even if he had no income. (If exact amount is not known, give best estimate.)*

a. How much did this person earn in 1969 in wages, salary, commissions, bonuses, or tips from all jobs?
(Before deductions for taxes, bonds, dues, or other items.)
$ _____ .00 *(Dollars only)*   OR ○ None

b. How much did he earn in 1969 from his own nonfarm business, professional practice, or partnership?
(Net after business expenses. If business lost money, write "Loss" above amount.)
$ _____ .00 *(Dollars only)*   OR ○ None

c. How much did he earn in 1969 from his own farm?
(Net after operating expenses. Include earnings as a tenant farmer or sharecropper. If farm lost money, write "Loss" above amount.)
$ _____ .00 *(Dollars only)*   OR ○ None

41. Income other than earnings in 1969— *Fill parts a, b, and c. (If exact amount is not known, give best estimate.)*

a. How much did this person receive in 1969 from Social Security or Railroad Retirement?
$ _____ .00 *(Dollars only)*   OR ○ None

b. How much did he receive in 1969 from public assistance or welfare payments?
Include aid for dependent children, old age assistance, general assistance, aid to the blind or totally disabled. Exclude separate payments for hospital or other medical care.
$ _____ .00 *(Dollars only)*   OR ○ None

c. How much did he receive in 1969 from all other sources?
Include interest, dividends, veterans' payments, pensions, and other regular payments. (See instruction sheet.)
$ _____ .00 *(Dollars only)*   OR ○ None

15 and 5 percent

15 and 5 percent

80, 15, and 5 percent (100 percent)

Please answer questions 10, 11, and 12 at the bottom of page 2.

A. How many living quarters, occupied and vacant, are at this address?

- ○ One
- ○ 2 apartments or living quarters
- ○ 3 apartments or living quarters
- ○ 4 apartments or living quarters
- ○ 5 apartments or living quarters
- ○ 6 apartments or living quarters
- ○ 7 apartments or living quarters
- ○ 8 apartments or living quarters
- ○ 9 apartments or living quarters
- ○ 10 or more apartments or living quarters
- ○ This is a mobile home or trailer

Answer these questions for your living quarters

H1. Is there a telephone on which people in your living quarters can be called?

- ○ Yes ──► What is
- ○ No   the number? _ _ _ _ _ _ _ _ _ _
  Phone number

H2. Do you enter your living quarters—

- ○ Directly from the outside or through a common or public hall?
- ○ Through someone else's living quarters?

H3. Do you have complete kitchen facilities?
Complete kitchen facilities are a sink with piped water, a range or cook stove, and a refrigerator.

- ○ Yes, for this household only
- ○ Yes, but also used by another household
- ○ No complete kitchen facilities for this household

H4. How many rooms do you have in your living quarters?
Do not count bathrooms, porches, balconies, foyers, halls, or half-rooms.

- ○ 1 room
- ○ 2 rooms
- ○ 3 rooms
- ○ 4 rooms
- ○ 5 rooms
- ○ 6 rooms
- ○ 7 rooms
- ○ 8 rooms
- ○ 9 rooms or more

H5. Is there hot and cold piped water in this building?

- ○ Yes, hot and cold piped water in this building
- ○ No, only cold piped water in this building
- ○ No piped water in this building

H6. Do you have a flush toilet?

- ○ Yes, for this household only
- ○ Yes, but also used by another household
- ○ No flush toilet

H7. Do you have a bathtub or shower?

- ○ Yes, for this household only
- ○ Yes, but also used by another household
- ○ No bathtub or shower

H8. Is there a basement in this building?

- ○ Yes
- ○ No, built on a concrete slab
- ○ No, built in another way *(include mobile homes and trailers)*

H9. Are your living quarters—

- ○ Owned or being bought by you or by someone else in this household? *Do not include cooperatives and condominiums here.*
- ○ A cooperative or condominium which is owned or being bought by you or by someone else in this household?
- ○ Rented for cash rent?
- ○ Occupied without payment of cash rent?

H10a. Is this building a one-family house?

- ○ Yes, a one-family house
- ○ No, a building for 2 or more families or a mobile home or trailer

b. If "Yes"— Is this house on a place of 10 acres or more, or is any part of this property used as a commercial establishment or medical office?

- ○ Yes, 10 acres or more
- ○ Yes, commercial establishment or medical office
- ○ No, none of the above

H11. If you live in a one-family house which you own or are buying—
What is the value of this property; that is, how much do you think this property (house and lot) would sell for if it were for sale?

- ○ Less than $5,000
- ○ $5,000 to $7,499
- ○ $7,500 to $9,999
- ○ $10,000 to $12,499
- ○ $12,500 to $14,999
- ○ $15,000 to $17,499
- ○ $17,500 to $19,999
- ○ $20,000 to $24,999
- ○ $25,000 to $34,999
- ○ $35,000 to $49,999
- ○ $50,000 or more

If this house is on a place of 10 acres or more, or if any part of this property is used as a commercial establishment or medical office, do not answer this question.

H12. Answer this question if you pay rent for your living quarters.
a. If rent is paid by the month—

What is the monthly rent?

Write amount here ──► $ _ _ _ _ _ _ _ _ _ .00 *(Nearest dollar)*

and

Fill one circle

- ○ Less than $30
- ○ $30 to $39
- ○ $40 to $49
- ○ $50 to $59
- ○ $60 to $69
- ○ $70 to $79
- ○ $80 to $89
- ○ $90 to $99
- ○ $100 to $119
- ○ $120 to $149
- ○ $150 to $199
- ○ $200 to $249
- ○ $250 to $299
- ○ $300 or more

b. If rent is not paid by the month—
What is the rent, and what period of time does it cover?

$ _ _ _ _ _ _ _ .00 per _ _ _ _ _ _ _ _ _ _
(Nearest dollar)   *(Week, half-month, year, etc.)*

FOR CENSUS ENUMERATOR'S USE ONLY

a4. Block number	a5. Serial number
Ø ○ ○ ○	Ø ○ ○ ○ Ø
1 ○ ○ ○	1 ○ ○ ○ 1
2 ○ ○ ○	2 ○ ○ ○ 2
3 ○ ○ ○	3 ○ ○ ○ 3
4 ○ ○ ○	4 ○ ○ ○ 4
5 ○ ○ ○	5 ○ ○ ○ 5
6 ○ ○ ○	6 ○ ○ ○ 6
7 ○ ○ ○	7 ○ ○ ○ 7
8 ○ ○ ○	8 ○ ○ ○ 8
9 ○ ○ ○	9 ○ ○ ○ 9

B. Type of unit or quarters

Occupied
- ○ First form
- ○ Continuation

Vacant
- ○ Regular
- ○ Usual residence elsewhere

Group quarters
- ○ First form
- ○ Continuation

For a vacant unit, also fill C, D, A, H2 to H8, and H10 to H12

C. Vacancy status
Year round—
- ○ For rent
- ○ For sale only
- ○ Rented or sold, not occupied
- ○ Held for occasional use
- ○ Other vacant
- ○ Seasonal
- ○ Migratory

D. Months vacant
- ○ Less than 1 month
- ○ 1 up to 2 months
- ○ 2 up to 6 months
- ○ 6 up to 12 months
- ○ 1 year up to 2 years
- ○ 2 years or more

C/O   ○   ○

Make no mark in this margin

Page 4

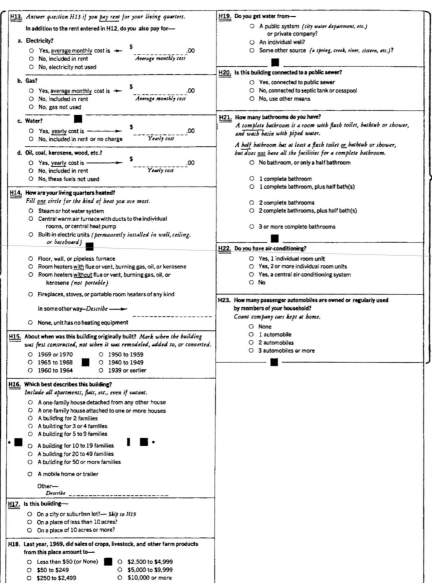

H13. *Answer question H13 if you pay rent for your living quarters.*

In addition to the rent entered in H12, do you also pay for—

a. Electricity?
- ○ Yes, average monthly cost is → $ _____ .00
  Average monthly cost
- ○ No, included in rent
- ○ No, electricity not used

b. Gas?
- ○ Yes, average monthly cost is → $ _____ .00
  Average monthly cost
- ○ No, included in rent
- ○ No, gas not used

c. Water?
- ○ Yes, yearly cost is → $ _____ .00
  Yearly cost
- ○ No, included in rent or no charge

d. Oil, coal, kerosene, wood, etc.?
- ○ Yes, yearly cost is → $ _____ .00
  Yearly cost
- ○ No, included in rent
- ○ No, these fuels not used

H14. How are your living quarters heated?
Fill one circle for the kind of heat you use most.
- ○ Steam or hot water system
- ○ Central warm air furnace with ducts to the individual rooms, or central heat pump
- ○ Built-in electric units *(permanently installed in wall, ceiling, or baseboard)*
- ○ Floor, wall, or pipeless furnace
- ○ Room heaters with flue or vent, burning gas, oil, or kerosene
- ○ Room heaters without flue or vent, burning gas, oil, or kerosene *(not portable)*
- ○ Fireplaces, stoves, or portable room heaters of any kind

In some other way—*Describe* → _____
- ○ None, unit has no heating equipment

H15. About when was this building originally built? *Mark when the building was first constructed, not when it was remodeled, added to, or converted.*
- ○ 1969 or 1970 ○ 1950 to 1959
- ○ 1965 to 1968 ○ 1940 to 1949
- ○ 1960 to 1964 ○ 1939 or earlier

H16. Which best describes this building?
Include all apartments, flats, etc., even if vacant.
- ○ A one-family house detached from any other house
- ○ A one-family house attached to one or more houses
- ○ A building for 2 families
- ○ A building for 3 or 4 families
- ○ A building for 5 to 9 families
- ○ A building for 10 to 19 families
- ○ A building for 20 to 49 families
- ○ A building for 50 or more families
- ○ A mobile home or trailer

Other—
Describe _____

H17. Is this building—
- ○ On a city or suburban lot?— *Skip to H19*
- ○ On a place of less than 10 acres?
- ○ On a place of 10 acres or more?

H18. Last year, 1969, did sales of crops, livestock, and other farm products from this place amount to—
- ○ Less than $50 (or None) ○ $2,500 to $4,999
- ○ $50 to $249 ○ $5,000 to $9,999
- ○ $250 to $2,499 ○ $10,000 or more

H19. Do you get water from—
- ○ A public system *(city water department, etc.)* or private company?
- ○ An individual well?
- ○ Some other source *(a spring, creek, river, cistern, etc.)?*

H20. Is this building connected to a public sewer?
- ○ Yes, connected to public sewer
- ○ No, connected to septic tank or cesspool
- ○ No, use other means

H21. How many bathrooms do you have?
A complete bathroom is a room with flush toilet, bathtub or shower, and wash basin with piped water.

A half bathroom has at least a flush toilet or bathtub or shower, but does not have all the facilities for a complete bathroom.
- ○ No bathroom, or only a half bathroom
- ○ 1 complete bathroom
- ○ 1 complete bathroom, plus half bath(s)
- ○ 2 complete bathrooms
- ○ 2 complete bathrooms, plus half bath(s)
- ○ 3 or more complete bathrooms

H22. Do you have air-conditioning?
- ○ Yes, 1 individual room unit
- ○ Yes, 2 or more individual room units
- ○ Yes, a central air-conditioning system
- ○ No

H23. How many passenger automobiles are owned or regularly used by members of your household?
Count company cars kept at home.
- ○ None
- ○ 1 automobile
- ○ 2 automobiles
- ○ 3 automobiles or more

The 15-percent form contains the questions shown on page 4. The 5-percent form contains the questions shown in the first column of page 4 and the questions on page 5.

 15 percent

15 and 5 percent

The 15-percent form contains the questions shown on page 4. The 5-percent form contains the questions shown in the first column of page 4 and the questions on page 5.

H24a. How many stories (floors) are in this building?

- ○ 1 to 3 stories
- ○ 4 to 6 stories
- ○ 7 to 12 stories
- ○ 13 stories or more ■

b. *If 4 or more stories—*
Is there a passenger elevator in this building?

○ Yes   ○ No

H25a. Which fuel is used most for cooking? ■

Gas { From underground pipes serving the neighborhood.	○	Coal or coke	○
Bottled, tank, or LP	○	Wood	○
Electricity..........................	○	Other fuel ..	○
Fuel oil, kerosene, etc.	○	No fuel used	○

b. Which fuel is used most for house heating? ■

Gas { From underground pipes serving the neighborhood.	○	Coal or coke	○
Bottled, tank, or LP	○	Wood	○
Electricity..........................	○	Other fuel ..	○
Fuel oil, kerosene, etc.	○	No fuel used	○

c. Which fuel is used most for water heating? ■

Gas { From underground pipes serving the neighborhood.	○	Coal or coke	○
Bottled, tank, or LP.........	○	Wood	○
Electricity..........................	○	Other fuel ..	○
Fuel oil, kerosene, etc.............	○	No fuel used	○

H26. How many bedrooms do you have?
Count rooms used mainly for sleeping even if used also for other purposes.

- ○ No bedroom
- ○ 1 bedroom ■
- ○ 2 bedrooms
- ○ 3 bedrooms
- ○ 4 bedrooms
- ○ 5 bedrooms or more

H27a. Do you have a clothes washing machine?

- ○ Yes, automatic or semi-automatic
- ○ Yes, wringer or separate spinner
- ○ No

b. Do you have a clothes dryer?

- ○ Yes, electrically heated
- ○ Yes, gas heated
- ○ No ■

c. Do you have a dishwasher *(built-in or portable)***?**

○ Yes   ○ No

d. Do you have a home food freezer which is separate from your refrigerator?

○ Yes   ○ No

H28a. Do you have a television set? *Count only sets in working order.*

- ○ Yes, one set
- ○ Yes, two or more sets
- ○ No

b. *If "Yes"—* **Is any set equipped to receive UHF broadcasts, that is, channels 14 to 83?**

○ Yes   ○ No ■

H29. Do you have a battery-operated radio?
Count car radios, transistors, and other battery-operated sets in working order or needing only a new battery for operation.

○ Yes, one or more   ○ No

H30. Do you (or any member of your household) own a second home or other living quarters which you occupy sometime during the year?

○ Yes   ○ No

5 percent

1980 Questionnaire

A separate questionnaire (a 10" X 11" booklet), containing both population and housing items, was used for each household, and completed by a respondent.

ALSO ANSWER THE HOUSING QUESTIONS ON PAGE 3 → ALSO ANSWER THE HOUSING QUESTIONS ON PAGE 3

Here are the QUESTIONS	These are the columns for ANSWERS — Please fill one column for each person listed in Question 1.	PERSON in column 1	PERSON in column 2	PERSON in column 3	PERSON in column 4	PERSON in column 5	PERSON in column 6
2. How is this person related to the person in column 1? Fill one circle. If "Other relative" of person in column 1, give exact relationship, such as mother-in-law, niece, grandson, etc.		*START* In this column with the household member (or one of the members) in whose name the home is owned or rented. If there is no such person, start in this column with any adult household member.	If relative of person in column 1: ○ Husband/wife ○ Father/mother ○ Son/daughter ○ Other relative ○ Brother/sister ▸ If not related to person in column 1: ○ Roomer, boarder ○ Other nonrelative ○ Partner, roommate ○ Paid employee	(same options)	(same options)	(same options)	(same options)
3. Sex Fill one circle.		○ Male ■ ○ Female	○ Male ■ ○ Female	○ Male ○ Female	○ Male ○ Female	○ Male ■ ○ Female	○ Male ○ Female
4. Is this person — Fill one circle.		○ White ○ Asian Indian ○ Black or Negro ○ Hawaiian ○ Japanese ○ Guamanian ○ Chinese ○ Samoan ○ Filipino ○ Eskimo ○ Korean ○ Aleut ○ Vietnamese ○ Other — Specify ○ Indian (Amer.) Print tribe	(same options)	(same options)	(same options)	(same options)	(same options)
5. Age, and month and year of birth a. Print age at last birthday. b. Print month and fill one circle. c. Print year in the spaces, and fill one circle below each number.		a. Age at last birthday / c. Year of birth b. Month of birth ○ Jan.—Mar. ○ Apr.—June ○ July—Sept. ○ Oct.—Dec.	(same)	(same)	(same)	(same)	(same)
6. Marital status Fill one circle.		○ Now married ○ Separated ○ Widowed ○ Never married ○ Divorced	(same)	(same)	(same)	(same)	(same)
7. Is this person of Spanish/Hispanic origin or descent? Fill one circle.		○ No (not Spanish/Hispanic) ○ Yes, Mexican, Mexican-Amer., Chicano ○ Yes, Puerto Rican ○ Yes, Cuban ○ Yes, other Spanish/Hispanic	(same)	(same)	(same)	(same)	(same)
8. Since February 1, 1980, has this person attended regular school or college at any time? Fill one circle. Count nursery school, kindergarten, elementary school, and schooling which leads to a high school diploma or college degree.		○ No, has not attended since February 1 ○ Yes, public school, public college ○ Yes, private, church-related ○ Yes, private, not church-related	(same)	(same)	(same)	(same)	(same)
9. What is the highest grade (or year) of regular school this person has ever attended? Fill one circle. If now attending school, mark grade person is in. If high school was finished by equivalency test (GED), mark "12."		Highest grade attended: ○ Nursery school ○ Kindergarten Elementary through high school (grade or year) 1 2 3 4 5 6 7 8 9 10 11 12 College (academic year) 1 2 3 4 5 6 7 8 or more ○ Never attended school — Skip question 10	(same)	(same)	(same)	(same)	(same)
10. Did this person finish the highest grade (or year) attended? Fill one circle.		○ Now attending this grade (or year) ○ Finished this grade (or year) ○ Did not finish this grade (or year)	(same)	(same)	(same)	(same)	(same)
CENSUS USE ONLY	A.	○ I ○ N ○ ○	○ I ○ N ○ ○	○ I ○ N ○ ○	○ I ○ N ○ ○	○ I ○ N ○ ○	

Name of Person 1 on page 2:

_____ | _____ | _____
Last name | First name | Middle initial

11. In what State or foreign country was this person born?
Print the State where this person's mother was living when this person was born. Do not give the location of the hospital unless the mother's home and the hospital were in the same State.

_____
Name of State or foreign country; or Puerto Rico, Guam, etc.

12. *If this person was born in a foreign country —*
a. Is this person a naturalized citizen of the United States?

- ○ Yes, a naturalized citizen
- ○ No, not a citizen
- ○ Born abroad of American parents

b. When did this person come to the United States to stay?

- ○ 1975 to 1980
- ○ 1965 to 1969
- ○ 1950 to 1959
- ○ 1970 to 1974
- ○ 1960 to 1964
- ○ Before 1950

13a. Does this person speak a language other than English at home?

- ○ Yes
- ○ No, only speaks English — *Skip to 14*

b. What is this language?

_____
(For example -- Chinese, Italian, Spanish, etc.)

c. How well does this person speak English?

- ○ Very well
- ○ Not well
- ○ Well
- ○ Not at all

14. What is this person's ancestry? *If uncertain about how to report ancestry, see instruction guide.*

_____

(For example: Afro-Amer., English, French, German, Honduran, Hungarian, Irish, Italian, Jamaican, Korean, Lebanese, Mexican, Nigerian, Polish, Ukrainian, Venezuelan, etc.)

15a. Did this person live in this house five years ago (April 1, 1975)?
If in college or Armed Forces in April 1975, report place of residence there.

- ○ Born April 1975 or later — *Turn to next page for next person*
- ○ Yes, this house — *Skip to 16*
- ○ No, different house

b. Where did this person live five years ago (April 1, 1975)?

(1) State, foreign country, Puerto Rico, Guam, etc.: _____

(2) County: _____

(3) City, town, village, etc.: _____

(4) Inside the incorporated (legal) limits of that city, town, village, etc.?

- ○ Yes
- ○ No, in unincorporated area

16. When was this person born?

- ○ Born before April 1965 — *Please go on with questions 17-33*
- ○ Born April 1965 or later — *Turn to next page for next person*

17. In April 1975 *(five years ago)* **was this person —**
a. On active duty in the Armed Forces?

- ○ Yes
- ○ No

b. Attending college?

- ○ Yes
- ○ No

c. Working at a job or business?

- ○ Yes, full time
- ○ No
- ○ Yes, part time

18a. Is this person a veteran of active-duty military service in the Armed Forces of the United States?
If service was in National Guard or Reserves only, see instruction guide.

- ○ Yes
- ○ No — *Skip to 19*

b. Was active-duty military service during —
Fill a circle for each period in which this person served.

- ○ May 1975 or later
- ○ Vietnam era *(August 1964–April 1975)*
- ○ February 1955—July 1964
- ○ Korean conflict *(June 1950–January 1955)*
- ○ World War II *(September 1940–July 1947)*
- ○ World War I *(April 1917–November 1918)*
- ○ Any other time

19. Does this person have a physical, mental, or other health condition which has lasted for 6 or more months and which . . .

	Yes	No
a. **Limits** the kind or amount of work this person can do at a job?	○	○
b. **Prevents** this person from working at a job?	○	○
c. **Limits** or prevents this person from using public transportation?	○	○

20. *If this person is a female —*
How many babies has she ever had, not counting stillbirths? Do not count her stepchildren or children she has adopted.

None 1 2 3 4 5 6
○ ○ ○ ○ ○ ○ ○

7 8 9 10 11 12 or more
○ ○ ○ ○ ○ ○

21. *If this person has ever been married —*
a. Has this person been married more than once?

- ○ Once
- ○ More than once

b. Month and year of marriage?

_____ _____
(Month) (Year)

Month and year of first marriage?

_____ _____
(Month) (Year)

c. *If married more than once* — Did the first marriage end because of the death of the husband (or wife)?

- ○ Yes
- ○ No

22a. Did this person work at any time last week?

- ○ Yes — *Fill this circle if this person worked full time or part time. (Count part-time work such as delivering papers, or helping without pay in a family business or farm. Also count active duty in the Armed Forces.)*
- ○ No — *Fill this circle if this person did not work, or did only own housework, school work, or volunteer work.*

Skip to 25

b. How many hours did this person work last week (at all jobs)?
Subtract any time off; add overtime or extra hours worked.

_____ Hours

23. At what location did this person work last week?
If this person worked at more than one location, print where he or she worked most last week.
If one location cannot be specified, see instruction guide.

a. Address *(Number and street)* _____

_____
If street address is not known, enter the building name, shopping center, or other physical location description.

b. Name of city, town, village, borough, etc.

_____

c. Is the place of work inside the incorporated (legal) limits of that city, town, village, borough, etc.?

- ○ Yes
- ○ No, in unincorporated area

d. County _____

e. State _____ **f. ZIP Code** _____

24a. Last week, how long did it usually take this person to get from home to work (one way)?

_____ Minutes

b. How did this person usually get to work last week?
If this person used more than one method, give the one usually used for most of the distance.

- ○ Car
- ○ Taxicab
- ○ Truck
- ○ Motorcycle
- ○ Van
- ○ Bicycle
- ○ Bus or streetcar
- ○ Walked only
- ○ Railroad
- ○ Worked at home
- ○ Subway or elevated
- ○ Other — *Specify*

If car, truck, or van in 24b, go to 24c.
Otherwise, skip to 28.

_____

FOR CENSUS USE ONLY

Per. No.	11.	13b.		14.		15b.		23.			○ VL	24a.
	⊘⊘⊘	⊘⊘⊘		⊘⊘⊘	⊘⊘⊘	⊘⊘⊘	⊘⊘⊘	⊘⊘⊘	⊘⊘⊘	⊘⊘⊘		⊘⊘
I	III	III		III	III	III	III	III	III	III		II
2	222	222		222	222	222	222	222	222	222		22
3	333	333		333	333	333	333	333	333	333		33
4	444	444		444	444	444	444	444	444	444		44
5	555	555		555	555	555	555	555	555	555		55
6	666	666		666	666	666	666	666	666	666		66
7	777	777		777	777	777	777	777	777	777		77
8	888	888		888	888	888	888	888	888	888		88
	999	999		999	999	999	999	999	999	999		99

Name of Person 1 on page 2:

Last name   First name   Middle initial

11. In what State or foreign country was this person born?
Print the State where this person's mother was living when this person was born. Do not give the location of the hospital unless the mother's home and the hospital were in the same State.

_____
Name of State or foreign country; or Puerto Rico, Guam, etc.

12. If this person was born in a foreign country —
a. Is this person a naturalized citizen of the United States?
- ○ Yes, a naturalized citizen
- ○ No, not a citizen
- ○ Born abroad of American parents

b. When did this person come to the United States to stay?
- ○ 1975 to 1980
- ○ 1965 to 1969
- ○ 1950 to 1959
- ○ 1970 to 1974
- ○ 1960 to 1964
- ○ Before 1950

13a. Does this person speak a language other than English at home?
- ○ Yes
- ○ No, only speaks English — *Skip to 14*

b. What is this language?

_____
(For example — Chinese, Italian, Spanish, etc.)

c. How well does this person speak English?
- ○ Very well
- ○ Well
- ○ Not well
- ○ Not at all

14. What is this person's ancestry? *If uncertain about how to report ancestry, see instruction guide.*

_____
(For example: Afro-Amer., English, French, German, Honduran, Hungarian, Irish, Italian, Jamaican, Korean, Lebanese, Mexican, Nigerian, Polish, Ukrainian, Venezuelan, etc.)

15a. Did this person live in this house five years ago (April 1, 1975)?
If in college or Armed Forces in April 1975, report place of residence there.
- ○ Born April 1975 or later — *Turn to next page for next person*
- ○ Yes, this house — *Skip to 16*
- ○ No, different house

b. Where did this person live five years ago (April 1, 1975)?

(1) State, foreign country, Puerto Rico, Guam, etc.: _____

(2) County: _____

(3) City, town, village, etc.: _____

(4) Inside the incorporated (legal) limits of that city, town, village, etc.?
- ○ Yes
- ○ No, in unincorporated area

---

16. When was this person born?
- ○ Born before April 1965 — *Please go on with questions 17-33*
- ○ Born April 1965 or later — *Turn to next page for next person*

17. In April 1975 (five years ago) was this person —
a. On active duty in the Armed Forces?
- ○ Yes
- ○ No

b. Attending college?
- ○ Yes
- ○ No

c. Working at a job or business?
- ○ Yes, full time
- ○ No
- ○ Yes, part time

18a. Is this person a veteran of active-duty military service in the Armed Forces of the United States?
If service was in National Guard or Reserves only, see instruction guide.
- ○ Yes
- ○ No — *Skip to 19*

b. Was active-duty military service during —
Fill a circle for each period in which this person served.
- ○ May 1975 or later
- ○ Vietnam era (August 1964—April 1975)
- ○ February 1955—July 1964
- ○ Korean conflict (June 1950—January 1955)
- ○ World War II (September 1940—July 1947)
- ○ World War I (April 1917—November 1918)
- ○ Any other time

19. Does this person have a physical, mental, or other health condition which has lasted for 6 or more months and which . . .

	Yes	No
a. <u>Limits</u> the kind or amount of work this person can do at a job?	○	○
b. <u>Prevents</u> this person from working at a job?	○	○
c. <u>Limits or prevents</u> this person from using public transportation?	○	○

20. If this person is a female —
How many babies has she ever had, not counting stillbirths?
Do not count her stepchildren or children she has adopted.
- None 1 2 3 4 5 6
- ○ ○ ○ ○ ○ ○ ○
- 7 8 9 10 11 12 or more
- ○ ○ ○ ○ ○ ○

21. If this person has ever been married —
a. Has this person been married more than once?
- ○ Once
- ○ More than once

b. Month and year of marriage?   **Month and year of first marriage?**

(Month) (Year)   (Month) (Year)

c. If married more than once — Did the first marriage end because of the death of the husband (or wife)?
- ○ Yes
- ○ No

22a. Did this person work at any time last week?
- ○ Yes — *Fill this circle if this person worked full time or part time. (Count part-time work such as delivering papers, or helping without pay in a family business or farm. Also count active duty in the Armed Forces.)*
- ○ No — *Fill this circle if this person did not work, or did only own housework, school work, or volunteer work.*

Skip to 25

b. How many hours did this person work last week (at all jobs)?
Subtract any time off; add overtime or extra hours worked.

_____ Hours

23. At what location did this person work last week?
If this person worked at more than one location, print where he or she worked most last week.
If one location cannot be specified, see instruction guide.

a. Address *(Number and street)* _____

If street address is not known, enter the building name, shopping center, or other physical location description.

b. Name of city, town, village, borough, etc.

_____

c. Is the place of work inside the incorporated (legal) limits of that city, town, village, borough, etc.?
- ○ Yes
- ○ No, in unincorporated area

d. County _____

e. State _____ **f. ZIP Code** _____

24a. Last week, how long did it usually take this person to get from home to work (one way)?

_____ Minutes

b. How did this person usually get to work last week?
If this person used more than one method, give the one usually used for most of the distance.
- ○ Car
- ○ Taxicab
- ○ Truck
- ○ Motorcycle
- ○ Van
- ○ Bicycle
- ○ Bus or streetcar
- ○ Walked only
- ○ Railroad
- ○ Worked at home
- ○ Subway or elevated
- ○ Other — *Specify*

If car, truck, or van in 24b, go to 24c.
Otherwise, skip to 28.

_____

FOR CENSUS USE ONLY

Per. No.	11.	13b.	14.	15b.	23.	○ VL	24a.
	0 0	0 0	0 0 | 0 0	0 0 0 0	0 0 0 0 0 0		0 0
1	1 1 1	1 1 1	1 1 1 | 1 1 1	1 1 1 1 1 1	1 1 1 1 1 1 1 1 1		1 1
2	2 2 2	2 2 2	2 2 2 | 2 2 2	2 2 2 2 2 2	2 2 2 2 2 2 2 2 2		2 2
3	3 3 3	3 3 3	3 3 3 | 3 3 3	3 3 3 3 3 3	3 3 3 3 3 3 3 3 3		3 3
4	4 4 4	4 4 4	4 4 4 | 4 4 4	4 4 4 4 4 4	4 4 4 4 4 4 4 4 4		4 4
5	5 5 5	5 5 5	5 5 5 | 5 5 5	5 5 5 5 5 5	5 5 5 5 5 5 5 5 5		5 5
6	6 6 6	6 6 6	6 6 6 | 6 6 6	6 6 6 6 6 6	6 6 6 6 6 6 6 6 6		6 6
7	7 7 7	7 7 7	7 7 7 | 7 7 7	7 7 7 7 7 7	7 7 7 7 7 7 7 7 7		7 7
8	8 8 8	8 8 8	8 8 8 | 8 8 8	8 8 8 8 8 8	8 8 8 8 8 8 8 8 8		8 8
9	9 9 9	9 9 9	9 9 9 | 9 9 9	9 9 9 9 9 9	9 9 9 9 9 9 9 9 9		9 9

    Page 7

---

c. When going to work last week, did this person usually —

- ○ Drive alone — Skip to 28
- ○ Share driving
- ○ Drive others only
- ○ Ride as passenger only

d. How many people, including this person, usually rode to work in the car, truck, or van last week?

- ○ 2
- ○ 3
- ○ 4
- ○ 5
- ○ 6
- ○ 7 or more ■

After answering 24d, skip to 28.

25. Was this person temporarily absent or on layoff from a job or business last week?

- ○ Yes, on layoff
- ○ Yes, on vacation, temporary illness, labor dispute, etc.
- ○ No

26a. Has this person been looking for work during the last 4 weeks?

- ○ Yes
- ○ No — Skip to 27

b. Could this person have taken a job last week?

- ○ No, already has a job ■
- ○ No, temporarily ill
- ○ No, other reasons (in school, etc.)
- ○ Yes, could have taken a job ■

27. When did this person last work, even for a few days?

- ○ 1980
- ○ 1979
- ○ 1978
- ○ 1975 to 1977
- ○ 1970 to 1974
- ○ 1969 or earlier
- ○ Never worked

} Skip to 31d

28–30. Current or most recent job activity

Describe clearly this person's chief job activity or business last week. If this person had more than one job, describe the one at which this person worked the most hours. If this person had no job or business last week, give information for last job or business since 1975.

28. Industry

a. For whom did this person work? *If now on active duty in the Armed Forces, print "AF" and skip to question 31.*

_____

(Name of company, business, organization, or other employer)

b. What kind of business or industry was this? *Describe the activity at location where employed.*

_____

(For example: Hospital, newspaper publishing, mail order house, auto engine manufacturing, breakfast cereal manufacturing) ■

c. Is this mainly — (Fill one circle)

- ○ Manufacturing
- ○ Wholesale trade
- ○ Retail trade
- ○ Other — (agriculture, construction, service, government, etc.)

29. Occupation

a. What kind of work was this person doing?

_____

(For example: Registered nurse, personnel manager, supervisor of order department, gasoline engine assembler, grinder operator)

b. What were this person's most important activities or duties?

_____

(For example: Patient care, directing hiring policies, supervising order clerks, assembling engines, operating grinding mill)

30. Was this person — (Fill one circle)

Employee of private company, business, or individual, for wages, salary, or commissions ..... ○ ■

- Federal government employee .... ○
- State government employee .... ○
- Local government employee (city, county, etc.)...... ○

Self-employed in own business, professional practice, or farm —
- Own business not incorporated .... ○
- Own business incorporated .... ○

Working without pay in family business or farm ..... ○

CENSUS USE

21b.

I	⊘ ⊘
	I I
	2 2
II	3 3
	4 4
III	5 5
	6 6
	7 7
IV	8 8
	9 9

22b.

⊘ ⊘
I I
2 2
3 3
4 4
5 5
6 6
7 7
8 8
9 9

28.

A	B	C
○	○	○
D	E	F
○	○	○
G	H	J
○	○	○
K	L	M
○	○	○

⊘ ⊘ ⊘
I I I
2 2 2
3 3
4 4
5 5
6 6
7 7
8 8
9 9

AF ○
NW ○

29.

N	P	Q
○	○	○
R	S	T
○	○	○
U	V	W
○	○	○
X	Y	Z
○	○	○

⊘ ⊘
I I
2 2
3 3 3
4 4 4
5 5 5
6 6 6
7 7 7
8 8 8
9 9 9

31a. Last year (1979), did this person work, even for a few days, at a paid job or in a business or farm?

    ○ Yes ■   ○ No — Skip to 31d

b. How many weeks did this person work in 1979?
Count paid vacation, paid sick leave, and military service.

_____ Weeks

c. During the weeks worked in 1979, how many hours did this person usually work each week?

_____ Hours

d. Of the weeks not worked in 1979 (if any), how many weeks was this person looking for work or on layoff from a job?

_____ Weeks

32. Income in 1979 —
Fill circles and print dollar amounts.
If net income was a loss, write "Loss" above the dollar amount. If exact amount is not known, give best estimate. For income received jointly by household members, see instruction guide.

During 1979 did this person receive any income from the following sources?

If "Yes" to any of the sources below — How much did this person receive for the entire year?

a. Wages, salary, commissions, bonuses, or tips from all jobs . . . *Report amount before deductions for taxes, bonds, dues, or other items.*

- ○ Yes → $ _____ .00
- ○ No   *(Annual amount – Dollars)*

b. Own nonfarm business, partnership, or professional practice . . . *Report net income after business expenses.*

- ○ Yes → $ _____ .00 ■
- ○ No   *(Annual amount – Dollars)*

c. Own farm . . .
Report net income after operating expenses. Include earnings as a tenant farmer or sharecropper.

- ○ Yes → $ _____ .00
- ○ No   *(Annual amount – Dollars)*

d. Interest, dividends, royalties, or net rental income . . .
Report even small amounts credited to an account.

- ○ Yes → $ _____ .00
- ○ No   *(Annual amount – Dollars)*

e. Social Security or Railroad Retirement . . .

- ○ Yes → $ _____ .00 ■
- ○ No   *(Annual amount – Dollars)*

f. Supplemental Security (SSI), Aid to Families with Dependent Children (AFDC), or other public assistance or public welfare payments . . .

- ○ Yes → $ _____ .00
- ○ No   *(Annual amount – Dollars)*

g. Unemployment compensation, veterans' payments, pensions, alimony or child support, or any other sources of income received regularly . . .
Exclude lump-sum payments such as money from an inheritance or the sale of a home.

- ○ Yes → $ _____ .00 ■
- ○ No   *(Annual amount – Dollars)*

33. What was this person's total income in 1979?
Add entries in questions 32a through g; subtract any losses. $ _____ .00
If total amount was a loss, write "Loss" above amount.   *(Annual amount – Dollars)*   OR ○ None

---

CENSUS USE ONLY

31b.	31c.	31d.
⊘ ⊘	⊘ ⊘	⊘ ⊘
I I	I I	I I
2 2	2 2	2 2
3 3	3 3	3 3
4 4	4 4	4 4
5 5	5 5	5 5
6	6 6	6
7	7 7	7
8	8 8	8
9	9 9	9

■

32a.	■	32b.
⊘ ⊘ ⊘ ⊘		⊘ ⊘ ⊘ ⊘
I I I I		I I I I
2 2 2 2		2 2 2 2
3 3 3 3		3 3 3 3
4 4 4 4		4 4 4 4
5 5 5 5		5 5 5 5
6 6 6 6		6 6 6 6
7 7 7 7		7 7 7 7
8 8 8 8		8 8 8 8
9 9 9 9		9 9 9 9
A ○		A ○

32c.	32d.
⊘ ⊘ ⊘ ⊘	⊘ ⊘ ⊘ ⊘
I I I I	I I I I
2 2 2 2	2 2 2 2
3 3 3 3	3 3 3 3
4 4 4 4	4 4 4 4
5 5 5 5	5 5 5 5
6 6 6 6	6 6 6 6
7 7 7 7	7 7 7 7
8 8 8 8	8 8 8 8
9 9 9 9	9 9 9 9
○ A ○	○ A ○

32e.	32f.
⊘ ⊘ ⊘ ⊘	⊘ ⊘ ⊘ ⊘
I I I	I I I
2 2 2	2 2 2
3 3 3	3 3 3
4 4 4	4 4 4
5 5 5	5 5 5
6 6 6	6 6 6
7 7 7	7 7 7
8 8 8	8 8 8
9 9 9	9 9 9

32g.	33.
⊘ ⊘ ⊘ ⊘	⊘ ⊘ ⊘ ⊘
I I I I	I I I I
2 2 2 2	2 2 2 2
3 3 3 3	3 3 3 3
4 4 4 4	4 4 4 4
5 5 5 5	5 5 5 5
6 6 6 6	6 6 6 6
7 7 7 7	7 7 7 7
8 8 8 8	8 8 8 8
9 9 9 9	9 9 9 9
	○ A ○
I I	I I
2 2	2 2
3 3	3 3
4 4	4 4
5 5	5 5
6 6	6 6
7 7	7 7
8 8	8 8
9 9	9 9

Right margin column:
⊘
9
8
7
6
5
4
3
●
I
■

⊘
9
8
7
6
5
4
3
2
1
■

→ *Please turn to the next page and answer the questions for Person 2 on page 2*

NOW PLEASE ANSWER QUESTIONS H1—H12

FOR YOUR HOUSEHOLD

PERSON in column 7	
Last name	
First name	Middle initial

If you listed more than 7 persons in Question 1, please see note on page 20.

If relative of person in column 1:
- ○ Husband/wife
- ○ Son/daughter
- ○ Brother/sister
- ○ Father/mother
- ○ Other relative

If not related to person in column 1:
- ○ Roomer, boarder
- ○ Partner, roommate
- ○ Paid employee
- ○ Other nonrelative

- ○ Male   ○ Female

- ○ White
- ○ Black or Negro
- ○ Japanese
- ○ Chinese
- ○ Filipino
- ○ Korean
- ○ Vietnamese
- ○ Indian (Amer.)
  Print tribe →
- ○ Asian Indian
- ○ Hawaiian
- ○ Guamanian
- ○ Samoan
- ○ Eskimo
- ○ Aleut
- ○ Other — Specify

a. Age at last birthday

c. Year of birth

			1					
1 ●	8 ○	0 ○	0 ○	0 ○				
9 ○	1 ○	1 ○						
	2 ○	2 ○						
	3 ○	3 ○						
	4 ○	4 ○						
	5 ○	5 ○						
	6 ○	6 ○						
	7 ○	7 ○						
	8 ○	8 ○						
	9 ○	9 ○						

b. Month of birth
- ○ Jan.—Mar.
- ○ Apr.—June
- ○ July—Sept.
- ○ Oct.—Dec.

- ○ Now married   ○ Separated
- ○ Widowed   ○ Never married
- ○ Divorced

- ○ No (not Spanish/Hispanic)
- ○ Yes, Mexican, Mexican-Amer., Chicano
- ○ Yes, Puerto Rican
- ○ Yes, Cuban
- ○ Yes, other Spanish/Hispanic

- ○ No, has not attended since February 1
- ○ Yes, public school, public college
- ○ Yes, private, church-related
- ○ Yes, private, not church-related

Highest grade attended:
- ○ Nursery school   ○ Kindergarten

Elementary through high school (grade or year)
1 2 3 4 5 6 7 8 9 10 11 12
○ ○ ○ ○ ○ ○ ○ ○ ○ ○ ○ ○

College (academic year)
1 2 3 4 5 6 7 8 or more
○ ○ ○ ○ ○ ○ ○ ○
- ○ Never attended school!—Skip question 10

- ○ Now attending this grade (or year)
- ○ Finished this grade (or year)
- ○ Did not finish this grade (or year)

CENSUS USE ONLY	A.	○ I	○ N	○ ○

H1. Did you leave anyone out of Question 1 because you were not sure if the person should be listed — for example, a new baby still in the hospital, a lodger who also has another home, or a person who stays here once in a while and has no other home?
- ○ Yes — On page 20 give name(s) and reason left out.
- ○ No

H2. Did you list anyone in Question 1 who is away from home now — for example, on a vacation or in a hospital?
- ○ Yes — On page 20 give name(s) and reason person is away.
- ○ No

H3. Is anyone visiting here who is not already listed?
- ○ Yes — On page 20 give name of each visitor for whom there is no one at the home address to report the person to a census taker.
- ○ No

H4. How many living quarters, occupied and vacant, are at this address?
- ○ One
- ○ 2 apartments or living quarters
- ○ 3 apartments or living quarters
- ○ 4 apartments or living quarters
- ○ 5 apartments or living quarters
- ○ 6 apartments or living quarters
- ○ 7 apartments or living quarters
- ○ 8 apartments or living quarters
- ○ 9 apartments or living quarters
- ○ 10 or more apartments or living quarters
- ○ This is a mobile home or trailer

H5. Do you enter your living quarters —
- ○ Directly from the outside or through a common or public hall?
- ○ Through someone else's living quarters?

H6. Do you have complete plumbing facilities in your living quarters, that is, hot and cold piped water, a flush toilet, and a bathtub or shower?
- ○ Yes, for this household only
- ○ Yes, but also used by another household
- ○ No, have some but not all plumbing facilities
- ○ No plumbing facilities in living quarters

H7. How many rooms do you have in your living quarters?
Do not count bathrooms, porches, balconies, foyers, halls, or half-rooms.
- ○ 1 room   ○ 4 rooms   ○ 7 rooms
- ○ 2 rooms   ○ 5 rooms   ○ 8 rooms
- ○ 3 rooms   ○ 6 rooms   ○ 9 or more rooms

H8. Are your living quarters —
- ○ Owned or being bought by you or by someone else in this household?
- ○ Rented for cash rent?
- ○ Occupied without payment of cash rent?

H9. Is this apartment (house) part of a condominium?
- ○ No
- ○ Yes, a condominium

H10. If this is a one-family house —

a. Is the house on a property of 10 or more acres?
- ○ Yes   ○ No

b. Is any part of the property used as a commercial establishment or medical office?
- ○ Yes   ○ No

H11. If you live in a one-family house or a condominium unit which you own or are buying —

What is the value of this property, that is, how much do you think this property (house and lot or condominium unit) would sell for if it were for sale?

Do not answer this question if this is —
- A mobile home or trailer
- A house on 10 or more acres
- A house with a commercial establishment or medical office on the property

- ○ Less than $10,000
- ○ $10,000 to $14,999
- ○ $15,000 to $17,499
- ○ $17,500 to $19,999
- ○ $20,000 to $22,499
- ○ $22,500 to $24,999
- ○ $25,000 to $27,499
- ○ $27,500 to $29,999
- ○ $30,000 to $34,999
- ○ $35,000 to $39,999
- ○ $40,000 to $44,999
- ○ $45,000 to $49,999
- ○ $50,000 to $54,999
- ○ $55,000 to $59,999
- ○ $60,000 to $64,999
- ○ $65,000 to $69,999
- ○ $70,000 to $74,999
- ○ $75,000 to $79,999
- ○ $80,000 to $89,999
- ○ $90,000 to $99,999
- ○ $100,000 to $124,999
- ○ $125,000 to $149,999
- ○ $150,000 to $199,999
- ○ $200,000 or more

H12. If you pay rent for your living quarters —
What is the monthly rent?
If rent is not paid by the month, see the instruction guide on how to figure a monthly rent.
- ○ Less than $50
- ○ $50 to $59
- ○ $60 to $69
- ○ $70 to $79
- ○ $80 to $89
- ○ $90 to $99
- ○ $100 to $109
- ○ $110 to $119
- ○ $120 to $129
- ○ $130 to $139
- ○ $140 to $149
- ○ $150 to $159
- ○ $160 to $169
- ○ $170 to $179
- ○ $180 to $189
- ○ $190 to $199
- ○ $200 to $224
- ○ $225 to $249
- ○ $250 to $274
- ○ $275 to $299
- ○ $300 to $349
- ○ $350 to $399
- ○ $400 to $499
- ○ $500 or more

FOR CENSUS USE ONLY

A4. Block number	A6. Serial number	B. Type of unit or quarters	For vacant units	D. Months vacant	F. Total persons
		Occupied	**C1.** Is this unit for —	○ Less than 1 month	
		○ First form	○ Year round use	○ 1 up to 2 months	
0 0 0	0 0 0 0	○ Continuation	○ Seasonal/Mig. — Skip C2, C3, and D.	○ 2 up to 6 months	0 0 0
I I I	I I I I	**Vacant**	**C2.** Vacancy status	○ 6 up to 12 months	I I I
2 2 2	2 2 2 2	○ Regular	○ For rent	○ 1 year up to 2 years	2 2 2
3 3 3	3 3 3 3	○ Usual home elsewhere	○ For sale only	○ 2 or more years	3 3 3
4 4 4	4 4 4 4		○ Rented or sold, not occupied	**E. Indicators**	4 4 4
5 5 5	5 5 5 5	**Group quarters**	○ Held for occasional use	1. ○ ○ Mail return	5 5 5
6 6 6	6 6 6 6	○ First form	○ Other vacant	2. ○ ○ Pop./F	6 6 6
7 7 7	7 7 7 7	○ Continuation	**C3.** Is this unit boarded up?		7 7 7
8 8 8	8 8 8 8		○ Yes ○ No	○ ○	8 8 8
9 9 9	9 9 9 9				9 9 9

Column indicators (right margin): 0 9 8 7 6 5 4 3 ● I   0 9 8 7 6 5 4 ● 2 I

Page 4

H13. Which best describes this building?
Include all apartments, flats, etc., even if vacant.

- ○ A mobile home or trailer
- ○ A one-family house detached from any other house
- ○ A one-family house attached to one or more houses
- ○ A building for 2 families
- ○ A building for 3 or 4 families
- ○ A building for 5 to 9 families
- ○ A building for 10 to 19 families
- ○ A building for 20 to 49 families
- ○ A building for 50 or more families
- ○ A boat, tent, van, etc. ■

H14a. How many stories (floors) are in this building?
Count an attic or basement as a story if it has any finished rooms for living purposes.

- ○ 1 to 3 — *Skip to H15*
- ○ 4 to 6
- ○ 7 to 12
- ○ 13 or more stories

b. Is there a passenger elevator in this building?

- ○ Yes
- ○ No

H15a. Is this building —

- ○ On a city or suburban lot, or on a place of less than 1 acre? — *Skip to H16*
- ○ On a place of 1 to 9 acres?
- ○ On a place of 10 or more acres?

b. Last year, 1979, did sales of crops, livestock, and other farm products from this place amount to —

- ○ Less than $50 (or None)
- ○ $50 to $249 ■
- ○ $250 to $599
- ○ $600 to $999
- ○ $1,000 to $2,499
- ○ $2,500 or more

H16. Do you get water from —

- ○ A public system *(city water department, etc.)* or private company?
- ○ An individual drilled well?
- ○ An individual dug well?
- ○ Some other source *(a spring, creek, river, cistern, etc.)?*

H17. Is this building connected to a public sewer?

- ○ Yes, connected to public sewer
- ○ No, connected to septic tank or cesspool
- ○ No, use other means

H18. About when was this building originally built? *Mark when the building was first constructed, not when it was remodeled, added to, or converted.*

- ○ 1979 or 1980
- ○ 1975 to 1978
- ○ 1970 to 1974 ■
- ○ 1960 to 1969
- ○ 1950 to 1959
- ○ 1940 to 1949
- ○ 1939 or earlier

H19. When did the person listed in column 1 move into this house (or apartment)?

- ○ 1979 or 1980
- ○ 1975 to 1978
- ○ 1970 to 1974
- ○ 1960 to 1969
- ○ 1950 to 1959
- ○ 1949 or earlier
- ○ Always lived here

H20. How are your living quarters heated?
Fill one circle for the kind of heat used most.

- ○ Steam or hot water system
- ○ Central warm-air furnace with ducts to the individual rooms
  (Do not count electric heat pumps here)
- ○ Electric heat pump
- ○ Other built-in electric units *(permanently installed in wall, ceiling, or baseboard)* ■
- ○ Floor, wall, or pipeless furnace
- ○ Room heaters <u>with</u> flue or vent, burning gas, oil, or kerosene
- ○ Room heaters <u>without</u> flue or vent, burning gas, oil, or kerosene *(not portable)*
- ○ Fireplaces, stoves, or portable room heaters of any kind
- ○ No heating equipment

H21a. Which fuel is used most for house heating?

- ○ Gas: from underground pipes serving the neighborhood
- ○ Gas: bottled, tank, or LP
- ○ Electricity
- ○ Fuel oil, kerosene, etc. ■
- ○ Coal or coke
- ○ Wood
- ○ Other fuel
- ○ No fuel used

b. Which fuel is used most for water heating?

- ○ Gas: from underground pipes serving the neighborhood
- ○ Gas: bottled, tank, or LP
- ○ Electricity
- ○ Fuel oil, kerosene, etc.
- ○ Coal or coke ■
- ○ Wood
- ○ Other fuel
- ○ No fuel used

c. Which fuel is used most for cooking?

- ○ Gas: from underground pipes serving the neighborhood
- ○ Gas: bottled, tank, or LP
- ○ Electricity
- ○ Fuel oil, kerosene, etc. ■
- ○ Coal or coke
- ○ Wood
- ○ Other fuel
- ○ No fuel used

H22. What are the costs of utilities and fuels for your living quarters?

a. Electricity
$ _____ .00 OR
- ○ Included in rent or no charge
- ○ Electricity not used

Average monthly cost

b. Gas
$ _____ .00 OR
- ○ Included in rent or no charge
- ○ Gas not used

Average monthly cost

c. Water
$ _____ .00 OR
- ○ Included in rent or no charge

Yearly cost

d. Oil, coal, kerosene, wood, etc.
$ _____ .00 OR
- ○ Included in rent or no charge
- ○ These fuels not used

Yearly cost

H23. Do you have complete kitchen facilities? *Complete kitchen facilities are a sink with piped water, a range or cookstove, and a refrigerator.*

- ○ Yes ■
- ○ No

H24. How many bedrooms do you have?
Count rooms used mainly for sleeping even if used also for other purposes.

- ○ No bedroom
- ○ 1 bedroom
- ○ 2 bedrooms
- ○ 3 bedrooms
- ○ 4 bedrooms
- ○ 5 or more bedrooms

H25. How many bathrooms do you have?

A complete bathroom is a room with flush toilet, bathtub or shower, and wash basin with piped water.

A half bathroom has at least a flush toilet <u>or</u> bathtub or shower, but does not have all the facilities for a complete bathroom.

- ○ No bathroom, or only a half bathroom
- ○ 1 complete bathroom
- ○ 1 complete bathroom, plus half bath(s)
- ○ 2 or more complete bathrooms

H26. Do you have a telephone in your living quarters?

- ○ Yes ■
- ○ No

H27. Do you have air conditioning?

- ○ Yes, a central air-conditioning system
- ○ Yes, 1 individual room unit
- ○ Yes, 2 or more individual room units
- ○ No

H28. How many automobiles are kept at home for use by members of your household?

- ○ None ■
- ○ 1 automobile
- ○ 2 automobiles
- ○ 3 or more automobiles ■

H29. How many vans or trucks of one-ton capacity or less are kept at home for use by members of your household?

- ○ None
- ○ 1 van or truck
- ○ 2 vans or trucks
- ○ 3 or more vans or trucks

CENSUS USE

H22a.
0 0 0 / 1 1 1 / 2 2 2 / 3 3 3 / 4 4 4 / 5 5 5 / 6 6 6 / 7 7 7 / 8 8 8 / 9 9 9

H22b.
0 0 0 / 1 1 1 / 2 2 2 / 3 3 3 / 4 4 4 / 5 5 5 / 6 6 6 / 7 7 7 / 8 8 8 / 9 9 9

H22c.
0 0 0 / 1 1 1 / 2 2 2 / 3 3 3 / 4 4 4 / 5 5 5 / 6 6 6 / 7 7 7 / 8 8 8 / 9 9 9

H22d.
0 0 0 0 / 1 1 1 1 / 2 2 2 2 / 3 3 3 3 / 4 4 4 4 / 5 5 5 5 / 6 6 6 6 / 7 7 7 7 / 8 8 8 8 / 9 9 9 9

0 0 0 0 / 1 1 1 1 / 2 2 2 2 / 3 3 3 3 / 4 4 4 4 / 5 5 5 5 / 6 6 6 6 / 7 7 7 7 / 8 8 8 8 / 9 9 9 9

0 0 0 0 / 1 1 1 1 / 2 2 2 2 / 3 3 3 3 / 4 4 4 4 / 5 5 5 5 / 6 6 6 6 / 7 7 7 7 / 8 8 8 8 / 9 9 9 9

FOR YOUR HOUSEHOLD

Please answer H30–H32 if you live in a one-family house which you own or are buying, <u>unless</u> this is —

- A mobile home or trailer . . . .
- A house on 10 or more acres . . . .
- A condominium unit . . . .
- A house with a commercial establishment or medical office on the property . . . . .

If any of these, or if you rent your unit or this is a multi-family structure, skip H30 to H32 and turn to page 6.

H30. What were the real estate taxes on <u>this</u> property last year?

$ _____ .00   OR   ○ None

H31. What is the annual premium for fire and hazard insurance on <u>this</u> property?

$ _____ .00   OR   ○ None

H32a. Do you have a mortgage, deed of trust, contract to purchase, or similar debt on <u>this</u> property?

○ Yes, mortgage, deed of trust, or similar debt

○ Yes, contract to purchase

○ No — *Skip to page 6*

b. Do you have a second or junior mortgage on <u>this</u> property?

○ Yes   ○ No

c. How much is your total regular monthly payment to the lender?
Also include payments on a contract to purchase and to lenders holding second or junior mortgages on this property.

$ _____ .00   OR   ○ No regular payment required — *Skip to page 6*

d. Does your regular monthly payment (amount entered in H32c) include payments for real estate taxes on <u>this</u> property?

○ Yes, taxes included in payment

○ No, taxes paid separately or taxes not required

e. Does your regular monthly payment (amount entered in H32c) include payments for fire and hazard insurance on <u>this</u> property?

○ Yes, insurance included in payment

○ No, insurance paid separately or no insurance

Please turn to page 6 →

FOR CENSUS USE ONLY

1990 QUESTIONNAIRE

The "short form" questionnaire for 1990, contained the 100-percent inquiries those asked of each member of each household. The "long form" or sample questionnaire (pictured here) included the 100-percent inquires plus a series of population, housing, social, and economic questions asked of a sample of households.

Page 2 | QUESTIONS ASKED OF ALL PERSONS

PLEASE ALSO ANSWER HOUSING QUESTIONS ON PAGE 3 → PLEASE ALSO ANSWER HOUSING QUESTIONS ON PAGE 3 →

Please fill one column for each person listed in Question 1a on page 1.

2. How is this person related to PERSON 1?
Fill ONE circle for each person.
If Other relative of person in column 1, fill circle and print exact relationship, such as mother-in-law, grandparent, son-in-law, niece, cousin, and so on.

PERSON 1: START in this column with the household member (or one of the members) in whose name the home is owned, being bought, or rented. If there is no such person, start in this column with any adult household member.

If a RELATIVE of Person 1:
○ Husband/wife ○ Brother/sister
○ Natural-born or adopted son/daughter ○ Father/mother ○ Grandchild
○ Stepson/stepdaughter ○ Other relative
If NOT RELATED to Person 1:
○ Roomer, boarder, or foster child ○ Unmarried partner
○ Housemate, roommate ○ Other nonrelative

3. Sex — Fill ONE circle for each person.
○ Male ○ Female

4. Race — Fill ONE circle for the race that the person considers himself/herself to be.
If Indian (Amer.), print the name of the enrolled or principal tribe.
○ White
○ Black or Negro
○ Indian (Amer.) (Print the name of the enrolled or principal tribe.)
○ Eskimo
○ Aleut
Asian or Pacific Islander (API)
○ Chinese ○ Japanese
○ Filipino ○ Asian Indian
○ Hawaiian ○ Samoan
○ Korean ○ Guamanian
○ Vietnamese ○ Other API

If Other Asian or Pacific Islander (API), print one group, for example: Hmong, Fijian, Laotian, Thai, Tongan, Pakistani, Cambodian, and so on.
If Other race, print race.
○ Other race (Print race.)

5. Age and year of birth
a. Print each person's age at last birthday. Fill in the matching circle below each box.
b. Print each person's year of birth and fill the matching circle below each box.

6. Marital status — Fill ONE circle for each person.
○ Now married ○ Separated
○ Widowed ○ Never married
○ Divorced

7. Is this person of Spanish/Hispanic origin? — Fill ONE circle for each person.
○ No (not Spanish/Hispanic)
○ Yes, Mexican, Mexican-Am., Chicano
○ Yes, Puerto Rican
○ Yes, Cuban
○ Yes, other Spanish/Hispanic (Print one group, for example: Argentinean, Colombian, Dominican, Nicaraguan, Salvadoran, Spaniard, and so on.)
If Yes, other Spanish/Hispanic, print one group.

FOR CENSUS USE →

EXPLANATORY NOTES

This booklet shows the content of the two 1990 census questionnaires being delivered by mail. The content of these forms was determined after review of the 1980 census experience, extensive consultation with many government and private users of census data, and a series of experimental censuses and surveys in which various alternatives were tested.

Two principal types of data-collection forms — a 100-percent questionnaire (or "short form") and a sample questionnaire (or "long form") — are being used in the census. Each household receives one of the two questionnaires.

Short form — This questionnaire contains 7 population questions and 7 housing questions, shown on pages 1–3 of this booklet. On average, about 5 in every 6 households will receive the short form. For the average household, this form will take an estimated 14 minutes to complete.

Long form — This questionnaire has all of the short-form questions plus housing questions H8 through H26, shown on pages 4 and 5, and population questions 8 through 33, shown on pages 6 and 7. The population questions are repeated for each member of the household but these pages were not reproduced in this booklet. A statistical sample of approximately 1 in every 6 households will receive the long form. For the average household, this form will take an estimated 43 minutes to complete.

An instruction guide accompanies each questionnaire to help the respondents complete the form, and a preaddressed envelope is provided for returning the questionnaire.

For additional information about the 1990 U.S. Census, please write the Director, Bureau of the Census, Washington, DC 20233.

QUESTIONS ASKED OF A SAMPLE OF HOUSEHOLDS

PLEASE ANSWER THESE QUESTIONS

PERSON 1

Last name   First name   Middle Initial

8. In what U.S. State or foreign country was this person born?

(Name of State or foreign country; or Puerto Rico, Guam, etc.)

9. Is this person a CITIZEN of the United States?

- ○ Yes, born in the United States — *Skip to 11*
- ○ Yes, born in Puerto Rico, Guam, the U.S. Virgin Islands, or Northern Marianas
- ○ Yes, born abroad of American parent or parents
- ○ Yes, U.S. citizen by naturalization
- ○ No, not a citizen of the United States

10. When did this person come to the United States to stay?

- ○ 1987 to 1990
- ○ 1985 or 1986
- ○ 1982 to 1984
- ○ 1980 or 1981
- ○ 1975 to 1979
- ○ 1970 to 1974
- ○ 1965 to 1969
- ○ 1960 to 1964
- ○ 1950 to 1959
- ○ Before 1950

11. At any time since February 1, 1990, has this person attended regular school or college? Include only nursery school, kindergarten, elementary school, and schooling which leads to a high school diploma or a college degree.

- ○ No, has not attended since February 1
- ○ Yes, public school, public college
- ○ Yes, private school, private college

12. How much school has this person COMPLETED? Fill ONE circle for the highest level COMPLETED or degree RECEIVED. If currently enrolled, mark the level of previous grade attended or highest degree received.

- ○ No school completed
- ○ Nursery school
- ○ Kindergarten
- ○ 1st, 2nd, 3rd, or 4th grade
- ○ 5th, 6th, 7th, or 8th grade
- ○ 9th grade
- ○ 10th grade
- ○ 11th grade
- ○ 12th grade, NO DIPLOMA
- ○ HIGH SCHOOL GRADUATE - high school DIPLOMA or the equivalent (For example: GED)
- ○ Some college but no degree
- ○ Associate degree in college - Occupational program
- ○ Associate degree in college - Academic program
- ○ Bachelor's degree (For example: BA, AB, BS)
- ○ Master's degree (For example: MA, MS, MEng, MEd, MSW, MBA)
- ○ Professional school degree (For example: MD, DDS, DVM, LLB, JD)
- ○ Doctorate degree (For example: PhD, EdD)

13. What is this person's ancestry or ethnic origin? (See instruction guide for further information.)

(For example: German, Italian, Afro-Amer., Croatian, Cape Verdean, Dominican, Ecuadoran, Haitian, Cajun, French Canadian, Jamaican, Korean, Lebanese, Mexican, Nigerian, Irish, Polish, Slovak, Taiwanese, Thai, Ukrainian, etc.)

14a. Did this person live in this house or apartment 5 years ago (on April 1, 1985)?

- ○ Born after April 1, 1985 — *Go to questions for the next person*
- ○ Yes — *Skip to 15a*
- ○ No

b. Where did this person live 5 years ago (on April 1, 1985)?

(1) Name of U.S. State or foreign country

(If outside U.S., print answer above and skip to 15a.)

(2) Name of county in the U.S.

(3) Name of city or town in the U.S.

(4) Did this person live inside the city or town limits?

- ○ Yes
- ○ No, lived outside the city/town limits

15a. Does this person speak a language other than English at home?

- ○ Yes
- ○ No — *Skip to 16*

b. What is this language?

(For example: Chinese, Italian, Spanish, Vietnamese)

c. How well does this person speak English?

- ○ Very well
- ○ Well
- ○ Not well
- ○ Not at all

16. When was this person born?

- ○ Born before April 1, 1975 — *Go to 17a*
- ○ Born April 1, 1975 or later — *Go to questions for the next person*

17a. Has this person ever been on active-duty military service in the Armed Forces of the United States or ever been in the United States military Reserves or the National Guard? If service was in Reserves or National Guard only, see instruction guide.

- ○ Yes, now on active duty
- ○ Yes, on active duty in past, but not now
- ○ Yes, service in Reserves or National Guard only — *Skip to 18*
- ○ No — *Skip to 18*

b. Was active-duty military service during — Fill a circle for each period in which this person served.

- ○ September 1980 or later
- ○ May 1975 to August 1980
- ○ Vietnam era (August 1964—April 1975)
- ○ February 1955—July 1964
- ○ Korean conflict (June 1950—January 1955)
- ○ World War II (September 1940—July 1947)
- ○ World War I (April 1917—November 1918)
- ○ Any other time

c. In total, how many years of active-duty military service has this person had?

_____ Years

18. Does this person have a physical, mental, or other health condition that has lasted for 6 or more months and which —

a. Limits the kind or amount of work this person can do at a job?

- ○ Yes
- ○ No

b. Prevents this person from working at a job?

- ○ Yes
- ○ No

19. Because of a health condition that has lasted for 6 or more months, does this person have any difficulty —

a. Going outside the home alone, for example, to shop or visit a doctor's office?

- ○ Yes
- ○ No

b. Taking care of his or her own personal needs, such as bathing, dressing, or getting around inside the home?

- ○ Yes
- ○ No

If this person is a female —

20. How many babies has she ever had, not counting stillbirths? Do not count her stepchildren or children she has adopted.

None 1 2 3 4 5 6 7 8 9 10 11 12 or more
○ ○ ○ ○ ○ ○ ○ ○ ○ ○ ○ ○ ○

21a. Did this person work at any time LAST WEEK?

- ○ Yes — Fill this circle if this person worked full time or part time. (Count part-time work such as delivering papers, or helping without pay in a family business or farm. Also count active duty in the Armed Forces.)
- ○ No — Fill this circle if this person did not work, or did only own housework, school work, or volunteer work. — *Skip to 25*

b. How many hours did this person work LAST WEEK (at all jobs)? Subtract any time off; add overtime or extra hours worked.

_____ Hours

22. At what location did this person work LAST WEEK? If this person worked at more than one location, print where he or she worked most last week.

a. Address (Number and street)

(If the exact address is not known, give a description of the location such as the building name or the nearest street or intersection.)

b. Name of city, town, or post office

c. Is the work location inside the limits of that city or town?

- ○ Yes
- ○ No, outside the city/town limits

d. County

e. State

f. ZIP Code

The sample questionnaire also contains population questions 8 to 33, shown here on pages 6 and 7. These questions appear on pairs of facing pages of the sample form (i.e., 6 and 7, 8 and 9, etc.) for each person in the household. Note that questions 17a to 33 do not apply to persons under 15 years of age.

Measuring America

U.S. Census Bureau

FOR PERSON 1 ON PAGE 2

QUESTIONS ASKED OF A SAMPLE OF HOUSEHOLDS

23a. How did this person usually get to work LAST WEEK? If this person usually used more than one method of transportation during the trip, fill the circle of the one used for most of the distance.

- ○ Car, truck, or van
- ○ Bus or trolley bus
- ○ Streetcar or trolley car
- ○ Subway or elevated
- ○ Railroad
- ○ Ferryboat
- ○ Taxicab
- ○ Motorcycle
- ○ Bicycle
- ○ Walked
- ○ Worked at home — *Skip to 28*
- ○ Other method

If "car, truck, or van" is marked in 23a, go to 23b. Otherwise, skip to 24a.

b. How many people, including this person, usually rode to work in the car, truck, or van LAST WEEK?

- ○ Drove alone
- ○ 2 people
- ○ 3 people
- ○ 4 people
- ○ 5 people
- ○ 6 people
- ○ 7 to 9 people
- ○ 10 or more people

24a. What time did this person usually leave home to go to work LAST WEEK?

- ○ a.m.
- ○ p.m.

b. How many minutes did it usually take this person to get from home to work LAST WEEK?

Minutes — *Skip to 28*

25. Was this person TEMPORARILY absent or on layoff from a job or business LAST WEEK?

- ○ Yes, on layoff
- ○ Yes, on vacation, temporary illness, labor dispute, etc.
- ○ No

26a. Has this person been looking for work during the last 4 weeks?

- ○ Yes
- ○ No — *Skip to 27*

b. Could this person have taken a job LAST WEEK if one had been offered?

- ○ No, already has a job
- ○ No, temporarily ill
- ○ No, other reasons (in school, etc.)
- ○ Yes, could have taken a job

27. When did this person last work, even for a few days?

- ○ 1990
- ○ 1989
- ○ 1988
- ○ 1985 to 1987
Go to 28
- ○ 1980 to 1984
- ○ 1979 or earlier
- ○ Never worked
Skip to 32

28–30. CURRENT OR MOST RECENT JOB ACTIVITY. Describe clearly this person's chief job activity or business last week. If this person had more than one job, describe the one at which this person worked the most hours. If this person had no job or business last week, give information for his/her last job or business since 1985.

28. Industry or Employer

a. For whom did this person work? If now on active duty in the Armed Forces, fill this circle → ○ and print the branch of the Armed Forces.

(Name of company, business, or other employer)

b. What kind of business or industry was this? Describe the activity at location where employed.

(For example: hospital, newspaper publishing, mail order house, auto engine manufacturing, retail bakery)

c. Is this mainly — Fill ONE circle

- ○ Manufacturing
- ○ Wholesale trade
- ○ Retail trade
- ○ Other (agriculture, construction, service, government, etc.)

29. Occupation

a. What kind of work was this person doing?

(For example: registered nurse, personnel manager, supervisor of order department, gasoline engine assembler, cake icer)

b. What were this person's most important activities or duties?

(For example: patient care, directing hiring policies, supervising order clerks, assembling engines, icing cakes)

30. Was this person — Fill ONE circle

- ○ Employee of a PRIVATE FOR PROFIT company or business or of an individual, for wages, salary, or commissions
- ○ Employee of a PRIVATE NOT-FOR-PROFIT, tax-exempt, or charitable organization
- ○ Local GOVERNMENT employee (city, county, etc.)
- ○ State GOVERNMENT employee
- ○ Federal GOVERNMENT employee
- ○ SELF-EMPLOYED in own NOT INCORPORATED business, professional practice, or farm
- ○ SELF-EMPLOYED in own INCORPORATED business, professional practice, or farm
- ○ Working WITHOUT PAY in family business or farm

31a. Last year (1989), did this person work, even for a few days, at a paid job or in a business or farm?

- ○ Yes
- ○ No — *Skip to 32*

b. How many weeks did this person work in 1989? Count paid vacation, paid sick leave, and military service.

Weeks

c. During the weeks WORKED in 1989, how many hours did this person usually work each week?

Hours

32. INCOME IN 1989 —
Fill the "Yes" circle below for each income source received during 1989. Otherwise, fill the "No" circle. If "Yes," enter the total amount received during 1989.
For income received jointly, see instruction guide.
If exact amount is not known, please give best estimate.
If net income was a loss, write "Loss" above the dollar amount.

a. Wages, salary, commissions, bonuses, or tips from all jobs — Report amount before deductions for taxes, bonds, dues, or other items.

- ○ Yes →
- ○ No
$ .00
Annual amount — Dollars

b. Self-employment income from own nonfarm business, including proprietorship and partnership — Report NET income after business expenses.

- ○ Yes →
- ○ No
$ .00
Annual amount — Dollars

c. Farm self-employment income — Report NET income after operating expenses. Include earnings as a tenant farmer or sharecropper.

- ○ Yes →
- ○ No
$ .00
Annual amount — Dollars

d. Interest, dividends, net rental income or royalty income, or income from estates and trusts — Report even small amounts credited to an account.

- ○ Yes →
- ○ No
$ .00
Annual amount — Dollars

e. Social Security or Railroad Retirement

- ○ Yes →
- ○ No
$ .00
Annual amount — Dollars

f. Supplemental Security Income (SSI), Aid to Families with Dependent Children (AFDC), or other public assistance or public welfare payments.

- ○ Yes →
- ○ No
$ .00
Annual amount — Dollars

g. Retirement, survivor, or disability pensions — Do NOT include Social Security.

- ○ Yes →
- ○ No
$ .00
Annual amount — Dollars

h. Any other sources of income received regularly such as Veterans' (VA) payments, unemployment compensation, child support, or alimony — Do NOT include lump-sum payments such as money from an inheritance or the sale of a home.

- ○ Yes →
- ○ No
$ .00
Annual amount — Dollars

33. What was this person's total income in 1989? Add entries in questions 32a through 32h; subtract any losses. If total amount was a loss, write "Loss" above amount.

- ○ None   OR $ .00
Annual amount — Dollars

Please turn to the next page and answer questions for Person 2 on page 2. If this is the last person listed in question 1a on page 1, go to the back of the form.

QUESTIONS ASKED OF ALL HOUSEHOLDS
NOW PLEASE ANSWER QUESTIONS H1a—H26 FOR YOUR HOUSEHOLD

PERSON 7

Last name

First name _____ Middle initial

If a RELATIVE of Person 1:
- O Husband/wife
- O Brother/sister
- O Natural-born or adopted son/daughter
- O Father/mother
- O Grandchild
- O Stepson/ stepdaughter
- O Other relative

If NOT RELATED to Person 1:
- O Roomer, boarder, or foster child
- O Unmarried partner
- O Housemate, roommate ■
- O Other nonrelative

- O Male
- O Female

- O White
- O Black or Negro
- O Indian (Amer.) (Print the name of the enrolled or principal tribe.)
- O Eskimo
- O Aleut

Asian or Pacific Islander (API)
- O Chinese
- O Japanese
- O Filipino ■
- O Asian Indian
- O Hawaiian
- O Samoan
- O Korean
- O Guamanian
- O Vietnamese
- O Other API

- O Other race (Print race)

a. Age

b. Year of birth 1

```
0 0 0 0 0 0      1 ● 8 0 0 0 0 0
1 0 1 0 1 0          9 0 1 0 1 0
  2 0 2 0              2 0 2 0
  3 0 3 0              3 0 3 0
  4 0 4 0              4 0 4 0
  5 0 5 0              5 0 5 0
  6 0 6 0              6 0 6 0
  7 0 7 0              7 0 7 0
  8 0 8 0              8 0 8 0
  9 0 9 0              9 0 9 0
```

- O Now married
- O Separated
- O Widowed
- O Never married
- O Divorced

- O No (not Spanish/Hispanic)
- O Yes, Mexican, Mexican-Am., Chicano
- O Yes, Puerto Rican
- O Yes, Cuban ■
- O Yes, other Spanish/Hispanic (Print one group, for example: Argentinean, Colombian, Dominican, Nicaraguan, Salvadoran, Spaniard, and so on.)

- O
- O

H1a. Did you leave anyone out of your list of persons for Question 1a on page 1 because you were not sure if the person should be listed — for example, someone temporarily away on a business trip or vacation, a newborn baby still in the hospital, or a person who stays here once in a while and has no other home?

- O Yes, please print the name(s) and reason(s).
- O No

b. Did you include anyone in your list of persons for Question 1a on page 1 even though you were not sure that the person should be listed — for example, a visitor who stays here temporarily or a person who usually lives somewhere else?

- O Yes, please print the name(s) and reason(s).
- O No

H2. Which best describes this building? Include all apartments, flats, etc., even if vacant.
- O A mobile home or trailer
- O A one-family house detached from any other house
- O A one-family house attached to one or more houses
- O A building with 2 apartments
- O A building with 3 or 4 apartments
- O A building with 5 to 9 apartments
- O A building with 10 to 19 apartments
- O A building with 20 to 49 apartments
- O A building with 50 or more apartments
- O Other

H3. How many rooms do you have in this house or apartment? Do NOT count bathrooms, porches, balconies, foyers, halls, or half-rooms.
- O 1 room ■
- O 4 rooms
- O 7 rooms
- O 2 rooms
- O 5 rooms
- O 8 rooms
- O 3 rooms
- O 6 rooms
- O 9 or more rooms

H4. Is this house or apartment —
- O Owned by you or someone in this household with a mortgage or loan?
- O Owned by you or someone in this household free and clear (without a mortgage)?
- O Rented for cash rent?
- O Occupied without payment of cash rent?

If this is a ONE-FAMILY HOUSE —

H5a. Is this house on ten or more acres?
- O Yes
- O No

b. Is there a business (such as a store or barber shop) or a medical office on this property?
- O Yes
- O No

Answer only if you or someone in this household OWNS OR IS BUYING this house or apartment —

H6. What is the value of this property; that is, how much do you think this house and lot or condominium unit would sell for if it were for sale?
- O Less than $10,000
- O $70,000 to $74,999
- O $10,000 to $14,999
- O $75,000 to $79,999
- O $15,000 to $19,999
- O $80,000 to $89,999
- O $20,000 to $24,999
- O $90,000 to $99,999
- O $25,000 to $29,999
- O $100,000 to $124,999
- O $30,000 to $34,999
- O $125,000 to $149,999
- O $35,000 to $39,999
- O $150,000 to $174,999
- O $40,000 to $44,999
- O $175,000 to $199,999
- O $45,000 to $49,999
- O $200,000 to $249,999
- O $50,000 to $54,999
- O $250,000 to $299,999
- O $55,000 to $59,999
- O $300,000 to $399,999
- O $60,000 to $64,999
- O $400,000 to $499,999
- O $65,000 to $69,999
- O $500,000 or more

Answer only if you PAY RENT for this house or apartment —

H7a. What is the monthly rent?
- O Less than $80
- O $375 to $399
- O $80 to $99
- O $400 to $424
- O $100 to $124
- O $425 to $449
- O $125 to $149
- O $450 to $474
- O $150 to $174
- O $475 to $499
- O $175 to $199
- O $500 to $524
- O $200 to $224 ■
- O $525 to $549
- O $225 to $249
- O $550 to $599
- O $250 to $274
- O $600 to $649
- O $275 to $299
- O $650 to $699
- O $300 to $324
- O $700 to $749
- O $325 to $349
- O $750 to $999
- O $350 to $374
- O $1,000 or more

b. Does the monthly rent include any meals?
- O Yes
- O No

FOR CENSUS USE

A. Total persons

```
0 0
I I
2 2
3
4 ■
5
6
7
8
9
```

B. Type of unit

Occupied	Vacant
O First born	O Regular
O Cont'n	O Usual home elsewhere

C1. Vacancy status
- O For rent
- O For seas/ rec/occ
- O For sale only
- O Rented or sold, not occupied
- O For migrant workers
- O Other vacant

C2. Is this unit boarded up?
- O Yes
- O No

D. Months vacant
- O Less than 1
- O 6 up to 12
- O 1 up to 2
- O 12 up to 24
- O 2 up to 6
- O 24 or more

E. Complete after
- O LR
- O TC
- O QA   JIC 1
- O P/F
- O RE
- O I/T
- O MV
- O ED
- O EN ■
- O P0
- O P3
- O P6
- O P1
- O P4
- O IA   JIC 2
- O P2
- O P5
- O SM   O

F. Cov.
- O 1b
- O 1a
- O 7
- O H1

G. DO

ID

```
0 0 0 0 0 0 0 0 0 0
I I I I I I I I I I
2 2 2 2 2 2 2 2 2 2
3 3 3 3 3 3 3 3 3 3
4 4 4 4 4 4 4 4 4 4
5 5 5 5 5 5 5 5 5 5
6 6 6 6 6 6 6 6 6 6
7 7 7 7 7 7 7 7 7 7
8 8 8 8 8 8 8 8 8 8
9 9 9 9 9 9 9 9 9 9
```

QUESTIONS ASKED OF A SAMPLE OF HOUSEHOLDS

Page 4

H8. When did the person listed in column 1 on page 2 move into this house or apartment?

- ○ 1989 or 1990
- ○ 1985 to 1988
- ○ 1980 to 1984
- ○ 1970 to 1979
- ○ 1960 to 1969
- ○ 1959 or earlier

H9. How many bedrooms do you have; that is, how many bedrooms would you list if this house or apartment were on the market for sale or rent?

- ○ No bedroom
- ○ 1 bedroom
- ○ 2 bedrooms
- ○ 3 bedrooms
- ○ 4 bedrooms
- ○ 5 or more bedrooms

H10. Do you have COMPLETE plumbing facilities in this house or apartment; that is, 1) hot and cold piped water, 2) a flush toilet, and 3) a bathtub or shower?

- ○ Yes, have all three facilities
- ○ No

H11. Do you have COMPLETE kitchen facilities; that is, 1) a sink with piped water, 2) a range or cookstove, and 3) a refrigerator?

- ○ Yes
- ○ No

H12. Do you have a telephone in this house or apartment?

- ○ Yes
- ○ No

H13. How many automobiles, vans, and trucks of one-ton capacity or less are kept at home for use by members of your household?

- ○ None
- ○ 1
- ○ 2
- ○ 3
- ○ 4
- ○ 5
- ○ 6
- ○ 7 or more

H14. Which FUEL is used MOST for heating this house or apartment?

- ○ Gas: from underground pipes serving the neighborhood
- ○ Gas: bottled, tank, or LP
- ○ Electricity
- ○ Fuel oil, kerosene, etc.
- ○ Coal or coke
- ○ Wood
- ○ Solar energy
- ○ Other fuel
- ○ No fuel used

H15. Do you get water from —

- ○ A public system such as a city water department, or private company?
- ○ An individual drilled well?
- ○ An individual dug well?
- ○ Some other source such as a spring, creek, river, cistern, etc.?

H16. Is this building connected to a public sewer?

- ○ Yes, connected to public sewer
- ○ No, connected to septic tank or cesspool
- ○ No, use other means

H17. About when was this building first built?

- ○ 1989 or 1990
- ○ 1985 to 1988
- ○ 1980 to 1984
- ○ 1970 to 1979
- ○ 1960 to 1969
- ○ 1950 to 1959
- ○ 1940 to 1949
- ○ 1939 or earlier
- ○ Don't know

H18. Is this house or apartment part of a condominium?

- ○ Yes
- ○ No

If you live in an apartment building, skip to H20.

H19a. Is this house on less than 1 acre?

- ○ Yes — *Skip to H20*
- ○ No

b. In 1989, what were the actual sales of all agricultural products from this property?

- ○ None
- ○ $1 to $999
- ○ $1,000 to $2,499
- ○ $2,500 to $4,999
- ○ $5,000 to $9,999
- ○ $10,000 or more

H20. What are the yearly costs of utilities and fuels for this house or apartment?
If you have lived here less than 1 year, estimate the yearly cost.

a. Electricity

$ _____ .00
Yearly cost — Dollars

OR

- ○ Included in rent or in condominium fee
- ○ No charge or electricity not used

b. Gas

$ _____ .00
Yearly cost — Dollars

OR

- ○ Included in rent or in condominium fee
- ○ No charge or gas not used

c. Water

$ _____ .00
Yearly cost — Dollars

OR

- ○ Included in rent or in condominium fee
- ○ No charge

d. Oil, coal, kerosene, wood, etc.

$ _____ .00
Yearly cost — Dollars

OR

- ○ Included in rent or in condominium fee
- ○ No charge or these fuels not used

The sample questionnaire contains housing questions H8 to H26 shown here on pages 4 and 5.

QUESTIONS FOR YOUR HOUSEHOLD

QUESTIONS ASKED OF A SAMPLE OF HOUSEHOLDS

INSTRUCTION:

Answer questions H21 TO H26, if this is a one-family house, a condominium, or a mobile home that someone in this household OWNS OR IS BUYING; otherwise, go to page 6.

H21. What were the real estate taxes on THIS property last year?

$ |_____.00|
Yearly amount — Dollars

OR

○ None

H22. What was the annual payment for fire, hazard, and flood insurance on THIS property?

$ |_____.00|
Yearly amount — Dollars

OR

○ None

H23a. Do you have a mortgage, deed of trust, contract to purchase, or similar debt on THIS property?

○ Yes, mortgage, deed of trust, or similar debt } *Go to H23b*
○ Yes, contract to purchase }
○ No — *Skip to H24a*

b. How much is your regular monthly mortgage payment on THIS property? Include payment only on first mortgage or contract to purchase.

$ |_____.00|
Monthly amount — Dollars

OR

○ No regular payment required — *Skip to H24a*

c. Does your regular monthly mortgage payment include payments for real estate taxes on THIS property?

○ Yes, taxes included in payment
○ No, taxes paid separately or taxes not required

d. Does your regular monthly mortgage payment include payments for fire, hazard, or flood insurance on THIS property?

○ Yes, insurance included in payment
○ No, insurance paid separately or no insurance

H24a. Do you have a second or junior mortgage or a home equity loan on THIS property?

○ Yes
○ No — *Skip to H25*

b. How much is your regular monthly payment on all second or junior mortgages and all home equity loans?

$ |_____.00|
Monthly amount — Dollars

OR

○ No regular payment required

Answer ONLY if this is a CONDOMINIUM —

H25. What is the monthly condominium fee?

$ |_____.00|
Monthly amount — Dollars

Answer ONLY if this is a MOBILE HOME —

H26. What was the total cost for personal property taxes, site rent, registration fees, and license fees on this mobile home and its site last year? Exclude real estate taxes.

$ |_____.00|
Yearly amount — Dollars

Please turn to page 6. ➔

2000 QUESTIONNAIRE

Census 2000 used two questionnaires—a long-form (sample) and a short-form (100 percent) questionnaire. The short-form questionnaire consisted of 7 questions that could be answered by up to 6 persons within a household (see questions 1-6 and 33 on long-form questionnaire reproduced here). Space was provided to identify 6 additional members of the household. The U.S. Census Bureau would collect data on persons 7-12 by telephone interview.

The long-form questionnaire (pictured here), sent to a sample of households throughout the United States and territories, contained 29 inquiries in addition to the 8 questions asked on the short-form questionnaire. These additional quesitons, as in the past, collected information on the population, housing, economic, and social characteristics of the Nation's households.

U.S. Census Bureau

United States Census 2000

**U.S. Department of Commerce
Bureau of the Census**

This is the official form for all the people at this address. It is quick and easy, and your answers are protected by law. Complete the Census and help your community get what it needs — today and in the future!

The "Informational Copy" shows the content of the United States Census 2000 "long" form questionnaire. Each household will receive either a short form (100-percent questions) or a long form (100-percent and sample questions). The long form questionnaire includes the same 6 population questions and 1 housing question that are on the Census 2000 short form, plus 26 additional population questions, and 20 additional housing questions. On average, about 1 in every 6 households will receive the long form. The content of the forms resulted from reviewing the 1990 census data, consulting with federal and non-federal data users, and conducting tests.

For additional information about Census 2000, visit our website at **www.census.gov** or write to the Director, Bureau of the Census, Washington, DC 20233.

Start Here

Please use a black or blue pen.

1 How many people were living or staying in this house, apartment, or mobile home on April 1, 2000?

☐☐ Number of people

INCLUDE in this number:

- foster children, roomers, or housemates
- people staying here on April 1, 2000 who have no other permanent place to stay
- people living here most of the time while working, even if they have another place to live

DO NOT INCLUDE in this number:

- college students living away while attending college
- people in a correctional facility, nursing home, or mental hospital on April 1, 2000
- Armed Forces personnel living somewhere else
- people who live or stay at another place most of the time

➡ **Please turn the page and print the names of all the people living or staying here on April 1, 2000.**

If you need help completing this form, *call 1–800–XXX–XXXX between 8:00 a.m. and 9:00 p.m., 7 days a week. The telephone call is free.*

TDD – *Telephone display device for the hearing impaired. Call 1–800–XXX–XXXX between 8:00 a.m. and 9:00 p.m., 7 days a week. The telephone call is free.*

¿NECESITA AYUDA? *Si usted necesita ayuda para completar este cuestionario llame al 1–800–XXX–XXXX entre las 8:00 a.m. y las 9:00 p.m., 7 días a la semana. La llamada telefónica es gratis.*

The Census Bureau estimates that, for the average household, this form will take about 38 minutes to complete, including the time for reviewing the instructions and answers. Comments about the estimate should be directed to the Associate Director for Finance and Administration, Attn: Paperwork Reduction Project 0607-0856, Room 3104, Federal Building 3, Bureau of the Census, Washington, DC 20233.

Respondents are not required to respond to any information collection unless it displays a valid approval number from the Office of Management and Budget.

Form **D-61B**

OMB No. 0607-0856: Approval Expires 12/31/2000

List of Persons

→ **Please be sure you answered question 1 on the front page before continuing.**

2 **Please print the names of all the people who you indicated in question 1 were living or staying here on April 1, 2000.**

Example — Last Name

J O H N S O N

First Name   MI

R O B I N   J

Start with the person, or one of the people living here who owns, is buying, or rents this house, apartment, or mobile home. If there is no such person, start with any adult living or staying here.

Person 1 — Last Name

First Name   MI

Person 2 — Last Name

First Name   MI

Person 3 — Last Name

First Name   MI

Person 4 — Last Name

First Name   MI

Person 5 — Last Name

First Name   MI

Person 6 — Last Name

First Name   MI

Person 7 — Last Name

First Name   MI

Person 8 — Last Name

First Name   MI

Person 9 — Last Name

First Name   MI

Person 10 — Last Name

First Name   MI

Person 11 — Last Name

First Name   MI

Person 12 — Last Name

First Name   MI

→ **Next, answer questions about Person 1.**

FOR OFFICE USE ONLY			
A. JIC1	**B. JIC2**	**C. JIC3**	**D. JIC4**

Form D-61B

2

Person 1

Your answers are important! Every person in the Census counts.

☞ **1** **What is this person's name?** *Print the name of Person 1 from page 2.*

Last Name

First Name   MI

2 **What is this person's telephone number?** *We may contact this person if we don't understand an answer.*

Area Code + Number

☞ **3** **What is this person's sex?** *Mark* X *ONE box.*

☐ Male
☐ Female

☞ **4** **What is this person's age and what is this person's date of birth?**

Age on April 1, 2000

Print numbers in boxes.

Month   Day   Year of birth

→ **NOTE: Please answer BOTH Questions 5 and 6.**

☞ **5** **Is this person Spanish/Hispanic/Latino?** *Mark* X *the "No" box if* **not** *Spanish/Hispanic/Latino.*

☐ **No,** not Spanish/Hispanic/Latino
☐ Yes, Mexican, Mexican Am., Chicano
☐ Yes, Puerto Rican
☐ Yes, Cuban
☐ Yes, other Spanish/Hispanic/Latino — *Print group.* ↙

☞ **6** **What is this person's race?** *Mark* X *one or more races to indicate what this person considers himself/herself to be.*

☐ White
☐ Black, African Am., or Negro
☐ American Indian or Alaska Native — *Print name of enrolled or principal tribe.* ↙

☐ Asian Indian   ☐ Native Hawaiian
☐ Chinese   ☐ Guamanian or Chamorro
☐ Filipino
☐ Japanese   ☐ Samoan
☐ Korean   ☐ Other Pacific Islander —
☐ Vietnamese   *Print race.* ↙
☐ Other Asian — *Print race.* ↙

☐ Some other race — *Print race.* ↙

7 **What is this person's marital status?**

☐ Now married
☐ Widowed
☐ Divorced
☐ Separated
☐ Never married

8 **a. At any time since February 1, 2000, has this person attended regular school or college?** *Include only nursery school or preschool, kindergarten, elementary school, and schooling which leads to a high school diploma or a college degree.*

☐ No, has not attended since February 1 → *Skip to 9*
☐ Yes, public school, public college
☐ Yes, private school, private college

☞ Question is asked of all persons on the short (100-percent) and long (sample) forms.

2043

Form D-61B

3

Measuring America

U.S. Census Bureau

Person 1 (continued)

8 b. What grade or level was this person attending?
Mark [X] ONE box.

☐ Nursery school, preschool
☐ Kindergarten
☐ Grade 1 to grade 4
☐ Grade 5 to grade 8
☐ Grade 9 to grade 12
☐ College undergraduate years (freshman to senior)
☐ Graduate or professional school (*for example: medical, dental, or law school*)

9 What is the highest degree or level of school this person has COMPLETED? *Mark [X] ONE box.*
If currently enrolled, mark the previous grade or highest degree received.

☐ No schooling completed
☐ Nursery school to 4th grade
☐ 5th grade or 6th grade
☐ 7th grade or 8th grade
☐ 9th grade
☐ 10th grade
☐ 11th grade
☐ 12th grade, **NO DIPLOMA**
☐ **HIGH SCHOOL GRADUATE** — high school DIPLOMA or the equivalent (*for example: GED*)
☐ Some college credit, but less than 1 year
☐ 1 or more years of college, no degree
☐ Associate degree (*for example: AA, AS*)
☐ Bachelor's degree (*for example: BA, AB, BS*)
☐ Master's degree (*for example: MA, MS, MEng, MEd, MSW, MBA*)
☐ Professional degree (*for example: MD, DDS, DVM, LLB, JD*)
☐ Doctorate degree (*for example: PhD, EdD*)

10 What is this person's ancestry or ethnic origin?

| | | | | | | | | | | | | | | | | | | | |

| | | | | | | | | | | | | | | | | | | | |

(*For example: Italian, Jamaican, African Am., Cambodian, Cape Verdean, Norwegian, Dominican, French Canadian, Haitian, Korean, Lebanese, Polish, Nigerian, Mexican, Taiwanese, Ukrainian, and so on.*)

11 a. Does this person speak a language other than English at home?

☐ Yes
☐ No → *Skip to 12*

b. What is this language?

| | | | | | | | | | | | | | | | | | | |

(*For example: Korean, Italian, Spanish, Vietnamese*)

c. How well does this person speak English?

☐ Very well
☐ Well
☐ Not well
☐ Not at all

12 Where was this person born?

☐ In the United States — *Print name of state.*

| | | | | | | | | | | | | | | | | | | |

☐ Outside the United States — *Print name of foreign country, or Puerto Rico, Guam, etc.*

| | | | | | | | | | | | | | | | | | | |

13 Is this person a CITIZEN of the United States?

☐ Yes, born in the United States → *Skip to 15a*
☐ Yes, born in Puerto Rico, Guam, the U.S. Virgin Islands, or Northern Marianas
☐ Yes, born abroad of American parent or parents
☐ Yes, a U.S. citizen by naturalization
☐ No, not a citizen of the United States

14 When did this person come to live in the United States? *Print numbers in boxes.*

Year

| | | | |

15 a. Did this person live in this house or apartment 5 years ago (on April 1, 1995)?

☐ Person is under 5 years old → *Skip to 33*
☐ Yes, this house → *Skip to 16*
☐ No, outside the United States — *Print name of foreign country, or Puerto Rico, Guam, etc., below; then skip to 16.*

| | | | | | | | | | | | | | | | | | | |

☐ No, different house in the United States

Person 1 (continued)

15 b. Where did this person live 5 years ago?

Name of city, town, or post office

Did this person live inside the limits of the city or town?
- ☐ Yes
- ☐ No, outside the city/town limits

Name of county

Name of state

ZIP Code

16 Does this person have any of the following long-lasting conditions:

	Yes	No
a. Blindness, deafness, or a severe vision or hearing impairment?	☐	☐
b. A condition that substantially limits one or more basic physical activities such as walking, climbing stairs, reaching, lifting, or carrying?	☐	☐

17 Because of a physical, mental, or emotional condition lasting 6 months or more, does this person have any difficulty in doing any of the following activities:

	Yes	No
a. Learning, remembering, or concentrating?	☐	☐
b. Dressing, bathing, or getting around inside the home?	☐	☐
c. (Answer if this person is 16 YEARS OLD OR OVER.) Going outside the home alone to shop or visit a doctor's office?	☐	☐
d. (Answer if this person is 16 YEARS OLD OR OVER.) Working at a job or business?	☐	☐

18 Was this person under 15 years of age on April 1, 2000?
- ☐ Yes → *Skip to 33*
- ☐ No

19 a. Does this person have any of his/her own grandchildren under the age of 18 living in this house or apartment?
- ☐ Yes
- ☐ No → *Skip to 20a*

b. Is this grandparent currently responsible for most of the basic needs of any grandchild(ren) under the age of 18 who live(s) in this house or apartment?
- ☐ Yes
- ☐ No → *Skip to 20a*

c. How long has this grandparent been responsible for the(se) grandchild(ren)? *If the grandparent is financially responsible for more than one grandchild, answer the question for the grandchild for whom the grandparent has been responsible for the longest period of time.*
- ☐ Less than 6 months
- ☐ 6 to 11 months
- ☐ 1 or 2 years
- ☐ 3 or 4 years
- ☐ 5 years or more

20 a. Has this person ever served on active duty in the U.S. Armed Forces, military Reserves, or National Guard? *Active duty does not include training for the Reserves or National Guard, but DOES include activation, for example, for the Persian Gulf War.*
- ☐ Yes, now on active duty
- ☐ Yes, on active duty in past, but not now
- ☐ No, training for Reserves or National Guard only → *Skip to 21*
- ☐ No, never served in the military → *Skip to 21*

b. When did this person serve on active duty in the U.S. Armed Forces? *Mark ☒ a box for EACH period in which this person served.*
- ☐ April 1995 or later
- ☐ August 1990 to March 1995 (including Persian Gulf War)
- ☐ September 1980 to July 1990
- ☐ May 1975 to August 1980
- ☐ Vietnam era (August 1964—April 1975)
- ☐ February 1955 to July 1964
- ☐ Korean conflict (June 1950—January 1955)
- ☐ World War II (September 1940—July 1947)
- ☐ Some other time

c. In total, how many years of active-duty military service has this person had?
- ☐ Less than 2 years
- ☐ 2 years or more

2045

Form D-61B

5

Person 1 (continued)

21 **LAST WEEK, did this person do ANY work for either pay or profit?** Mark ☒ the "Yes" box even if the person worked only 1 hour, or helped without pay in a family business or farm for 15 hours or more, or was on active duty in the Armed Forces.

☐ Yes
☐ No → *Skip to 25a*

22 **At what location did this person work LAST WEEK?** *If this person worked at more than one location, print where he or she worked most last week.*

a. Address (Number and street name)

| | | | | | | | | | | | | | | | | | | | | |

| | | | | | | | | | | | | | | | | | | | | |

(If the exact address is not known, give a description of the location such as the building name or the nearest street or intersection.)

b. Name of city, town, or post office

| | | | | | | | | | | | | | | | | | | |

c. Is the work location inside the limits of that city or town?

☐ Yes
☐ No, outside the city/town limits

d. Name of county

| | | | | | | | | | | | | | | | | | | |

e. Name of U.S. state or foreign country

| | | | | | | | | | | | | | | | | | | |

f. ZIP Code

| | | | | |

23 **a. How did this person usually get to work LAST WEEK?** *If this person usually used more than one method of transportation during the trip, mark ☒ the box of the one used for most of the distance.*

☐ Car, truck, or van
☐ Bus or trolley bus
☐ Streetcar or trolley car
☐ Subway or elevated
☐ Railroad
☐ Ferryboat
☐ Taxicab
☐ Motorcycle
☐ Bicycle
☐ Walked
☐ Worked at home → *Skip to 27*
☐ Other method

→ If "Car, truck, or van" is marked in 23a, go to 23b. Otherwise, skip to 24a.

23 **b. How many people, including this person, usually rode to work in the car, truck, or van LAST WEEK?**

☐ Drove alone
☐ 2 people
☐ 3 people
☐ 4 people
☐ 5 or 6 people
☐ 7 or more people

24 **a. What time did this person usually leave home to go to work LAST WEEK?**

| | : | | ☐ a.m.   ☐ p.m.

b. How many minutes did it usually take this person to get from home to work LAST WEEK?

Minutes

→ **Answer questions 25–26 for persons who did not work for pay or profit last week. Others skip to 27.**

25 **a. LAST WEEK, was this person on layoff from a job?**

☐ Yes → *Skip to 25c*
☐ No

b. LAST WEEK, was this person TEMPORARILY absent from a job or business?

☐ Yes, on vacation, temporary illness, labor dispute, etc. → *Skip to 26*
☐ No → *Skip to 25d*

c. Has this person been informed that he or she will be recalled to work within the next 6 months OR been given a date to return to work?

☐ Yes → *Skip to 25e*
☐ No

d. Has this person been looking for work during the last 4 weeks?

☐ Yes
☐ No → *Skip to 26*

e. LAST WEEK, could this person have started a job if offered one, or returned to work if recalled?

☐ Yes, could have gone to work
☐ No, because of own temporary illness
☐ No, because of all other reasons *(in school, etc.)*

26 **When did this person last work, even for a few days?**

☐ 1995 to 2000
☐ 1994 or earlier, or never worked → *Skip to 31*

Form D-61B

6

Person 1 (continued)

27 **Industry or Employer** — *Describe clearly this person's chief job activity or business last week. If this person had more than one job, describe the one at which this person worked the most hours. If this person had no job or business last week, give the information for his/her last job or business since 1995.*

a. For whom did this person work? *If now on active duty in the Armed Forces, mark ☒ this box →* ☐ *and print the branch of the Armed Forces.*

Name of company, business, or other employer

☐☐☐☐☐☐☐☐☐☐☐☐☐☐☐☐☐☐☐☐☐☐

☐☐☐☐☐☐☐☐☐☐☐☐☐☐☐☐☐☐☐☐☐☐

☐☐☐☐☐☐☐☐☐☐☐☐☐☐☐☐☐☐☐☐☐☐

b. What kind of business or industry was this?
Describe the activity at location where employed. (For example: hospital, newspaper publishing, mail order house, auto repair shop, bank)

☐☐☐☐☐☐☐☐☐☐☐☐☐☐☐☐☐☐☐☐☐☐

☐☐☐☐☐☐☐☐☐☐☐☐☐☐☐☐☐☐☐☐☐☐

☐☐☐☐☐☐☐☐☐☐☐☐☐☐☐☐☐☐☐☐☐☐

c. Is this mainly — *Mark ☒ ONE box.*
☐ Manufacturing?
☐ Wholesale trade?
☐ Retail trade?
☐ Other (agriculture, construction, service, government, etc.)?

28 **Occupation**

a. What kind of work was this person doing?
(For example: registered nurse, personnel manager, supervisor of order department, auto mechanic, accountant)

☐☐☐☐☐☐☐☐☐☐☐☐☐☐☐☐☐☐☐☐☐☐

☐☐☐☐☐☐☐☐☐☐☐☐☐☐☐☐☐☐☐☐☐☐

☐☐☐☐☐☐☐☐☐☐☐☐☐☐☐☐☐☐☐☐☐☐

b. What were this person's most important activities or duties? *(For example: patient care, directing hiring policies, supervising order clerks, repairing automobiles, reconciling financial records)*

☐☐☐☐☐☐☐☐☐☐☐☐☐☐☐☐☐☐☐☐☐☐

☐☐☐☐☐☐☐☐☐☐☐☐☐☐☐☐☐☐☐☐☐☐

☐☐☐☐☐☐☐☐☐☐☐☐☐☐☐☐☐☐☐☐☐☐

29 **Was this person** — *Mark ☒ ONE box.*
☐ Employee of a PRIVATE-FOR-PROFIT company or business or of an individual, for wages, salary, or commissions
☐ Employee of a PRIVATE NOT-FOR-PROFIT, tax-exempt, or charitable organization
☐ Local GOVERNMENT employee *(city, county, etc.)*
☐ State GOVERNMENT employee
☐ Federal GOVERNMENT employee
☐ SELF-EMPLOYED in own NOT INCORPORATED business, professional practice, or farm
☐ SELF-EMPLOYED in own INCORPORATED business, professional practice, or farm
☐ Working WITHOUT PAY in family business or farm

30 **a. LAST YEAR, 1999, did this person work at a job or business at any time?**
☐ Yes
☐ No → *Skip to 31*

b. How many weeks did this person work in 1999?
Count paid vacation, paid sick leave, and military service.
Weeks
☐☐

c. During the weeks WORKED in 1999, how many hours did this person usually work each WEEK?
Usual hours worked each WEEK
☐☐

31 **INCOME IN 1999** — *Mark ☒ the "Yes" box for each income source received during 1999 and enter the total amount received during 1999 to a maximum of $999,999. Mark ☒ the "No" box if the income source was not received. If net income was a loss, enter the amount and mark ☒ the "Loss" box next to the dollar amount.*

For income received jointly, report, if possible, the appropriate share for each person; otherwise, report the whole amount for only one person and mark ☒ the "No" box for the other person. If exact amount is not known, please give best estimate.

a. Wages, salary, commissions, bonuses, or tips from all jobs — *Report amount before deductions for taxes, bonds, dues, or other items.*
☐ Yes   Annual amount — *Dollars*
$ ☐☐☐,☐☐☐ .00
☐ No

b. Self-employment income from own nonfarm businesses or farm businesses, including proprietorships and partnerships — *Report NET income after business expenses.*
☐ Yes   Annual amount — *Dollars*
$ ☐☐☐,☐☐☐ .00   ☐ Loss
☐ No

2047

Form D-61B

7

Person 1 (continued)

31. c. Interest, dividends, net rental income, royalty income, or income from estates and trusts — *Report even small amounts credited to an account.*

☐ Yes   Annual amount — *Dollars*

$ |___|___|___,|___|___|___|.00   ☐ Loss

☐ No

d. Social Security or Railroad Retirement

☐ Yes   Annual amount — *Dollars*

$ |___|___|___,|___|___|.00

☐ No

e. Supplemental Security Income (SSI)

☐ Yes   Annual amount — *Dollars*

$ |___|___|___,|___|___|.00

☐ No

f. Any public assistance or welfare payments from the state or local welfare office

☐ Yes   Annual amount — *Dollars*

$ |___|___|___,|___|___|.00

☐ No

g. Retirement, survivor, or disability pensions — *Do NOT include Social Security.*

☐ Yes   Annual amount — *Dollars*

$ |___|___|___,|___|___|.00

☐ No

h. Any other sources of income received regularly such as Veterans' (VA) payments, unemployment compensation, child support, or alimony — *Do NOT include lump-sum payments such as money from an inheritance or sale of a home.*

☐ Yes   Annual amount — *Dollars*

$ |___|___|___,|___|___|.00

☐ No

32. What was this person's total income in 1999? *Add entries in questions 31a—31h; subtract any losses. If net income was a loss, enter the amount and mark* ☒ *the "Loss" box next to the dollar amount.*

Annual amount — *Dollars*

☐ None   OR $ |___|___|___,|___|___|.00   ☐ Loss

> ☞ Question is asked of all households on the short (100-percent) and long (sample) forms.

HOUSING QUESTIONS

➡ **Now, please answer questions 33—53 about your household.**

☞ **33. Is this house, apartment, or mobile home —**

☐ Owned by you or someone in this household with a mortgage or loan?

☐ Owned by you or someone in this household free and clear (without a mortgage or loan)?

☐ Rented for cash rent?

☐ Occupied without payment of cash rent?

34. Which best describes this building? *Include all apartments, flats, etc., even if vacant.*

☐ A mobile home

☐ A one-family house detached from any other house

☐ A one-family house attached to one or more houses

☐ A building with 2 apartments

☐ A building with 3 or 4 apartments

☐ A building with 5 to 9 apartments

☐ A building with 10 to 19 apartments

☐ A building with 20 to 49 apartments

☒ A building with 50 or more apartments

☐ Boat, RV, van, etc.

35. About when was this building first built?

☐ 1999 or 2000

☐ 1995 to 1998

☐ 1990 to 1994

☐ 1980 to 1989

☐ 1970 to 1979

☐ 1960 to 1969

☐ 1950 to 1959

☐ 1940 to 1949

☐ 1939 or earlier

36. When did this person move into this house, apartment, or mobile home?

☐ 1999 or 2000

☐ 1995 to 1998

☐ 1990 to 1994

☐ 1980 to 1989

☐ 1970 to 1979

☐ 1969 or earlier

37. How many rooms do you have in this house, apartment, or mobile home? *Do NOT count bathrooms, porches, balconies, foyers, halls, or half-rooms.*

☐ 1 room   ☐ 6 rooms

☐ 2 rooms   ☐ 7 rooms

☐ 3 rooms   ☐ 8 rooms

☐ 4 rooms   ☐ 9 or more rooms

☐ 5 rooms

Form D-61B

8

Person 1 (continued)

38 How many bedrooms do you have; that is, how many bedrooms would you list if this house, apartment, or mobile home were on the market for sale or rent?

- ☐ No bedroom
- ☐ 1 bedroom
- ☐ 2 bedrooms
- ☐ 3 bedrooms
- ☐ 4 bedrooms
- ☐ 5 or more bedrooms

39 Do you have COMPLETE plumbing facilities in this house, apartment, or mobile home; that is, 1) hot and cold piped water, 2) a flush toilet, and 3) a bathtub or shower?

- ☐ Yes, have all three facilities
- ☐ No

40 Do you have COMPLETE kitchen facilities in this house, apartment, or mobile home; that is, 1) a sink with piped water, 2) a range or stove, and 3) a refrigerator?

- ☐ Yes, have all three facilities
- ☐ No

41 Is there telephone service available in this house, apartment, or mobile home from which you can both make and receive calls?

- ☐ Yes
- ☐ No

42 Which FUEL is used MOST for heating this house, apartment, or mobile home?

- ☐ Gas: from underground pipes serving the neighborhood
- ☐ Gas: bottled, tank, or LP
- ☐ Electricity
- ☐ Fuel oil, kerosene, etc.
- ☐ Coal or coke
- ☐ Wood
- ☐ Solar energy
- ☐ Other fuel
- ☐ No fuel used

43 How many automobiles, vans, and trucks of one-ton capacity or less are kept at home for use by members of your household?

- ☐ None
- ☐ 1
- ☐ 2
- ☐ 3
- ☐ 4
- ☐ 5
- ☐ 6 or more

44 Answer ONLY if this is a ONE-FAMILY HOUSE OR MOBILE HOME — All others skip to 45.

a. Is there a business (such as a store or barber shop) or a medical office on this property?

- ☐ Yes
- ☐ No

b. How many acres is this house or mobile home on?

- ☐ Less than 1 acre → *Skip to 45*
- ☐ 1 to 9.9 acres
- ☐ 10 or more acres

c. In 1999, what were the actual sales of all agricultural products from this property?

- ☐ None
- ☐ $1 to $999
- ☐ $1,000 to $2,499
- ☒ $2,500 to $4,999
- ☐ $5,000 to $9,999
- ☐ $10,000 or more

45 What are the annual costs of utilities and fuels for this house, apartment, or mobile home? *If you have lived here less than 1 year, estimate the annual cost.*

a. Electricity

Annual cost — *Dollars*

$ | , | | | .00

OR

- ☐ Included in rent or in condominium fee
- ☐ No charge or electricity not used

b. Gas

Annual cost — *Dollars*

$ | , | | | .00

OR

- ☐ Included in rent or in condominium fee
- ☐ No charge or gas not used

c. Water and sewer

Annual cost — *Dollars*

$ | , | | | .00

OR

- ☐ Included in rent or in condominium fee
- ☐ No charge

d. Oil, coal, kerosene, wood, etc.

Annual cost — *Dollars*

$ | , | | | .00

OR

- ☐ Included in rent or in condominium fee
- ☐ No charge or these fuels not used

2049

Form D-61B

9

Person 1 (continued)

46 Answer ONLY if you PAY RENT for this house, apartment, or mobile home — All others skip to 47.

a. What is the monthly rent?

Monthly amount — *Dollars*

$ ___,___.00

b. Does the monthly rent include any meals?

☐ Yes
☐ No

47 Answer questions 47a—53 if you or someone in this household owns or is buying this house, apartment, or mobile home; otherwise, skip to questions for Person 2.

a. Do you have a mortgage, deed of trust, contract to purchase, or similar debt on THIS property?

☐ Yes, mortgage, deed of trust, or similar debt
☐ Yes, contract to purchase
☐ No → *Skip to 48a*

b. How much is your regular monthly mortgage payment on THIS property? *Include payment only on first mortgage or contract to purchase.*

Monthly amount — *Dollars*

$ ___,___.00

OR

☐ No regular payment required → *Skip to 48a*

c. Does your regular monthly mortgage payment include payments for real estate taxes on THIS property?

☐ Yes, taxes included in mortgage payment
☐ No, taxes paid separately or taxes not required

d. Does your regular monthly mortgage payment include payments for fire, hazard, or flood insurance on THIS property?

☐ Yes, insurance included in mortgage payment
☐ No, insurance paid separately or no insurance

48 **a. Do you have a second mortgage or a home equity loan on THIS property?** *Mark ☒ all boxes that apply.*

☐ Yes, a second mortgage
☐ Yes, a home equity loan
☐ No → *Skip to 49*

b. How much is your regular monthly payment on all second or junior mortgages and all home equity loans on THIS property?

Monthly amount — *Dollars*

$ ___,___.00

OR

☐ No regular payment required

49 **What were the real estate taxes on THIS property last year?**

Yearly amount — *Dollars*

$ ___,___.00

OR

☐ None

50 **What was the annual payment for fire, hazard, and flood insurance on THIS property?**

Annual amount — *Dollars*

$ ___,___.00

OR

☐ None

51 **What is the value of this property; that is, how much do you think this house and lot, apartment, or mobile home and lot would sell for if it were for sale?**

☐ Less than $10,000
☐ $10,000 to $14,999
☐ $15,000 to $19,999
☐ $20,000 to $24,999
☐ $25,000 to $29,999
☐ $30,000 to $34,999
☐ $35,000 to $39,999
☐ $40,000 to $49,999
☐ $50,000 to $59,999
☐ $60,000 to $69,999
☐ $70,000 to $79,999
☐ $80,000 to $89,999
☐ $90,000 to $99,999
☐ $100,000 to $124,999
☐ $125,000 to $149,999
☐ $150,000 to $174,999
☐ $175,000 to $199,999
☐ $200,000 to $249,999
☐ $250,000 to $299,999
☐ $300,000 to $399,999
☐ $400,000 to $499,999
☐ $500,000 to $749,999
☐ $750,000 to $999,999
☐ $1,000,000 or more

52 Answer ONLY if this is a CONDOMINIUM —

What is the monthly condominium fee?

Monthly amount — *Dollars*

$ ___,___.00

53 Answer ONLY if this is a MOBILE HOME —

a. Do you have an installment loan or contract on THIS mobile home?

☐ Yes
☐ No

b. What was the total cost for installment loan payments, personal property taxes, site rent, registration fees, and license fees on THIS mobile home and its site last year? *Exclude real estate taxes.*

Yearly amount — *Dollars*

$ ___,___.00

➜ **Are there more people living here? If yes, continue with Person 2.**

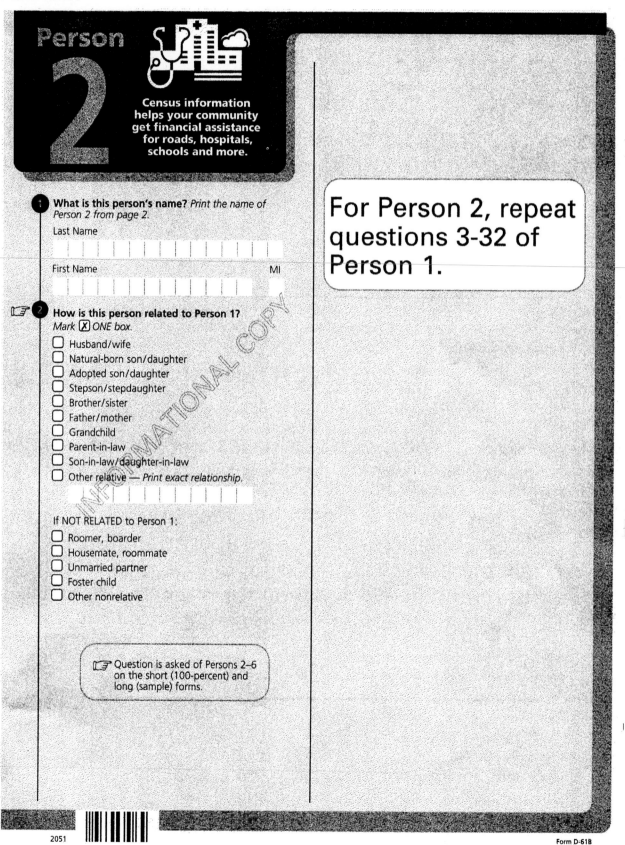

Person 2

Census information helps your community get financial assistance for roads, hospitals, schools and more.

1 **What is this person's name?** *Print the name of Person 2 from page 2.*

Last Name

First Name · MI

☞ 2 **How is this person related to Person 1?**
Mark **X** *ONE box.*

☐ Husband/wife
☐ Natural-born son/daughter
☐ Adopted son/daughter
☐ Stepson/stepdaughter
☐ Brother/sister
☐ Father/mother
☐ Grandchild
☐ Parent-in-law
☐ Son-in-law/daughter-in-law
☐ Other relative — *Print exact relationship.*

If NOT RELATED to Person 1:

☐ Roomer, boarder
☐ Housemate, roommate
☐ Unmarried partner
☐ Foster child
☐ Other nonrelative

☞ Question is asked of Persons 2–6 on the short (100-percent) and long (sample) forms.

For Person 2, repeat questions 3-32 of Person 1.

2051

Form D-61B

11

Measuring America

U.S. Census Bureau

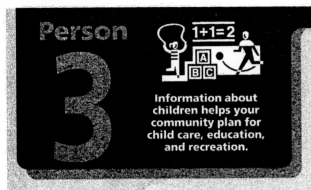

Person 3

Information about children helps your community plan for child care, education, and recreation.

For Persons 3–6. repeat questions 1-32 of Person 2.

NOTE – *The content for Question 2 varies between Person 1 and Persons 2–6.*

Thank you for completing your official U.S. Census form. If there are more than six people at this address, the Census Bureau may contact you for the same information about these people.

Form D-61B

12

AVAILABILITY OF POPULATION SCHEDULES

Microfilmed copies of the Census schedules from 1790 to 1920 (1930 after April 1, 2002) are available at the National Archives Building, 700 Pennsylvania Avenue, NW, Washington, DC; at the National Archives Regional Offices (see Appendix A); and through the National Archives Microfilm Rental Program.

Title 44, U.S. Code, allows the public to use the National Archives' census record holdings after 72 years, thus the 1790 to 1920 records are available to the public on microfilm from the National Archives. After April 1, 2002, individual records from the 1930 census will be made available. The U.S. Census Bureau holds only the records for 1930 through 2000 (after April 1, 2000, the Census Bureau will hold census records from 1940 to 2000). The agency's Personal Census Search Unit, in Jeffersonville, IN, maintains and searches these records, which are confidential by law (Title 13, U.S. Code).[1]

As a result of fire, damage, or other loss, census records on microfilm are not entirely complete. The most notable gap in coverage is for 1890. As a result of a 1921 fire at the Department of Commerce, surviving records are limited to portions of Alabama, the District of Columbia,

Georgia, Illinois, Minnesota, New Jersey, New York, North Carolina, Ohio, South Dakota, and Texas plus the special 1890 schedules enumerating Union veterans of the Civil War and their widows for Kentucky and Wyoming (See Appendix C).

Figure 1 shows the decennial population schedules from 1790 through 1920, together with SOUNDEX indexes for 1880, 1900, 1910, and 1920, for which microfilmed copies are available for public use through the National Archives, its regional branches, and at libraries in various parts of the country. (Pursuant to Title 44, U.S. Code, the National Archives will open the 1930 records to the public after April 1, 2002). The National Archives sells or rents the microfilm publications listed on the chart to individuals and institutions, and some libraries are willing to release copies through interlibrary loan. The National Archives periodically issues catalogs for use in ordering the microfilm and publishes checklists of institutional holdings. See the bibliography

Electronic data processing. In the mid-1940s, the Census Bureau and scientists from the National Bureau of Standards began studying the use of electronic computers for large-scale data processing. In 1951, the Census Bureau acquired the UNIVAC 1 built according to the Census Bureau's requirements and experimental processing began following the 1950 census. Together with a second UNIVAC, tabulations were successfully completed for a number of programs, including the majority of the 1954 Economic Census.

---

[1]A form BC-600, "Application for Search of Census Records," is required to obtain census records still held by the Census Bureau. This application can be downloaded, using Adobe Acrobat from the following address: www.census.gov/genealogy/www/bc-600.pdf.

To meet the needs of the 1960 Census, the Census Bureau obtained two new 1105 computers in October and December, 1959. As a result of a cooperative agreement between the Census Bureau and the University of North Carolina and the Armour Research Foundation of the Illinois Institute of Technology, a UNIVAC 1105 was installed at each university that was compatible with those housed at the Census Bureau. Each university allocated two-thirds of the "productive" time on its computers to the census, with additional time (in lesser amount) being afforded the Census Bureau upon completion of the 1960 Census processing.

The Census Bureau also employed the film optical sensing device for input to computers (FOSDIC). The FOSDIC scanned microfilm copies of appropriately designed questionnaires, read the marks entered by enumerators, and transcribed the information to reels of magnetic tape readable by computer. When installed on the computers, the data on these tapes were reviewed, tabulated, and finally transferred to other tapes used by high speed printers[2]—speeding the compilation of census data and making the hiring and training of 2,000 people dedicated to the manual preparation of punch cards obsolete.

---

[2]High-speed printers received data for printing from the magnetic tape reels created by the electronic computers. Data represented by the magnetized "spots" on the tape were printed as tabulations (600 lines per minute) which could be photographed and reproduced by the offset printing process.

Microfilm. In most cases, census schedules and questionnaires were microfilmed many years after they originated, by which time the ink often had faded and the pages were brittle. To save valuable storage space after filming, the paper copies were destroyed or (as was the case with the 1880 census) offered to state archives. While schedules from the period from 1790 to 1880 usually were stored flat in binders secured by cloth tape, later ones, such as the 1890 through 1920, were bound for safekeeping and ready use (for age search, etc.) in large volumes. When microfilming began around 1940, it was impractical to remove and rebind the pages in those volumes, so they were photographed in place. The pages were turned for filming, and their legibility, poor at best, sometimes was reduced even further by the camera's inability to focus on the curved surfaces of some pages.

For the years beginning in 1890, when punch card tabulation came into use, clerks used red ink to add alphabetical or numerical codes in certain schedule columns (such as the one for veteran status) for the keypunch operators' guidance. These codes represent occupation, number of persons in the household, and the like information already appearing on the schedule. As the microfilm is only in black and white, this color cannot be distinguished. The reader should recognize and ignore these codes as extraneous when transcribing or interpreting what appears on the film.

Figure 1.
Census Microfilm Publication and Roll Numbers

(A dash (—) in the column means that no census was taken or Soundex prepared. "No" in the column means that the census was taken, but no manuscript copies are known to exist)

State	1790 M637	1800 M32	1810 M252	1820 M33	1830 M19	1840 M704	1850 M432	1860 M653	1870 M593	1880 T9	1880 Soundex	1890* (M407) M123	1900 T623	1900 Soundex	1910 T624	1910 Soundex or Miracode	1920 T625	1920 Soundex
Alabama	-	No	No	(1)No	36528	36540	36548	1-36	1-45	1-35	T734 1-74	-1	1-44	T1030 1-180	1-37	T1259 1-14	1-45	M1548
Alaska	-						-	-	-	No	No	No	1828-1832	T1031 1-15	1748-1750	-	2030-2031	M1597
Arizona	-						See New Mexico 468	(2)See New Mexico 712	46	36,37	T735 1-2	No	45-48	T1032 1-22	38-42	-	46-52	M1549
Arkansas	-	-	-	No	5	17-20	25-32	37-54	47-67	38-60	T736 1-48	No	49-80	T1033 1-132	43-68	T1260 1-139	53-86	M1550
California	-	-	-	-	-	-	33-36	55-72	68-93	61-86	T737 1-34	No	81-116	T1034 1-198	69-111	T1261 1-272	87-154	M1551
Colorado	-	-	-	-	-	-	-	See Kansas 348	94-95	87-93	T738 1-7	No	117-130	T1035 1-68	112-126	-	155-173	M1552
Connecticut	1 (T498)1	36527	36527	36527	36687	21-32	37-51	73-93	96-117	94-110	T739 1-25	No	131-152	T1036 1-107	127-144	-	174-199	M1553
Delaware	(3)No	4	4	4	36872	33-34	52-55	95-100	199-122	111-120	T741 1-9	No	153-157	T1037 1-21	145-148	-	200-204	M1554
District of Columbia	See MD&VA	5	No	5	14	35	56-57	101-105	123-127	121-124	T742 1-9	(2)118	158-164	T1038 1-42	149-155	-	205-213	M1555
Florida	-	-	-	-	15	36	58-60	106-110	128-133	125-132	T743 1-16	No	165-177	T1039 1-59	156-169	T1262 1-84	214-232	M1556
Georgia	No	(4)No	No	36686	16-21	37-53	61-96	111-153	134-184	133-172	T744 1-86	-3	178230	T1040 1-211	170-220	T1263 1-174	233-286	M1557
Hawaii	-	-	-	-	-	-	-	-	-	-	-	No	1833-1837	T1041 1-30	1751-1755	-	2033-2039	M1598
Idaho	-	-	-	-	-	-	-	-	185	173	T746 1-2	No	231-234	T1042 1-19	221-228	-	287-295	M1558
Illinois	-	-	(5)No	36841	22-25	54-73	97-134	154-241	186-295	174-262	T746 1-143	-3	235-356	T1043 1-479	229-337	T1264 1-491	296-419	M1559
Indiana	-	No	No	36905	26-32	74-100	135-181	242-309	296-373	263-324	T747 1-98	No	357-414	T1044 1-252	338-389	-	420-475	M1560
Iowa	-	-	-	-	See Missouri 72, 73	101-102	182-189	310-345	374-427	325-371	T748 1-78	No	415-468	T1045 1-198	390-430	-	476-521	M1561
Kansas	-	-	-	-	-	-	-	346-352	428-443	372-400	T749 1-51	No	469-505	T1046 1-147	431-461	T1265 1-205	522-556	M1562
Kentucky	(7)No	(7)No	36654	16-29	33-42	103-126	190-228	353-406	444-504	401-446	T750 1-83	36527	506555	T1047 1-198	462-506	T1266 1-194	557-602	M1563
Louisiana	-	-	10	30-32	43-45	127-135	229-247	407-431	505-535	447-474	T751 1-55	36620	556-586	T1048 1-146	507-535	T1267 1-132	603-636	M1564
Maine	2 (T491)1	36684	36841	33-39	46-52	136-155	248-276	432-455	536-565	475-492	T752 1-29	36683	587-603	T1049 1-79	536-548	-	637-651	M1565
Maryland	3 (T498)1	36780	36906	40-46	53-58	156-172	277-302	456-485	566-599	493-518	T753 1-47	36747	604-630	T1050 1-127	549-570	-	652-678	M1566
Massachusetts	4 (T498)1	36909	17-22	47-55	59-68	173-202	303-345	485-534	600-659	519-568	T754 1-70	36845	631-697	T1051 1-314	571-633	-	679-752	M1567
Michigan	-	-	No	56	69	203-212	346-366	535-566	660-715	569-614	T755 1-73	17-21	698-755	T1052 1-259	634-688	T1268 1-253	753-821	M1568

Figure 1.
Census Microfilm Publication and Roll Numbers—Con.

(A dash (—) in the column means that no census was taken or Soundex prepared. "No" in the column means that the census was taken, but no manuscript copies are known to exist)

State	1790 M637	1800 M32	1810 M252	1820 M33	1830 M19	1840 M704	1850 M432	1860 M653	1870 M593	1880 T9	1880 Soundex	1890* (M407) M123	1900 T623	1900 Soundex	1910 T624	1910 Soundex or Miracode	1920 T625	1920 Soundex
Minnesota	-	-	-	-	-	-	367	567-576 (1857: T1175 1-5)	716-719 (T132) 1-13	615-638	T756 1-37	(3) 22-25	756-798	T1053 1-181	689-730	-	822-867	M1569
Mississippi	-	No	No	57-58	70-71	213-219	368-390	577-604	720-754	639-670	T757 1-69	26	799-835	T1054 1-155	731-765	T1269 1-118	868-901	M1570
Missouri	-	-	No	No	72-73	220-233	391-424	605-664	755-826	671-741	T758 1-114	27-34	836-908	T1055 1-300	766-828	T1270 1-285	902-966	M1571
Montana	-	-	-	-	-	-	-	See Nebraska	827	742	T759 1-2	35	909-915	T1056 1-40	829-837	-	967-978	M1572
Nebraska	-	-	-	-	-	-	-	665	828-833	743-757	T760 1-22	36-38	916-942	T1057 1-107	838-857	-	979-1003	M1573
Nevada	-	-	-	-	-	-	See Utah 991	See Utah 1314	834-835	758-759	T761 1-3	39	943	T1058 1-7	858-859	-	1004-1005	M1574
New Hampshire	5 (T498)1	20	23-25	59-61	74-78	234-246	425-441	666-681	836-850	760-789	T762 1-13	40	944-952	T1059 1-52	860-866	-	1006-1014	M1575
New Jersey	(8)No	No	No	No	79-83	247-263	442-466	682-711	851-892	770-801	T763 1-49	(3) 41-43	953-998	T1060 1-203	867-912	-	1015-1073	M1576
New Mexico	-	-	-	-	-	-	467-470	712-716	893-897	802-804	T764 1-6	44	999-1003	T1061 1-23	913-919	-	1074-1080	M1577
New York	6 (T498)2	21-28	26-37	62-79	84-117	263-353	471-618	717-885	898-1120	805-949	T765 1-187	(3) 45-57	1004-1179	T1062 1-766	920-1094	-	1081-1281	M1578
North Carolina	7 (T498)2	29-34	38-43	80-85	118-125	354-374	619-656	886-927	1121-1166	950-988	T766 1-79	(3) 58	1180-1225	T1003 1-168	1095-1137	T1271 1-178	1282-1329	M1579
North Dakota	-	-	-	-	-	-	-	94	118	(9)11 1-115	T740 1-6	59	1226-1234	T1064 1-36	1138-1149	-	1330-1343	M1580
Ohio	-	No	No	86-95	126-142	375-434	657-741	928-1054	1167-1284	989-1079	T767 1-143	(3) 60-75	1235-1334	T1065 1-195	1150-1241	T1272 1-418	1344-1450	M1581
Oklahoma	-	-	-	-	-	-	-	See Arkansas 52-54	No	-	No	(10)76	1335-1344	T1066 1-43	1242-1277	T1273 1-143	1451-1490	M1582
Oregon	-	-	-	-	-	-	742	1055-1056	36653	1080-1084	T768 1-8	77	1345-1353	T1067 1-53	1278-1291	-	1491-1506	M1583
Pennsylvania	8, 9 (T498)2	35-44	44-57	96-114	143-166	435-503	743-840	1057-1201	1289-1470	1085-1208	T769 1-168	78-91	1354-1503	T1068 1-590	1292-1435	T1274 1-688	1507-1669	M1584
Rhode Island	10 (T498)3	45-46	58-59	115-117	167-168	504-506	841-847	1202-1211	1471-1480	1209-1216	T770 1-11	92	1504-1513	T1069 1-49	1436-1445	-	1670-1681	M1585
South Carolina	11 (T498)3	47-50	60-62	118-121	169-173	507-516	848-868	1212-1238	1481-1512	1217-1243	T771 1-56	93	1514-1545	T1070 1-124	1446-1474	T1275 1-93	1682-1713	M1586
South Dakota	-	-	-	-	-	-	-	94	118	(9)11 1-115	T740 1-6	(3) 94	36818	T1071 1-44	1475-1489	-	1714-1727	M1587
Tennessee	No	(11)No	63	(12)122-125	174-182	36670	869-907	1239-1286	1513-1572	1244-1287	T772 1-86	95-98	1557-1606	T1072 1-187	1490-1526	T1276 1-142	1728-1771	M1588
Texas	-	-	-	(13)-	-	-	908-918	1287-1312	1573-1609	1288-1334	T773 1-77	(3) 99-102	1607-1681	T1073 1-286	1527-1601	T1277 1-262	1772-1860	M1589
Utah	-	-	-	-	-	-	919	1313-1314	1610-1613	1335-1339	T774 1-7	103	1682-1688	T1074 1-29	1602-1611	-	1861-1869	M1590

Figure 1.
Census Microfilm Publication and Roll Numbers—Con.

(A dash (—) in the column means that no census was taken or Soundex prepared. "No" in the column means that the census was taken, but no manuscript copies are known to exist)

State	1790 M637	1800 M32	1810 M252	1820 M33	1830 M19	1840 M704	1850 M432	1860 M653	1870 M593	1880 T9	1880 Soundex	1890* (M407) M123	1900 T623	1900 Soundex	1910 T624	1910 Soundex or Miracode	1920 T625	1920 Soundex
Vermont	12 (T498)3	51-52	64-65	126-128	183-188	538-548	920-931	1315-1329	1614-1629	1340-1350	T775 1-15	105	1689-1696	T1075 1-41	1612-1618	-	1870-1876	M1591
Virginia	(T498)3	(14)No	66-71	129-142	189-201	549-579	932-993	1330-1397	1630-1682	1351-1395	T776 1-82	106-107	1697-1740	T1076 1-164	1619-1652	T1278 1-183	-	1877-1919	M1592
Washington	-	-	-	-	-	-	742	1398	1683	1396-1398	T777 1-4	108	1741-1754	T1077 1-70	1653-1675	-	1920-1946	M1593
West Virginia	See Virginia	See Virginia	See Virginia	See Virginia	See Virginia	See Virginia	See Virginia	See Virginia	1684-1702	1399-1416	T778 1-32	109-110	1755-1776	T1078+ 1-92	1676-1699	T1279 1-108	1947-1974	M1594
Wisconsin	-	-	-	See Michigan	See Michigan	580	994-1009	1399-1438	1703-1747	1417-1453	T779 1-51	111-116	1777-1825	T1079 1-188	1700-1744	-	1975-2024	M1595
Wyoming	-	-	-	-	-	-	-	See Nebraska	1748	1454	T780 1	117	1826-1827	T1080 1-14	1745-1747	-	2025-2029	M1596
Military & Naval	-	-	-	-	-	-	-	-	-	-	-	104	1838-1842	T1081 1-32	1784	-	2040-2041 (16)	M1600
Indian Territory	-	-	-	-	-	-	-	-	-	-	-	76	1843-1854	T1082 1-42	See Oklahoma	See Oklahoma Institutions	T1083 1-8	M1601
Puerto Rico	-	-	-	-	-	-	-	-	-	-	-	-	No		1756-1783	No	2043-2075	
Guam	-	-	-	-	-	-	-	-	-	-	-	-	-	-	-	-	-	M1605
American Samoa	-	-	-	-	-	-	-	-	-	-	-	-	-	-	-	-	-	M1603
Virgin Islands	-	-	-	-	-	-	-	-	-	-	-	-	-	-	-	-	2076	M1604
Canal Zone	-	-	-	-	-	-	-	-	-	-	-	-	-	-	-	-	2042	M1599

1. Extant part in State Department Archives and History, Montgomery, AL.

2. 1864 territorial census schedules are in the custody of the Secretary of State, Phoenix, AZ; Those for 1866, 1867, and 1869 are at the National Archives.

3. See reconstruction in Leon de Valinger, Reconstructed 1790 Census of Delaware, Genealogical Publications of the National Genealogical Society, Vol. 10, Washington, DC, 1954.

4. Schedules for Ogelthorpe County are in the Georgia Department of Archives and History, Atlanta, GA.

5. Schedules for Randolph County are in the Illinois State Library, Springfield, IL.

6. See reconstruction in Charles Brunk Heinermann and Gaius Marcus Brumbaugh, First Census of Kentucky, 1790, Washington, DC, 1940.

7. See reconstruction in Garrett Glenn Clift, comp., Second Census of Kentucky, 1800, Frankfort, KY, 1954.

8. County tax lists for 1783 exist on microfilm.

9. 1885 Dakota Territory census schedules are at the State Historical Society Library, Bismark, ND.

10. 1890 territorial census records are at the Oklahoma Historical Society Library, Oklahoma City, OK.

11. 1885 Dakota Territory census schedules are in the State Historical Society Library, Bismark, ND.

12. See reconstruction in Pollyanna Creekmore, Early East Tennessee Tax Payers, The East Tennessee Historical Society Publications 23, 24, 26, 27, 28, 30, and 31 (1951-1959).

13. See also Compilation of Tennessee Census Reports, 1820 (microfilm publication T911, 1 roll).

14. The Texas State Archives, Austin, TX, has extant Texas census schedules for 1829-1836, reprinted in Marion Day Mullins, "The First Census of Texas, 1829-1836," National Genealogical Society Quarterly, Vol. 40, No. 49 (June 1952) and following.

15. Schedules for Accomack County only in the Virginia State Library, Richmond, VA. 16. Overseas.

AVAILABILITY OF THE 1930 CENSUS RECORDS

The 1930 census and all existing soundex indexes will become available after April 1, 2002, at the National Archives in Washington, DC, and its thirteen regional facilities. Indexes using the soundex indexing system will be available for the states of Alabama, Arkansas, Florida, Georgia, Kentucky (Bell, Floyd, Harlan, Kenton, Muhlenberg, Perry, and Pike counties only), Louisiana, Mississippi, North Carolina, South Carolina, Tennessee, Virginia, and West Virginia (Fayette, Harrison, Kanawha, Logan, McDowell, Mercer, and Raleigh counties only). Additional information about the 1930 census records, soundex index, and ordering information will be available from the National Archives after April 1, 2002.

FINDING GUIDES

All decennial census schedules are arranged geographically, not by name, so an address or an index generally is necessary to find a particular record. In 1908, the U.S. Census Bureau prepared a 12-volume work entitled *Heads of Families at the First Census of the United States Taken in the Year 1790 [state]* that reproduces the completed 1790 schedules in printed form with indexes. Various individuals and organizations have compiled alphabetical indexes for 19th century censuses, generally through 1870, and these can be found in many libraries and genealogical collections. There are SOUNDEX or MIRACODE indexes for 1880 (only households with children 10 years of age or younger), 1900, 1910 (21 states only, mainly in the South), and 1920. These indexes, based on the sound of the surname, originally were prepared to assist the Census Bureau in finding records for persons who needed official proof of age from a period before all states had a uniform system of registering births. There is a separate index for each of the above years for each state or territory. The U.S. Census Bureau also created an index for selected cities in the 1910 census that translates specific street addresses into the appropriate enumeration district number and corresponding volume number of the schedules.

The 1840 Census. This census included a special enumeration of military pensioners. The names and ages listed were printed in *A Census of Pensioners for Revolutionary or Military Services; With Their Names, Ages, Places of Residence,* Washington, DC: Department of State, 1841 (reprinted by the Genealogical Publishing Co., Baltimore, MD, in 1967) and reproduced at the end of roll 3 in National Archives microfilm publication T498.

The 1885 Census. Five states and territories chose to take an 1885 census with federal assistance. The schedules show the same type of information as those for 1880, but in many cases the initial letters of enumerated persons' given names appear instead for the names themselves. The relevant National Archives microfilm publication numbers are as follows:

- Colorado   M158, 8 rolls
- Florida   M845, 13 rolls
- Nebraska   M352, 56 rolls
- New Mexico   M846, 6 rolls
- Dakota Territory
  - North Dakota   In the collection of the state historical society not on microfilm
  - South Dakota   GR27, 3 rolls

The 1890 Records. The majority of 1890 census records were destroyed as a result of a fire in January 1921. The smoke, water, and other damage to the bound volumes was such that only fragments remained to be microfilmed in later years. The surviving records are available on three rolls, National Archives Publication M407. The three rolls cover the following areas:

1. *Alabama.* Perry County (Perryville Beat No. 11 and Severe Beat No. 8).

2. *District of Columbia.* Blocks bounded on the East and West by 13th and 15th streets, Northwest, on the South by Q Street, and on the North by S Street.

3. *Georgia.* Muscogee Country (Columbus).
   Illinois. McDonough County (Mound Twp.).
   Minnesota. Wright County (Rockford).
   New Jersey. Westchester County (Eastchester), Suffolk County (Brookhaven Twp.).
   North Carolina. Gaston County (South Point and River Bend Twps.), and Cleveland County (Twp. No. 2).
   Ohio. Hamilton County (Cincinnati) and Clinton County (Wayne Twp.).*South Dakota.* Union County (Jefferson Twp.).
   Texas. Ellis County (J.P. No. 6, Mountain Peak ad Ovilla Precinct), Hood County (Precinct No. 5), Rusk County (No. 6 and J.P. No. 7), Trinity County (Trinity town and Precinct No. 2), and Kaufman County (Kaufman).

A number of the special schedules of Union veterans of the Civil War and their widows were saved, including those for U.S. vessels and Navy yards. These were microfilmed as National Archives Publication M123.

State and Territorial Censuses

In addition to the 1885 censuses discussed above, many states and territories took their own censuses at various times. Some were fairly detailed; others contained little more than counts. They are not within the scope of this document, but they are described in *State Censuses: An Annotated Bibliography of Census of Population Taken After the Year 1790 by States and Territories of the United States,* prepared by Henry J. Dubester, Library of Congress, Washington, DC: Government Printing Office, 1948, 73 pages (reprinted by Burt Franklin, New York, NY; ISBN 0-83370-927-5). Also see, Lainhart, Ann S. *State Census Records*. Genealogical Publishing Company, 1992 (ISBN 0-8063-1362-5). Extant schedules are available on microfiche from KTO Microform, Millwood, NY.

Mortality Schedules

In 1850, 1860, 1870, 1880, and 1885 (where applicable), the census included inquiries about persons who had died in the year immediately preceding the enumeration (Figure 2). In general, the questions covered these topics—

- Name
- Age at last birthday
- Sex
- Race
- Marital Status
- Profession, occupation, or trade
- State, territory, or country of birth of person and parents
- Length of residence in county
- Month in which person died
- Disease or cause of death
- Place where disease contracted (if not at place of death)
- Name of attending physician

The following chart (Figure 2) is a checklist of existing schedules.

Figure 2.
Mortality Schedules

(This listing provides, by state and year, the available mortality schedules. Where the schedule has a National Archives publication number (M, T, GR, A, etc.) that number is listed. If the publication was issued by a state archives or other organization, that organization is listed as the originator. Where there is no microfilm publication and the mortality schedule is available in book form only, that is indicated in the individual entry. If "manuscript" is indicated, the schedule has not been published and is available only at the holding institution)

State	1850	1860	1870	1880	1885
Alabama	Alabama Dept. Of Archives and History (ADAH)	ADAH	ADAH	ADAH	
Arizona		New Mexico State Records Center and Archives (NMSRCA)	T655	T655	
Arkansas	Arkansas History Commission (AHC)	AHC	AHC	AHC	
California	UC Berkeley Bancroft Library (BL)	BL	BL	BL	
Colorado			T655	T655	M158
Connecticut	Connecticut State Library (CSL)	CSL	CSL	CSL	
Delaware	A1155	A1155	A1155	A1155	
District of Columbia	T655	T655	T655	T655	
Florida	T1168	T1168	T1168	T1168	M845
Georgia	T655	T655	T655	T655	
Idaho	(book form)		Idaho State Historical Society (ISHS)	ISHS	
Illinois	T1133	T1133	T1133	T1133	
Indiana	Indiana State Library (ISL)	ISL	ISL	ISL	
Iowa	A1156	A1156	A1156	A1156	
Kansas		T1130	T1130	T1130	
Kentucky	T655	T655	T655	T655	
Louisiana	T655	T655	T655	T655	
Maine	Maine State Archives (MSA)	MSA	MSA	MSA	
Maryland	Maryland State Law Library (MSLL)	MSLL	MSLL	MSLL	
Massachusetts	GR19 T1204	GR19 T1204	GR19 T1204	T1204	
Michigan	T1163	T1163	T1163	T1163	
Minnesota	Minnesota Historical Society (MHS) (manuscript)	MHS	MHS	MHS	
Mississippi	Mississippi Dept. of Archives and History (MDAH)	MDAH	MDAH	MDAH	
Missouri	State Historical Society of Missouri (SHSM)	SHSM	SHSM	SHSM	
Montana			GR6	GR6	

Figure 2.
Mortality Schedules—Con.

(This listing provides, by state and year, the available mortality schedules. Where the schedule has a National Archives publication number (M, T, GR, A, etc.) that number is listed. If the publication was issued by a state archives or other organization, that organization is listed as the originator. Where there is no microfilm publication and the mortality schedule is available in book form only, that is indicated in the individual entry. If "manuscript" is indicated, the schedule has not been published and is available only at the holding institution)

State	1850	1860	1870	1880	1885
Nebraska		T1128	T1128	T1128	M352
Nevada			Nevada Historical Society (NHS) (manuscript)	NHS (manuscript)	
New Hampshire	New Hampshire State Library (NHSL)	NHSL	NHSL	NHSL	
New Jersey	GR21	GR21	GR21	GR21	
New Mexico	NMSRCA	NMSRCA	NMSRCA	NMSRCA	M846
New York	New York State Archives (NYSA)	NYSA	NYSA	NYSA	
North Carolina	GR1	GR1	GR1	GR1	
North Dakota		South Dakota State Historical Society (SDSHS)	SDSHS	SDSHS	State Historical Society of North Dakota (manuscript)
Ohio	T1159	T1159	T1159	T1159	
Oregon	Oregon State Library (OSL)	OSL	OSL	OSL	
Pennsylvania	T956	T956	T956	T956	
Rhode Island			Rhode Island State Archives (manuscript)		
South Carolina	GR22	GR22	GR22	GR22	
South Dakota		SDSHS	SDSHS	SDSHS	GR27
Tennessee	T655	T655		T655	
Texas	T1134	T1134	T1134GR7	T1134	
Utah	(book form)	(book form)	GR7 State		
Vermont	Vermont Dept. of Libraries (VDL) (manuscript)	VDL (manuscript)	GR7	VDL (manuscript)	
Virginia	T1132	T1132	T1132	T1132	
Washington	OSL	A1154	A1154	A1154	
West Virginia	West Virginia Dept. of Archives and History (WVDAH)	WVDAH	WVDAH	WVDAH	
Wisconsin	State Historical Society of Wisconsin (SHSW)	SHSW	SHSW	SHSW	
Wyoming			(book form)	(book form)	

Population Items on Principal Census Questionnaires: 1790 to 1890

(Excludes identification items, screening questions, and other information collected, but not intended for tabulation)

Demographic characteristics	1790	1800	1810	1820	1830	1840	1850	1860	1870	1880	1890
Age	-	¹X	¹X	X	X	X	X	X	X	X	X
Sex	¹X	¹X	¹X	X	X	X	X	X	X	X	X
Color or Race	X	X	X	X	X	X	X	X	X	X	X
Ancestry/Ethnic Origin	-	-	-	-	-	-	-	-	-	-	-
If American Indian, proportions of Indian or other blood	-	-	-	-	-	-	-	-	-	-	-
If American Indian, name of Tribe	-	-	-	-	-	-	-	-	-	-	-
Relationship to head of family or household	-	-	-	-	-	-	-	-	-	X	X
Married in the past year	-	-	-	-	-	-	²X	²X	X	X	X
Marital status	-	-	-	-	-	-	-	-	-	X	X
Number of years married	-	-	-	-	-	-	-	-	-	-	-
Age at or date of first marriage	-	-	-	-	-	-	-	-	-	-	-
Married more than once	-	-	-	-	-	-	-	-	-	-	-
If remarried, was first marriage terminated by death?	-	-	-	-	-	-	-	-	-	-	-
Number of years widowed, divorced, or separated	-	-	-	-	-	-	-	-	-	-	-
Social Characteristics											
Free or slave	X	X	X	X	X	X	X	X	-	-	-
Per slave owner, number of fugitives	-	-	-	-	-	-	X	X	-	-	-
Per slave owner, number of manumitted	-	-	-	-	-	-	X	X	-	-	-
Physical and mental handicaps and infirmities:											
Deaf or deaf mutes	-	-	-	-	X	X	X	X	X	X	X
Blind	-	-	-	-	X	X	X	X	X	X	X
Insane	-	-	-	-	-	X	X	X	X	X	X
How supported (insane and idiotic only)	-	-	-	-	-	X	-	-	-	†	†
Feeble-minded (idiotic)	-	-	-	-	-	‡X	X	X	X	X	†X
Ill or disabled	-	-	-	-	-	-	-	-	-	‡X	†X
Duration of disability	-	-	-	-	-	-	-	-	-	-	†X
Paupers	-	-	-	-	-	-	²X	²X	-	†	†X
Convicts	-	-	-	-	-	-	²X	²X	-	†	†X
Homeless children	-	-	-	-	-	-	-	-	-	†	†X
Education:											
Literacy	-	-	-	-	-	¹X	²X	²X	X	X	X
School attendance	-	-	-	-	-	-	²X	²X	X	X	X
Educational attainment	-	-	-	-	-	-	-	-	-	-	-
Public or private school	-	-	-	-	-	-	-	-	-	-	-

Population Items on Principal Census Questionnaires: 1790 to 1890—Con.

(Excludes identification items, screening questions, and other information collected, but not intended for tabulation)

Social characteristics	1790	1800	1810	1820	1830	1840	1850	1860	1870	1880	1890
Vocational training	-	-	-	-	-	-	-	-	-	-	-
Place of birth	-	-	-	-	-	-	[2]X	[2]X	X	X	X
Place of birth of parents	-	-	-	-	-	-	-	-	[5]X	X	X
Citizenship	-	-	-	X	X	-	-	-	[6]X	-	X
Year of naturalization	-	-	-	-	-	-	-	-	-	-	-
Eligibility to vote	-	-	-	-	-	-	-	-	[6]X	-	-
If foreign born, year of immigration	-	-	-	-	-	-	-	-	-	-	X
Language	-	-	-	-	-	-	-	-	-	-	X
Language of parents	-	-	-	-	-	-	-	-	-	-	-
Spanish origin or descent	-	-	-	-	-	-	-	-	-	-	-
Number of children living	-	-	-	-	-	-	-	-	-	-	X
Number of children ever born to mother	-	-	-	-	-	-	-	-	-	-	X
For Grandparents' households											
Are grandchildren under 18 living within the household?	-	-	-	-	-	-	-	-	-	-	-
Are grandparents responsible for Grandchild's basic needs?	-	-	-	-	-	-	-	-	-	-	-
Length of responsibility of grandchild	-	-	-	-	-	-	-	-	-	-	-
Veteran status	-	-	-	-	-	X	-	-	-	-	†X
Length of service	-	-	-	-	-	-	-	-	-	-	-
In service date	-	-	-	-	-	-	-	-	-	-	-
Whether wife or widow of veteran	-	-	-	-	-	-	-	-	-	-	†X
If child of veteran, is father dead?	-	-	-	-	-	-	-	-	-	-	-
Farm residence	-	-	-	-	-	-	-	-	-	-	X
Farm residence in a previous year	-	-	-	-	-	-	-	-	-	-	-
Place of residence in a previous year	-	-	-	-	-	-	-	-	-	-	-
Year moved to present residence	-	-	-	-	-	-	-	-	-	-	-
Economic Characteristics											
Industry	-	-	-	X	-	X	-	-	-	-	-
Occupation	-	-	-	-	-	-	[2]X	[2]X	X	X	X
Class of worker	-	-	-	-	-	-	-	-	-	-	-
Private or public nonemergency work, or public emergency work	-	-	-	-	-	-	-	-	-	-	-
Employment status	-	-	-	-	-	-	-	-	-	-	-
Duration of unemployment	-	-	-	-	-	-	-	-	-	X	X
Year last worked	-	-	-	-	-	-	-	-	-	-	-
Weeks worked in preceding year	-	-	-	-	-	-	-	-	-	-	-
Hours worked in preceding week	-	-	-	-	-	-	-	-	-	-	-

Measuring America

Population Items on Principal Census Questionnaires: 1790 to 1890—Con.

(Excludes identification items, screening questions, and other information collected, but not intended for tabulation)

Economic characteristics	1790	1800	1810	1820	1830	1840	1850	1860	1870	1880	1890
Activity 5 years ago	-	-	-	-	-	-	-	-	-	-	-
Industry 5 years ago	-	-	-	-	-	-	-	-	-	-	-
Occupation 5 years ago	-	-	-	-	-	-	-	-	-	-	-
Class of worker 5 years ago	-	-	-	-	-	-	-	-	-	-	-
Value of real estate	-	-	-	-	-	-	^{2}X	^{2}X	X	-	-
Value of personal property	-	-	-	-	-	-	-	^{2}X	-	-	-
Income	-	-	-	-	-	-	-	-	-	-	-
Social Security:	-	-	-	-	-	-	-	-	-	-	-
Registered	-	-	-	-	-	-	-	-	-	-	-
Deductions from all or part of wages or salary	-	-	-	-	-	-	-	-	-	-	-
Place of work	-	-	-	-	-	-	-	-	-	-	-
Means of transportation to work	-	-	-	-	-	-	-	-	-	-	-

† Available on supplemental questionnaires at the National Archives and Records Administration.
s Sample question.
(1) Free White persons only.
(2) Question only asked of free inhabitants.
(3) Question was whether insane or idiotic.
(4) In 1960, place of birth was asked on a sample basis generally, but on a 100-percent basis in New York and Puerto Rico. Citizenship was asked only in New York and Puerto Rico, where it was a 100-percent item.
(5) Question was only whether parents were foreign born.
(6) For males 21 years of age or over.
(7) Whether person could speak English. In 1900, this was the only question; in 1920 and 1930 this question was in addition to request for mother tongue.
(8) Asked only outside cities.
(9) On housing portion of questionnaire.

Population Items on Principal Census Questionnaires: 1900 to 2000

Demographic characteristics	1900	1910	1920	1930	1940	1950	1960	1970	1980	1990	2000
Age	X	X	X	X	X	X	X	X	X	X	X
Sex	X	X	X	X	X	X	X	X	X	X	X
Color or Race	X	X	X	X	X	X	X	X	X	X	X
Ancestry/Ethnic Origin	-	-	-	-	-	-	-	-	sX	sX	sX
If American Indian, proportions of Indian or other blood	†	†	-	X	-	†	-	-	-	-	-
If American Indian, name of Tribe	†	†	-	X	-	†	-	X	X	X	X
Relationship to head of family or household	X	X	X	X	X	X	X	X	X	X	X
Married in the past year	-	-	-	-	-	-	-	-	-	-	-
Marital status	X	X	X	X	X	X	X	X	X	X	sX
Number of years married	X	X	-	-	-	sX	-	-	-	-	-
Age at or date of first marriage	-	-	-	X	sX	-	sX	sX	sX	-	-
Married more than once	-	-	-	-	sX	sX	sX	sX	sX	-	-
If remarried, was first marriage terminated by death?	-	-	-	-	-	-	-	sX	sX	-	-
Number of years widowed, divorced, or separated	-	-	-	-	-	sX	-	-	-	-	-
Social Characteristics											
Free or slave	-	-	-	-	-	-	-	-	-	-	-
Per slave owner, number of slaves	-	-	-	-	-	-	-	-	-	-	-
Per slave owner, number of fugitives	-	-	-	-	-	-	-	-	-	-	-
Per slave owner, number of manumitted	-	-	-	-	-	-	-	-	-	-	-
Physical/mental handicaps and infirmities:											
Deaf or deaf mute	†	†X	†	†	-	-	-	-	-	-	sX
Blind	†	†X	†	†	-	-	-	-	-	-	sX
Insane	-	†	-	-	-	-	-	-	-	-	-
How supported (insane and idiotic only)	-	-	-	-	-	-	-	-	-	-	-
Feeble-minded (idiotic)	-	†	-	-	-	-	-	-	-	-	-
Ill or disabled	-	†	-	-	-	-	-	sX	sX	sX	sX
Duration of disability	-	†	-	-	-	-	-	sX	-	-	-
Paupers	-	†	-	-	-	-	-	-	-	-	-
Convicts	†	†	-	-	-	-	-	-	-	-	-
Homeless children	-	†	-	-	-	-	-	-	-	-	-
Education:											
Literacy	X	X	X	X	-	-	-	-	-	-	-
School attendance	X	X	X	X	X	sX	sX	sX	sX	sX	sX
Educational attainment	-	-	-	-	X	sX	sX	sX	sX	sX	sX

Population Items on Principal Census Questionnaires: 1900 to 2000—Con.

Social characteristics	1900	1910	1920	1930	1940	1950	1960	1970	1980	1990	2000
Public or private school	-	-	-	-	-	-	ˢX	ˢX	-	-	-
Vocational training	-	-	-	-	-	-	-	ˢX	-	-	-
Place of birth	X	X	X	X	X	X	ˢ⁴X	ˢX	ˢX	ˢX	ˢX
Place of birth of parents	X	X	X	X	ˢX	ˢX	ˢX	ˢX	-	-	-
Citizenship	X	X	X	X	X	X	⁴X	ˢX	ˢX	ˢX	ˢX
Year of naturalization	-	-	X	-	-	-	-	-	-	-	-
Eligibility to vote	-	-	-	-	-	-	-	-	-	-	-
If foreign born, year of immigration	X	X	X	X	-	-	-	ˢX	ˢX	ˢX	ˢX
Language	⁷X	X	⁷X	⁷X	ˢX	-	ˢX	ˢX	ˢX	ˢX	ˢX
Language of parents	-	X	X	-	-	-	-	-	-	-	-
Spanish origin or descent	-	-	-	-	-	-	-	ˢX	ˢX	ˢX	ˢX
Number of children living	X	X	-	-	-	-	-	-	-	-	-
Number of children ever born to mother	X	X	-	-	ˢX	ˢX	ˢX	ˢX	ˢX	ˢX	-
For Grandparent households:											
Are grandchildren under 18 living within the household?	-	-	-	-	-	-	·ⁱ	-	-	-	ˢX
Are grandparents Responsible for a Grandchild's basic needs?	-	-	-	-	-	-	-	-	-	-	ˢX
Length of responsibility for grandchild	-	-	-	-	-	-	-	-	-	-	ˢX
Veteran status	-	X	-	X	ˢX	ˢX	ˢX	ˢX	ˢX	ˢX	ˢX
Length of service	-	-	-	-	-	-	-	-	-	ˢX	ˢX
Whether wife or widow of veteran	-	-	-	-	ˢX	-	-	-	-	-	-
If child of veteran, is father dead?	-	-	-	-	ˢX	-	-	-	-	-	-
In service date	-	-	-	-	-	-	-	-	ˢX	ˢX	ˢX
Farm residence	X	X	X	X	X	X	ˢ⁸⁹X	⁹X	-	-	-
Farm residence in a previous year	-	-	-	-	X	ˢX	-	-	-	-	-
Place of residence in a previous year	-	-	-	-	X	ˢX	ˢX	ˢX	ˢX	ˢX	ˢX
Year moved to present residence	-	-	-	-	-	-	ˢX	ˢX	ˢ⁹X	ˢ⁹X	ˢ⁹X
Industry	-	X	X	X	X	X	ˢX	ˢX	ˢX	ˢX	ˢX
Occupation	X	X	X	X	X	X	ˢX	ˢX	ˢX	ˢX	ˢX
Class of worker	-	X	X	X	X	X	ˢX	ˢX	ˢX	ˢX	ˢX
Private or public nonemergency work, or public emergency work	-	-	-	-	X	-	-	-	-	-	-
Employment status	-	-	-	†X	X	X	ˢX	ˢX	ˢX	ˢX	ˢX
Duration of unemployment	X	X	-	†	X	ˢX	-	-	ˢX	ˢX	ˢX
Year last worked	-	-	-	-	-	-	ˢX	ˢX	ˢX	ˢX	ˢX
Economic Characteristics											
Weeks worked in preceding year	-	-	-	†	X	ˢX	ˢX	ˢX	ˢX	ˢX	ˢX
Hours worked in preceding week	-	-	-	†	X	X	ˢX	ˢX	ˢX	ˢX	ˢX
Activity 5 years ago	-	-	-	-	-	-	-	ˢX	-	-	-

Population Items on Principal Census Questionnaires: 1900 to 2000—Con.

Economic characteristics	1900	1910	1920	1930	1940	1950	1960	1970	1980	1990	2000
Industry 5 years ago	-	-	-	-	-	-	-	-	-	-	sX
Occupation 5 years ago	-	-	-	-	-	-	-	sX	-	-	-
Class of worker 5 years ago	-	-	-	-	-	-	-	sX	-	-	-
Value of real estate	-	-	-	-	-	-	-	-	s 9X	s 9X	s 9X
Value of personal property	-	-	-	-	-	-	-	-	-	-	-
Income	-	-	-	-	X	sX	sX	sX	sX	sX	sX
Social Security:											
Registered	-	-	-	-	sX	-	-	-	-	-	-
Deductions from all or part of wages or salary	-	-	-	-	sX	-	-	-	-	-	-
Place of work	-	-	-	-	-	-	sX	sX	sX	sX	sX
Means of transportation to work	-	-	-	-	-	-	sX	sX	sX	sX	sX

See also supplemental questionnaires.

† Available on supplemental questionnaires at the National Archives and Records Administration.

s Sample question.

[1] Free White persons only.

[2] Question only asked of free inhabitants.

[3] Question was whether insane or idiotic.

[4] In 1960, place of birth was asked on a sample basis generally, but on a 100-percent basis in New York and Puerto Rico. Citizenship was asked only in New York and Puerto Rico, where it was a 100-percent item.

[5] Question was only whether parents were foreign born.

[6] For males 21 years of age or over.

[7] Whether person could speak English. In 1900, this was the only question; in 1920 and 1930 this question was in addition to request for mother tongue.

[8] Asked only outside cities.

[9] On housing portion of questionnaire.

A note about microfilmed schedules for genealogy.
Please note that the microfilmed images of schedules completed by an enumerator can have abbreviations, titles, comments, and even "doodles," that do not correspond to any information contained in the instructions given to each enumerator. In such cases, the meaning of this entry has been lost with the enumerator. Furthermore, schedules will frequently have entries (within the schedule or its margins) that seem to have no relation to the question asked. The meaning of these entries have been lost so many years since the marks were made. Although these entries may indeed relate to the household, they often are related to the administrative duties conducted during receipt and tabulation of the schedules by Census Bureau clerks. For example, the letters "JGG" (or any other letters, numbers, or words) next to or within an entry may have been the initials of a Census Bureau clerk, used to indicate where he/she stopped for lunch or the end of the workday, or a manager making an administrative note, such as a shift change. Thus, abbreviations/marks found on the microfilms that are not explicitly identified within the instructions to the enumerators are impossible to definitively understand.

A HISTORY OF THE DECENNIAL CENSUSES: 1790-2000

Censuses of 1790 to 1840

A nationwide population census on a regular basis dates from the establishment of the United States. Article I, Section 2, of the United States Constitution required that—

> "Representatives and direct taxes shall be apportioned among the several states which may be included within this union, according to their respective numbers, which shall be determined by adding to the whole number of free persons, including those bound to service for a term of years, and excluding Indians not taxed, three-fifths of all other persons. The actual Enumeration shall be made within three Years after the first Meeting of the Congress of the United States, and within every subsequent term of ten years, in such manner as they shall by law direct.[3]"

Starting with the 1800 census, the Secretary of State directed the enumeration and, from 1800 to 1840, the marshals reported the results to him. From 1850 through 1900, the Interior Department, established in 1849, had jurisdiction.

---

[3]In subsequent decades, the practice of "service for a term of years" died out. "Indians not taxes" were those not living in settled areas and paying taxes; by the 1940s, all American Indians were considered to be taxed. The 13th Amendment abolished slavery in 1865, and the 14th Amendment to the Constitution, ratified in 1868, officially ended Article 1's "three-fifths rule." Thus, the original census requirements were modified. Direct taxation based on the census never became practical.

The 1800 and 1810 population censuses were similar in scope and method to the 1790 census. However, the Congress, statisticians, and other scholars urged that while the populace was being enumerated, other information the new government needed also should be collected. The first inquiries on manufacturing were made in 1810 and, in later decades, censuses of agriculture, mining, governments, religious bodies (discontinued after 1946), business, housing, and transportation were added to the decennial census. (Legislation enacted in 1948 and later years specified that the various economic, agriculture, and government censuses would be taken at times that did not conflict with those in which the population and housing censuses occurred.)

The 1830 census related solely to population. The marshals and their assistants began using uniform printed schedules; before that, they had to use whatever paper was available, rule it, write in the headings, and bind the sheets together.

The census act for the 1840 census authorized the establishment of a centralized census office during each enumeration and provided for the collection of statistics pertaining to "the pursuits, industry, education, and resources of the country." The new population inquiries included school attendance, illiteracy, and type of occupation.

From 1790 through the 1840 census, the household, not the individual, was the unit of enumeration in the population census, and only the names of the household heads appeared on the schedules. There was no tabulation beyond the simple addition of the entries the marshals had submitted, and there was no attempt to publish details uniformly by cities or towns, or to summarize returns for each state, other than by county, unless the marshals had done so.

Censuses of 1850 to 1890

The act governing the Seventh, Eighth, and Ninth Decennial Censuses (1850-1870) made several changes in census procedures: Each marshal was responsible for subdividing his district into "known civil divisions," such as counties, townships, or wards, and for checking to ensure that his assistants' returns were completed properly. The number of population inquiries grew; every free person's name was to be listed, as were the items relating to each individual enumerated. Beginning in 1850, marshals collected additional "social statistics" (information about taxes, schools, crime, wages, value of estate, etc.) and data on mortality. [Decennial mortality schedules for some states and territories exist for 1850-1880 and for a few places in 1885; see Table 2.]

Noteworthy features of the 1870 census included the introduction of a rudimentary tally device to help the clerks in their work and the publications of maps, charts, and diagrams to illustrate the most significant census results.

The general scope of the 1880 census was expanded only slightly over that of 1870, but much greater detail was obtained for many of the items—so much more that, beyond the basic counts, which were released promptly, publication of these data was not completed until nearly 1890.

The census act of 1880 replaced the marshals and their assistants with specially appointed agents (experts assigned to collect technical data, such as on manufacturing processes), supervisors, and enumerators, every one of whom was forbidden to disclose census information. Maintaining the confidentiality of the data was a result of what some people regarded as the census' invasion of privacy, especially since prior to the 1880 census, there was no law limiting the extent to which the public could use or see the information on any schedule. (Subsequent demographic and economic censuses, as well as most surveys, have been carried out according to statutes that make compliance mandatory, with penalties for refusal; and responses confidential, with penalties for disclosure. Congress codified these laws in 1954 as Title 13, U.S. Code.) For the first time, enumerators were given detailed maps to follow, so they could account for every street or road and not stray beyond their assigned boundaries. (The National Archives' Cartographic and Architectural Branch maintains this map collection.[4])

Again, in 1890, there was an extension of the decennial census's scope, and some subjects were covered in even greater detail than in 1880. Data were collected in supplemental surveys on farm and home mortgages and private corporations' and individuals' indebtedness. The 1890 census also used, for the first time in history, a separate schedule for each family.

Herman Hollerith, who had been a special agent for the 1880 census, developed punch cards and electric tabulating machines to process the 1890 census returns, considerably reducing the time needed to complete the clerical work. (Hollerith's venture became part of what is now the IBM Corporation.) Both the cards and the machines were improved progressively over the next 50 years.[5]

The 1890 census was historic in another way. In the first volume of the results, the Superintendent of the Census wrote—

"Up to and including 1880, the country had a frontier of settlement, but at present the unsettled area has been so broken into by isolated bodies of settlement that there can hardly be said to be a frontier line. In

the discussion of its extent, its westward movement, etc., it can not, therefore, any longer have a place in the census reports.[6]

Commenting on this statement, historian Frederick Jackson Turner wrote in 1893 that, "up to our own day, American history has been in a large degree the history of the colonization of the Great West. The existence of an area of free land, its continuous recession, and the advance of American settlement westward, explain American development."[7] The censuses that followed 1890 reflected the filling in, rather than the expansion of, the colonized areas; symbolizing a turning point in America's development as a Nation.

Censuses of 1900 to 2000

Although the censuses in the early 1900s did not witness the expansion of inquiries as had been witnessed in the late nineteenth century, geographic coverage of the census reflected the Nation's growing status as a political and military power. As a result of the country's expanding global influence, the following areas saw their first censuses administered by the United States in the early 1900s:

- Following its annexation in 1898, Hawaii (where the local government took a census every 6 years from 1866 though 1896) was included in the 1900 census, which also had the first count of the U.S. population abroad (Armed Forces and Federal civilian employees, and their households).

- The War Department carried out an enumeration in Puerto Rico in 1899 following that island's acquisition from Spain in 1898 (there were periodic censuses from 1765 to 1887 under Spanish rule), and there have been decennial censuses conducted in Puerto Rico from 1910 to the present.

- The U.S. Census Bureau compiled and published one census of the Philippine Islands following their accession by the United States in 1898; this census was taken under the direction of the Philippine Commission in 1903. (Under Spanish rule, there had been censuses in 1818 and 1876. The Philippine legislature directed in 1918, and the Commonwealth's statistical office began periodic enumerations in 1939. The Philippines became an independent republic in 1946).

- The Isthmian Canal Commission ordered a general census of the Panama Canal Zone when the United States took control of the area in 1904; there was another general census in 1912 and several special censuses at various

---

[4]The National Archives Cartographic and Architectural Branch, 8601 Adelphi Road, College Park, MD 20740-6001, 301-713-7040.
[5]For more information, see "100 Years of Data Processing: The Punch card Century." U.S. Department of Commerce, Bureau of the Census, January 1991.

[6]U.S. Census Office, *Compendium of the Eleventh Census: 1890.* Part 1.—Population. Washing, DC: Government Printing Office, 1892, p. xlviii.
The Frontier in American History. New York: H. Holt & Company, 1958, p. 1.

times. The Canal Zone was included in the U.S. censuses from 1920 to 1970. (Sovereignty over the Zone was transferred to the Republic of Panama in 1979.)

- Following the United States' occupation of Guam in 1899, the local governor conducted a census there in 1901. The island has been included in U.S. censuses from 1920 onward.

- The governors of American Samoa conducted censuses at various times after the United States acquired the islands in 1900, and the population was enumerated in U.S. censuses from 1920 onward.

- Prior to the acquisition of the Danish Virgin Islands by the United States in 1917, the Danish government took periodic censuses between 1835 and 1911. The U.S. census was conducted in 1917 and the islands appeared in the 1930 and subsequent U.S. censuses.

- A census of Cuba was conducted under a provisional U.S. administration in 1907. There were earlier censuses under Spanish rule (which ended in 1898). The U.S. War Department conducted an enumeration in 1899, and subsequent censuses were overseen by the Republic (established in 1901) beginning in 1919.

- There had been quinquennial Japanese censuses from 1920 to 1940 for the islands that became the U.S. Trust Territory of the Pacific Islands. The U.S. Navy conducted a census in 1950, and the U.S. High Commissioner carried out a census in 1958, the results of which appeared in the 1960 U.S. census reports. The U.S. Census Bureau conducted the 1970 and 1980 censuses[8]; in 1980, 1990, and 2000, there was a separate census of the Northern Mariana Islands, which had been part of the Trust Territory.

A number of the censuses noted above collected data on agriculture, housing, and economic subjects and included enumerations on isolated islands, such as Truk and Yap, mainly in the Pacific.

Stateside Developments

From the 1840 through the 1900 censuses, a temporary census office had been established before each decennial enumeration and disbanded as soon as the results were compiled and published. Congress established a permanent Bureau of the Census in 1902, in the Department of the Interior, so there would be an ongoing organization capable of carrying out censuses throughout the decades instead of concentrating all the work in those years ending in "0." The Census Bureau moved to the new Department of Commerce

---

[8]In 1986, compacts of free association were implemented between the Federated States of Micronesia and the Marshall Islands, and the United States. Under the terms of Title 13, U.S. Code, the United States was no longer authorized to take the decennial censuses in those areas that were formerly part of the Trust Territory.

and Labor in 1903, and remained within the Department of Commerce when the Department of Labor was split off in 1913.

The 1910 census was the first for which prospective census employees took open competitive examinations throughout the country (since 1880, appointees had been given non-competitve tests). The way in which results were published also was changed, with those statistics that were ready first—especially those in greatest demand (such as the total population of individual cities and states, and of the United States as a whole)—issued first as press releases, then in greater detail as bulletins and abstracts, the latter appearing 6 months to 1 year before the final reports were issued.

In 1920 and 1930, there were minor changes in scope. A census of unemployment accompanied the 1930 census —data were collected for each person reported to have a gainful occupation, but who was not at work on the day preceding the enumerator's visit.

Sampling. In many ways, 1940 saw the first modern census. One of its major innovations was the use of statistical techniques, such as probability sampling, that had only been experimented with previously, such as in 1920s crop sampling, a Civil Works Administration trial census and surveys of retail stores conducted in the 1930s, and an official sample survey of unemployment in 1940 that covered about 20,000 households. Sampling in the 1940 census allowed the addition of several questions for just 5 percent of the persons enumerated, without unduly increasing the overall burden on respondents and on data processing. Sampling also made it possible to publish preliminary returns 8 months ahead of the complete tabulations. The Census Bureau was able to increase the number of detailed tables published and review of the quality of the data processing was more efficient.

Most population and housing inquiries included in the 1940 census were repeated in later years, and a few were added, including—

- Place of work and means of transportation to work (1960).

- Occupation 5 years before the census (1970 and 1980 only).

- Housing costs (1980).

- Inquiries relating to childcare by grandparents (2000).

In 1940 and 1950, the sample population questions were asked only for those persons whose names fell on the schedules' sample lines. Sampling was extended to the housing schedule in 1950, with a few questions asked on a cyclic basis: One pair of questions for household 1, another pair for household 2, etc., until household 6, when the cycle was started again with the first pair of questions.

In the 1960 census, the sampling pattern was changed for population and housing questions alike: If a housing unit was in the sample, all of the household members were in the sample, too. This scheme yielded sufficient data for accurate estimates of population and housing characteristics for areas as small as a census tract (an average of 4,000 people). The only population questions asked on a 100-percent basis (name and address, age, sex, race, and since 1980, Hispanic origin, marital status, and relationship to householder), were those necessary to identify the population and avoid duplication.

The sampling pattern changed in later censuses. For 1970, some sample questions were asked of either a 15-percent or a 5-percent sample of households, but some were asked for both, thus constituting a 20-percent sample. There was no "split sample" for 1980, but it was used at every other household (50 percent) in places with fewer than 2,500 inhabitants and at every sixth household (17 percent) elsewhere. For Census 2000, the overall sampling rate was 1-in-6 households, but the actual sampling rate for any given geographic entity depended on its estimated population density and included four rates: 1-in-2, 1-in-4, 1-in-6, and 1-in-8 households.

Reflecting the concerns of the Depression years, the 1940 census asked several questions to measure employment and unemployment, internal migration, and income. It was also the first to include a census of housing that obtained a variety of facts on the general condition of the Nation's housing and the need for public housing programs. (Prior to this, the housing data collected as part of the population censuses were generally limited to one or two items.)

At the time of the 1950 census, a survey of residential financing was conducted as a related, but separate, operation with information collected on a sample basis from owners of owner-occupied and rental properties and mortgage lenders. Similar surveys accompanied subsequent censuses. There also were surveys of components of housing change with the 1960, 1970, and 1980 censuses (but not 1990, when the survey was scheduled for 1989 and 1991). These measured the quantitative and qualitative impact of basic changes that occurred in the Nation's housing stock during the previous decade. The survey also offered a measure of "same" units, i.e., the preponderant part of the housing inventory that was not affected by the basic changes. (The first survey of this type had been a key part of the National Housing Inventory in 1956.)

Processing. The major innovation of the 1950 census was the use of an electronic computer—the Universal Automatic Computer I (UNIVAC I)—the first of a series delivered in 1951 to help tabulate some of the census data. Nearly all of the data processing was done by computer in the 1960 census. Beginning in 1960, census data were tabulated with the aid of the film optical sensing device for input to computers (FOSDIC)—an electronic device for "reading" the data on questionnaires. Special questionnaires were designed on which the answers could be indicated by marking small

circles. The completed questionnaires were photographed onto microfilm with automatic cameras. The FOSDIC then "read" the blackened dots (which appeared as clear holes on the negative film) and transferred the data they represented to magnetic tape to be processed by computer at speeds that ranged from 3,000 items a minute in 1960 to 70,000 items per minute by the time the 1990 census data were tabulated.[9]

Collecting the data. The 1960 census was the first in which population and housing data were extensively collected by mail. The field canvass was preceded by the delivery to every occupied housing unit of a questionnaire that contained the 100-percent questions (those asked for all persons and housing units). Householders were asked to complete the questionnaire and hold it until an enumerator visited.

The sample items were on a different questionnaire. In urban areas, containing about 80 percent of the Nation's population, the enumerators carried questionnaires containing the sample population and housing questions for every fourth housing unit. If the units were occupied, the householders were asked to fill out the sample questionnaires themselves and mail them to the census district office. The enumerators completed the questionnaires for vacant units. When these questionnaires were received in the district offices, the responses were transcribed to the special FOSDIC schedules. In rural areas, the enumerators obtained the sample information during their visits, and they recorded it directly on FOSDIC schedules.

The 1970 census marked the use nearly everywhere of separate, FOSDIC-readable household questionnaires—approximately 70 million of them—rather than the large schedules that contained information for four or more households. Thus, respondents could mark the appropriate answer circles on their questionnaires, which then could be processed directly without transcription.

Subsequent censuses were taken principally by mail—approximately 60 percent of the population in 1970, 90 percent in 1980, and 94 percent or more in 1990 and 2000. The questionnaires contained the 100-percent and, where appropriate, sample questions. In areas where the mailout/mailback procedure was used, enumerators contacted, either by telephone or personal visit, only those households that had not returned questionnaires or had given incomplete or inconsistent answers. For the remainder of the population, most of which was located in rural areas or small towns, postal carriers left a census form containing the 100-percent questions at each residential housing unit on their routes. An enumerator visited each of these households to collect the completed questionnaires

---

[9]The FOSDIC was replaced for Census 2000 with mark and optical character recognition (OMR and OCR) equipment.

and ask the additional questions for any household or housing unit in the sample. These procedures were continued, with modifications, for 1990 and 2000. In many rural areas, the enumerators, rather than the postal carriers, delivered the questionnaires and asked that they be completed and mailed back. In some inner-city areas, the enumerators took address lists with them, checked for additional units, and enumerated any persons they found living there.

Publishing. For 1970, extensive discussions with census data users led to a major increase in the amount of statistics tabulated, especially for small areas. As part of the 1970 census program, the Census Bureau published 100-percent (but not sample) data for each of 1.5 million census blocks (including all blocks in urbanized areas), as compared with 1960, when block data were provided for 750,000 blocks within the city limits of places with 50,000 or more inhabitants. For 1980, there were data for 1.8 million blocks, with the population limit lowered to include incorporated places with populations of 10,000 or more; several states were "blocked" in their entirety. For 1990 and 2000, the block statistics program was expanded to cover the entire country, or approximately 7.5 million blocks.

The 1970, 1980, and 1990 population and housing census data appear in series of printed reports—either on paper or microfiche, or both—similar to those issued after the 1960 census, with accompanying maps, where appropriate. In addition, the U.S. Census Bureau issued public-use microdata tapes, usually containing much more detail than the printed reports, for users with computer access. After 1980, some data were made available on diskettes, online, through commercial computer networks, and by 1990, on CD-ROMs. Following Census 2000, data were released via the Internet, on CD-ROMs, computer-assisted "print-on-demand," and for some publications, the traditional printed volumes.

INDIVIDUAL HISTORIES OF THE UNITED STATES CENSUSES

The First Census: 1790

The first enumeration began on Monday, August 2, 1790, little more than a year after the inauguration of President Washington and shortly before the second session of the first Congress ended. The Congress assigned responsibility for the 1790 census to the marshals of the U.S. judicial districts under an act that, with minor modifications and extensions, governed census-taking through 1840. The law required that every household be visited and that completed census schedules be posted in "two of the most public places within [each jurisdiction],there to remain for the inspection of all concerned . . ." and that "the aggregate amount of each description of persons" for every district be transmitted to the President. The six inquiries in 1790 called for the name of the head of the family and the number of persons in each household of the following descriptions: Free White males of 16 years and upward (to assess the country's industrial and military potential), free White males under 16 years, free White females, all other free persons (by sex and color), and slaves.

It is presumed that the Secretary of State (Thomas Jefferson), acting under the authority of the President, sent the marshals within each state, copies of the census act, and the required inquiries[10]. The marshals then incorporated these inquiries into "schedules" of their own design.

The Second Census: 1800

A February 28, 1800, act provided for the taking of the second census of the United States, which included the states and territories northwest of the Ohio River and Mississippi Territory. The guidelines for the 1800 enumeration followed those of the first enumeration, except that the work was to be carried on under the direction of the Secretary of State.

The enumeration was to begin, as in 1790, on the first Monday in August, and conclude in 9 calendar months. The marshals and secretaries were required to deposit the returns of their assistants, which were to be transmitted to the Secretary of State (not the President as in 1790), on or before September 1, 1801.

The Third Census: 1810

The third census, taken by the terms of an act of March 26, 1810, stipulated that the census was to be "an actual inquiry at every dwelling house, or of the head of every family within each district, and not otherwise" and commenced on the first Monday of August.

The results of the 1810 census were published in a 180-page volume. Data for the population were presented by counties and towns in the northern sections of the country (except New York, which was by counties only), and in Ohio, Kentucky, and Georgia. The returns for the southern states were limited to counties. Territories were generally returned by counties and townships.

No additional details concerning the population were collected by the census; however, an act of May 1, 1810, required marshals, secretaries, and assistants to take (under the Secretary of the Treasury), "an account of the several manufacturing establishments and manufactures within their several districts, territories, and divisions." The marshals collected and transmitted these data to the Secretary of the Treasury at the same time as the results of the population enumeration were transmitted to the Secretary of State. No schedule was prescribed for the collection of industrial data and the nature of the inquiries were at the discretion of the Secretary of the Treasury.

An act of May 16, 1812, provided for the publication of a digest of manufactures containing data on the kind, quality,

---

[10]Carrol D. Wright and William C. Hunt, *The History and Growth of the United States Census.* Government Printing Office: Washington, DC, 1900. p.17.

and value of goods manufactured, the number of establishments, and the number of machines of various kinds used in certain classes of manufactures. The report, containing incomplete returns covering these items for more than 200 kinds of goods and included several items that were principally agricultural, was published in 1813.

The Fourth Census: 1820

The fourth census was taken under the provisions of an act of March 14, 1820. The enumeration began on the first Monday of August, and was scheduled to conclude within 6 calendar months; however, the time prescribed for completing the enumeration was extended to September 1, 1821. The 1820 census act required that enumeration should be by an actual inquiry at every dwelling house, or of the head of every family within each district.

As in 1810, the 1820 census attempted to collect industrial statistics. Data relating to manufactures were collected by the assistants, sent to the marshals, and then transmitted to the Secretary of State at the same time as the population returns. The report on manufactures presented the data for manufacturing establishments by counties, but the results were not summarized for each district and an aggregate statement was compiled as a result of incomplete returns. (The poor quality of manufacturing data was blamed partly on insufficient compensation for the collection of the data and the refusal of manufacturers to supply it).

The Fifth Census: 1830

Prior to the passage of the census act authorizing the fifth census in 1830, President Adams, in his fourth address to the U.S. Congress on December 28, 1828, suggested the census commence earlier in the year than August 1. He also proposed that the collection of age data should be extended from infancy, in intervals of 10 years, to the "utmost boundaries of life". These changes were incorporated into the census act of March 23, 1830. As in the previous census, the enumeration was made by an actual inquiry by the marshals or assistants at every dwelling house, or, as the law stated, by "personal" inquiry of the head of every family, and began on June 1 (instead of the first Monday of August as in previous censuses.) The assistants were required to transmit their returns to the marshals of their respective districts by December 1, 1830. Marshals filed these returns and the aggregate counts for their respective districts to the Secretary of State, by February 1, 1831. However, because of delays in the compilation of the census returns, the filing date was extended to August 1, 1831.

The 1830 census concerned the population only. No attempt was made to collect additional data on the Nation's manufactures and industry.

The Sixth Census: 1840

The sixth census was governed by the same general provisions of law as in 1830. Under the provisions of an act of March 3, 1839 (and amended by an act of February 26,

1840), the enumeration began on June 1, 1840. Marshals were to receive two copies of the census receipts from enumerators by November 1, 1840, one of which was to be sent to the Secretary of State by December 1, 1840. Again, as a result of delays, the deadlines for assistants and marshals were extended to May 1 and June 1, 1841, respectively. (The January 14, 1841 act extending these deadlines also provided for the re-enumeration of Montgomery County, Maryland, [due to discrepencies in the reports], to begin on June 1, 1841, and to be completed, with receipts returned, by October 1, 1841.)

No population questionnaire was prescribed by the Congress—the design of the questionnaire was left to the discretion of the Secretary of State, and closely followed that used in 1830. The law did specify the inquiries to be made of each household.

The Seventh Census: 1850

In March 1849, Congress enacted a bill establishing a census board, whose membership consisted of the Secretary of State, the Attorney General, and the Postmaster General. This board was "to prepare and cause to be printed such forms and schedules as may be necessary for the full enumeration of the inhabitants of the United States; and also proper forms and schedules for collecting in statistical tables, under proper heads, such information as to mines, agriculture, commerce, manufactures, education, and other topics as will exhibit a full view of the pursuits, industry, education, and resources of the country."

The Congress also authorized the creation of the Department of the Interior in March 1849, and part of the enabling act provided that the Secretary of the Interior should "exercise all the supervisory and appellate powers now exercised by the Secretary of State in relation to all acts of marshals and others in taking and returning the census of the United States."

The seventh census was governed by the provisions of an act of May 23, 1850, which directed that six schedules be used to collect the information requested by the Congress. The enumeration began on June 1, 1850, and was to be completed, with the results returned to the Secretary of the Interior by November 1, 1850.

The Census Board prepared and printed six schedules for the 1850 census as follows:

- Schedule No. 1 - Free Inhabitants.

- Schedule No. 2 - Slave Inhabitants.

- Schedule No. 3 - Mortality. This schedule collected data—including name, age, sex, color, and place of birth—on persons having died during the year ending June 1, 1850. Additional data were collected on constitutional and marital status; profession, occupation, or trade; month of death; disease or cause of death; number of days ill; and any suitable remarks.

Measuring America

- Schedule No. 4 - Production of Agriculture. This schedule collected data on agricultural production for the year ending June 1, 1850.

- Schedule No. 5 - Products of Industry. This schedule collected data on the products of industry for the year ending June 1, 1850, and applied to all forms of productive industry, including manufactures (except household manufactures), mining, fisheries, and all kinds of mercantile, commercial, and trading businesses.

- Schedule No. 6 - Social Statistics. This schedule collected aggregate statistics for each subdivision enumerated on the following topics: valuation of real estate; annual taxes; colleges, academies, and schools; seasons and crops; libraries; newspapers and periodicals; religion; pauperism; crime; and wages.

Each of these schedules was supplemented by printed instructions in which the intention of each inquiry was explained. In addition, each assistant was supplied with a "sample" schedule that had been completed the way the Census Board had intended. Each schedule included a space at the head for the entry of the name of the civil division for which the enumeration was made and the date on which the inquiries were completed. Assistants were required to sign each completed schedule.

Joseph C.G. Kennedy supervised the enumeration and compilation of census data at the end of the 1850 Census. He served as "Secretary" of the Census Board from May 1, 1849 to May 31, 1850, before being appointed Superintendent Clerk, by the Secretary of the Interior. Kennedy was succeeded as Superintendent Clerk by James D. B. De Bow, on March 18, 1853. Upon completing the compilation of census results, De Bow resigned the office on December 31, 1854, and the census office was disbanded.

The Eighth Census: 1860

The Eighth Census of the United States was authorized by the previous census May 23, 1850 act. On the recommendation of the Secretary of the Interior, the provisions of this act were to be "adhered to, following the requirement for the taking of the eighth, or any subsequent census under its provisions, if no law, therefore, was passed before January 1 of the year in which the census was required.[11]" By an act of May 5, 1860, a clerical force was provided for the census office and on June 1, 1860, and Joseph C. G. Kennedy was appointed Superintendent.

The census office, and the position of Superintending Clerk were (for all practical purpose) abolished in May 1862. A portion of the clerks engaged in census work were transferred to the General Land Office, where the work of the 1860 census was completed, including the publication of a two-volume census report, under the direction of the Commissioner of the General Land Office.

The Ninth Census: 1870

The 1870 census commenced on June 1, 1870, and was taken under the provisions of the census act of May 23, 1850.[12]

The Secretary of Interior appointed General Francis A. Walker Superintendent of the Ninth Census on February 7, 1870.[13] Although the 1870 Census was under the 1850 act, a new bill approved on May 6, 1870, made the following changes:

- The marshals were to submit the returns from "schedule 1" (free inhabitants) to the Census Office by September 10, 1870. All other schedules were to be submitted by October 1, 1870.

- The 1850 law authorizing penalties for refusing to reply to the inquiries was expanded to apply to all inquiries made by enumerators.

Redesigned schedules used for 1870 and the omission of a "slave" schedule made possible several additional inquiries as follows:

Schedule No. 1 - General Population Schedule. This schedule collected data from the entire population of the United States.

Schedule No. 2 - Mortality. This schedule collected data on persons who died during the year. In addition to the 1860 inquiries, inquiries were modified to include Schedule 1's additions to collect data on parentage and to differentiate between Chinese and American Indians. Inquiries concerning "free or slave" status and "number of days ill" were discontinued.

Schedule No. 3 - Agriculture. The 1860 inquiries were used with additional requests for (1) acreage of woodland, (2) production of Spring and Winter wheat, (3) livestock sold for slaughter, (4) total tons of hemp produced, (5) total wages paid, (6) gallons of milk sold, (7) value of forest products, and (8) estimated value of all farm productions.

Schedule No. 4 - Products of Industry. Using the 1860 schedule as a basis, additional information was requested on (1) motive power and machinery, (2)

---

[11]Wright and Hunt, p. 50.

[12]Although a Congressional committee stated that the 1860 Census had been "the most complete census that any Nation has ever had," it was recognized that the 1850 act was inadequate to meet the changing conditions in which the 1870 Census would need to be conducted. A special committee of the U.S. House of Representatives (Second Session, Forty-First Congress) investigated and reported on the need for a new census act. The committee's report was submitted as a bill on January 18, 1870. This bill was passed by the U.S. House of Representatives, but defeated in the Senate, compelling the use of the 1850 Census act.

[13]General Walker was one of several "experts" participating in the U.S. House of Representatives' Committee deliberations on the 1870 Census. Prior to being appointed Superintendent of the Ninth Census, Walker was Chief of the Bureau of Statistics, which then was an agency within the Treasury Department.

hands employed by sex and specified age groups, (3) total annual salaries paid, and (4) time of full- and part-time operation.

Schedule No. 5 - Social Statistics. The 1860 schedule was modified to incorporate the questions on (1) bonded and other debt of counties, cities, towns, and townships, parishes, and boroughs, (2) pauperism and crime by race ("native black" and "native white"); (3) number of church organizations and church buildings; (4) number of teachers and students; (5) kinds of schools, libraries, and taxes, by type.

The 1870 enumeration was completed on August 23, 1871. The work of compiling the census data, a portion of which was tallied using a machine invented by Charles W. Seaton, was completed in 1872.

The Tenth Census: 1880

The 1880 census was carried out under a law enacted March 3, 1879. Additional amendments to the law were made on April 20, 1880, and appropriations made on June 16, 1880—16 days after the actual enumeration had begun.

The new census law specifically handed over the supervision of the enumeration to a body of officers, known as supervisors of the census, specifically chosen for the work of the census, and appointed in each state or territory, of which they should be residents before March 1, 1880.

Each supervisor was responsible for recommending the organization of his district for enumeration, choosing enumerators for the district and supervising their work, reviewing and transmitting the returns from the enumerators to the central census office, and overseeing the compensation for enumerators in each district.

Each enumerator was required by law "to visit personally each dwelling house in his subdivision, and each family therein, and each individual living out of a family in any place of abode, and by inquiry made of the head of such family, or of the member thereof deemed most credible and worthy of trust, or of such individual living out of a family, to obtain each and every item of information and all the particulars." In case no one was available at a family's usual place of abode, the enumerator was directed by the law "to obtain the required information, as nearly as may be practicable, from the family or families, or person or persons, living nearest to such place of abode."

The 1879 census act also provided for the collection of detailed data on the condition and operation of railroad corporations, incorporated express companies, and telegraph companies, and of life, fire, and marine insurance companies (using Schedule No. 4 - Social Statistics). In addition, the Superintendent of Census was required to collect and publish statistics of the population, industries, and

resources of Alaska, with as much detail as was practical. An enumeration was made of all untaxed Indians within the jurisdiction of the United States to collect as much information about their condition as possible.

The following five schedules were authorized by the 1880 census act:

Schedule No. 1 - Population. The 1880 schedule was similar to that used previously, with a few exceptions.

Schedule No. 2 - Mortality. The schedule used the same inquiries as in 1870, and added inquiries to record marital status, birthplace of parents, length of residence in the United States or territory, and name of place where the disease was contracted, if other than place of death.

The Superintendent of Census was authorized to withdraw the mortality schedule in those areas where an official registration of death was maintained, and the required statistics were then collected from these administrative records.

Schedule No. 3 - Agriculture. In addition to greatly expanded inquiries concerning various crops (including acreage for principal crop), questions were added to collect data on farm tenure, weeks of hired labor, annual cost for fence building and repair, fertilizer purchases, and the number of livestock as of June 1, 1880.

Schedule No. 4 - Social Statistics. Section 18 of the March 3, 1879, census act made the collection of social statistics the responsibility of experts and special agents, not the enumerators. Although some data were collected by enumerators using the general population schedule (Schedule No. 1), the majority of the data were collected through correspondence with officials of institutions providing care and treatment of certain members of the population. Experts and special agents also were employed to collect data on valuation, taxation, and indebtedness; religion; libraries; colleges, academies, and schools; newspapers and periodicals, and wages.

Schedule No. 5 - Relating to Manufactures. In addition to the inquiries made in 1870, this schedule contained new inquiries as to the greatest number of hands employed at any time during the year, the number of hours in the ordinary work day from May to November and November to May, the average daily wages paid to skilled mechanics and laborers, months of full- and part-time operation, and machinery used.

Special agents were charged with collecting data on specific industries throughout the country, and included the manufactures of iron and steel; cotton, woolen, and worsted goods; silk and silk goods;

chemical products and salt; coke and glass; shipbuilding; and all aspects of fisheries and mining, including the production of coal and petroleum.

Interdecennial Censuses of States and Territories: 1885

In addition to the 1880 Census, the 1879 census act also provided for interdecennial censuses by any state or territory, through their duly appointed officers, during the 2 months beginning with the first Monday of June 1885 (*State Censuses: An Annotated Bibliography of Census of Population Taken After the Year 1790 by States and Territories of the United States,* Prepared by Henry J. Dubester). The schedules used were to be similar in all respects to those used by the federal census. Upon completion of a state or territorial census, certified copies of the returns were to be forwarded to the Secretary of the Interior by September 1 of the interdecennial year. States or territories opting to conduct these censuses were provided 50 percent of the total cost to cover census operations. As a result, the states of Florida, Nebraska, and Colorado, and the territories of New Mexico and Dakota conducted censuses in 1885. Copies of the returns were sent to the Department of the Interior, but the data were not published.

The Eleventh Census: 1890

The census of 1890 was taken, under the supervision of Robert P. Porter,[14] according to an act of March 1, 1889, and modeled after that used for the 1880 Census.

The enumeration began on June 2, 1890, because June 1 was a Sunday. The census employed 175 supervisors, with one or more appointed to each state or territory, exclusive of Alaska and Indian territory. Each subdivision assigned to an enumerator was not to exceed 4,000 inhabitants. Enumeration was to be completed in cities with populations under 10,000 (according to the 1880 Census results) was to be completed within 2 weeks. Enumerators were required to collect all the information required by the act by a personal visit to each dwelling and family.

As in 1880, experts and special agents were hired to make special enumerations of manufactures,[15] Indians living within the jurisdiction of the United States, and a separate enumeration of Alaska. Furthermore, the schedule collecting social statistics was withdrawn from enumerators; the work of obtaining statistics concerning mines and mining, fisheries, churches, education, insurance, transportation, and wealth, debt, and taxation, also was conducted by experts and special agents.

Robert B. Porter served as Superintendant of Census until his resignation on July 31, 1893. On October 3, 1893, Congress enacted a law that directed census-related work to continue under the direction of the Commissioner of Labor. On March 2, 1895, a further act of Congress closed the census office and transferred the unfinished work to the office of the Secretary of the Interior, where it continued until July 1, 1897.[16]

The results of the 1890 Census are contained in 25 volumes, plus a three-part compendium, statistical atlas, and an abstract. The complete results from the special enumeration of survivors of the Civil War were not published (the schedules of which were turned over to the Bureau of Pensions); however, the special inquiry on Schedule 1 (general population schedule) regarding Union and Confederate veterans were published in the report on population.

The Twelfth Census: 1900

The twelfth census of the United States was conducted under the terms of the census act of March 3, 1899, and supervised by the Director of the Census, William R. Merriam. The enumeration was conducted in each state and organized territory, including Washington, DC, Alaska, Hawaii, and "Indian Territory."[17] The census was taken as of June 1, 1900, and was to be completed in 2 weeks in places of 8,000 inhabitants or more (as of the 1890 Census) and 1 month in rural districts. The United States and its territories were divided into 297 supervisors' districts, which were subdivided into 52,726 enumeration districts.

The enumeration of military and naval personnel (within the country and abroad) was conducted through the Departments of War and the Navy. Similarly, the enumeration of the "Indian Territory" was carried out in cooperation with the Commissioner of Indian Affairs. Large institutions (prisons, hospitals, etc.) were enumerated through the appointment of special "institution" enumerators.

Enumerators were much more closely supervised during the 1900 Census. In large cities, special agents were appointed to assist the census supervisor. Enumerators used "street books," in which a record of each enumerator's work was made on a daily basis. Enumerators used individual census slips for obtaining a correct return for any person (particularly lodgers and boarders) absent at the time of the enumerator's visit. Additionally, "absent family" schedules were used for securing a complete record for any person residing within the enumeration district, but temporarily absent.

---

[14]Robert P. Porter was appointed as Superintendent of Census by the President on April 17, 1889. He resigned the position on July 31, 1893.

[15]In 1890, the manufactures schedules were withdrawn from the general enumeration for 1,042 "important" manufacturing centers (opposed to 279 in 1880). Special agents were responsible for collecting the detailed data in these areas.

[16]The Commissioner of Labor continued his supervisory role of census-related work until October 5, 1897 (serving since October 1, 1865 without compensation), when upon his request, he was relieved by the Secretary of Interior.

[17]Censuses were not conducted until 1890 of Indian Territory. Alaska's first census was conducted in 1880. Hawaii was annexed by the United States on August 12, 1898. Therefore, the 1900 Census was the first census of the islands taken under the supervision of the United States. The Hawaiian Government, however, did conduct censuses every 6 years, from 1866 to 1896.

The Thirteenth Census: 1910

Under the provisions of the census act of July 2, 1909, the thirteenth census was administered. In accordance with the provisions of the act, general population and Indian population schedules were prepared. The schedules used for Hawaii and Puerto Rico, although similar to the general population schedule, differed slightly from those used within the United States.

Census enumerators began canvassing the Nation on April 15, 1910.[18] The law gave census takers 2 weeks to complete their work in cities of 5,000 inhabitants or more, while enumerators in smaller and rural areas were allotted 30 days to complete their task.

The Fourteenth Census: 1920

The Fourteenth Census Act of July 2, 1909, provided for the 1920 and subsequent censuses; however, numerous minor changes were sought prior to the census, so a new law was enacted on March 3, 1919. This act designated a 3-year decennial census period, beginning July 1, 1919. During this 3-year period, the act provided for an increased work force at the Census Bureau's headquarters in Washington, DC, and for the creation of a special field force to collect census data.

Section 20, of the Fourteenth Census Act, provided that the enumeration of the population should be made as of January 1, 1920.[19] Under the direction of the Director of the Census, Samuel L. Rogers, the work of actual enumeration began on January 2, 1920. The census covered the United States, the outlying possessions (excluding the Philippines and the Virgin Islands, the military, Red Cross, consular services abroad, and the naval service abroad or in American waters, but not on a fixed station.)[20]

For the country as a whole and for states and political subdivisions within the country, the population enumerated was the resident population. The enumerators (according to the census law), were instructed to enumerate persons at their "usual place of abode"—i.e., their permanent home or regular lodging place. Persons were not always counted in the places where they happened to be found by the enumerators or where they transacted their daily business. Persons temporarily absent from their usual places of abode (i.e., on business, traveling, attending school, or in hospitals) were enumerated at the places where they habitually resided and the information for these people was obtained from relatives or acquaintances. Persons having no fixed place of abode were required by the census law to be enumerated where they slept on the night of January 1, 1920.

The Fifteenth Census: 1930

Under the direction of William M. Steuart, Director of the Census, and in accordance with the Fifteenth Census Act, approved June 18, 1929, "a census of population, agriculture, irrigation, drainage, distribution, unemployment, and mines [was] taken by the Director of the Census" on April 1, 1930. The census encompassed each state and Washington, DC, Alaska, Hawaii, and Puerto Rico. A census of Guam, Samoa, and the Virgin Islands was taken in the same year by the islands' respective governors, and a census of the Panama Canal Zone was taken by the governor of that area.

In addition to population data, the 1930 census also collected the following statistics:

- *Agriculture.* Acreage of farm; value of land and buildings; mortgage debt; expenditures for labor, feed, and fertilizer; farm machinery and facilities; acreage, yield, and value of crops; quantity and value of livestock.

- *Manufacturing* (with similar data collected from mines and quarries). Quantity and value of products; the number of salaried employees and wage earners; aggregate payments for salaries and wages; the cost of materials and fuel.

- *Distribution.* Kind of business; type of operation; net sales; number of employees; total amount paid in salaries and wages; stocks on hand.

- *Construction.* Data was collected from general contractors, subcontractors, and operative builders regarding value of construction; wage payments; cost of materials; and subcontract work performed or let.

- *Unemployment.*

Data from families and establishments were transferred to punch cards—approximately 300,000,000 in all[21]— and were processed by electronic sorting and "automatic tabulating machine" at the rate of approximately 400 per minute. These tabulations provided the raw data necessary for the compilation of statistical tables prepared by clerks and statisticians.[22]

---

[18]The change of "census day" from June 1 to April 15 was made upon the suggestion of the Census Bureau. It was believed that the April 15 date would be more desirable, since a large number of people are away from their homes in June.

[19]The date was changed upon the request of the Department of Agriculture and users of agricultural statistics. The new date had advantages for the agricultural census—the past years work on all farms had been finished, and the new years work had not yet begun. The majority of farmers would have been occupying the farms they had the previous year, whereas, a few months later, many renters would have moved to other farms. Furthermore, the birth of livestock increases greatly during the Spring and early Summer. Therefore, a livestock census referring to January 1, 1920, would be far more valuable than one taken several months later.

[20]No provision was made by the Fourteenth Census Act for the enumeration of the Philippines. Censuses of the Philippines were conducted by the Philippine Commission in 1903. A second was conducted by the Philippines Government on December 31, 1918 (but called the "1919 Census"). A special census of the Virgin Islands was conducted by the United States, November 1, 1917.

[21]Approximately 125,000,000 punch cards were used to tabulate the data for the population. Fifteen or more cards were required for each farm, thus, the census of agriculture comprised an additional 150,000,000 cards.

[22]William L. Austin, "Bureau of the Census," reprinted from, *The United States Department of Commerce—How it Serves You on Land, And Sea, And in The Air.* Pp. 4-5.

1930 Census of Unemployment

A Census of Unemployment was conducted, in conjunction with the 1930 census, by an act of May 3, 1928. This special enumeration collected data on persons who usually worked for wages or a salary, but were not working at the time the census was taken.

William M. Steuart, Director of the Census, said "the results of the [unemployment] census will furnish a picture of the unemployment situation as indicated not only by the number of unemployed but by the attendant circumstance of unemployment. It will bring the answer to certain fundamental questions about which nothing definite is known at present. Obviously, something more than a mere knowledge of the number of persons out of work is needed, if we are to measure fairly and accurately, without exaggeration and without understatement, the gravity of the unemployment situation. We need the census to know the facts.[23]"

Enumerators were instructed to complete an unemployment schedule for every person responding "No" in column 25 of the general population schedule. The "unemployed" were grouped into two classes—those having a job but temporarily laid-off on account of a lack of orders, weather, sickness, etc.; and those who were unemployed but want to work.

The unemployment census provided data concerning the number of men and women unemployed, the average age of the unemployed, how many of the unemployed were married and single, how long they had been out of work, and the leading reasons for unemployment in the United States. Data were made available for the Nation, individual segments of the population (i.e., by age, race, marital status, etc.), and for the foreign-born and native populations.

The Sixteenth Census: 1940

The Sixteenth Census of the United States covered the continental United States, Alaska, American Samoa, Guam, Hawaii, the Panama Canal Zone, Puerto Rico, the Virgin Islands of the United States, the military and consular services abroad, and naval services abroad or in American waters, but not at a fixed station.[24] Persons in the military services were enumerated as residents of the states, counties, and minor civil divisions in which their posts of duty were located (members of their families were enumerated at the place in which they resided). The crews of American merchant marine vessels were enumerated as part of the population of the port from which the vessel operated.

No apportionment had been done after the 1920 Census—the 1910 apportionment remained in effect. Consequently, the 1929 act included provisions that, for the 1930 and subsequent censuses, (unless the Congress, within a specified time enacted legislation providing for apportionment on a different basis) the apportionment should automatically be made by the method last used. In accordance with this act, a report was submitted by the President to the Congress on December 4, 1930, showing the apportionment computations both by the method of major fractions (which was used in 1910) and by the method of equal proportions. In 1931, in the absence of additional legislation, the method of major fractions was automatically followed.[25]

In the application of this method, the Representatives are so assigned that the average population per Representative has the least possible variation as between one state and any other. As a result, California gained three Representatives between 1930 and 1940 and six other states—Arizona, Florida, New Mexico, North Carolina, Oregon, and Tennessee—each gained one. To balance these gains (since the number of Representatives in the House was not changed), nine states lost one Representative each—Illinois, Indiana, Iowa, Kansas, Massachusetts, Nebraska, Ohio, Oklahoma, and Pennsylvania.

Four notable changes were made to the 1940 Census, including the addition of the housing schedule, the sampling procedure (both discussed in further detail below), the incorporation of the questions on employment and unemployment onto the general population[26] schedule, and inquiries into migration.[27]

1940 Census of Housing

On August 11, 1939, a national census of housing was approved by the Congress, "to provide information concerning the number, characteristics (including utilities and equipment), and geographic distribution of dwelling structures and dwelling units in the United States. The Director of the Census shall take a census of housing in each state, the District of Columbia, Hawaii, Puerto Rico, the Virgin Islands, and Alaska, in the year 1940 in conjunction with, and at the same time, and as part of the population inquiry of the sixteenth decennial census."

The housing inquiries were collected via a separate census, partly because they were added by legislation late in the census planning, and partly because the nature of the questions so differed from those of the census of population.

---

[23]Undated memorandum, "The Census of Unemployment." Pp. 3-4.

[24]Again, the Philippine Islands were not included in the United States decennial census. The commonwealth of the Philippines conducted a census in 1939. The statistics from this census were then included in the data from the 1940 Census.

[25]In 1941, this law was amended to the effect that apportionment based on the 1940 and subsequent censuses should be made by the method of equal proportions.

[26]These inquiries had been made by special Census of Unemployment in 1930 (See 1930 Unemployment Census).

[27]A question was added asking, for each person 5 years old and above, the residence on April 1, 1935. These data were coded and compared to the place of residence in 1940, thus providing, for the first time, statistics on population movement.

The information collected by the two schedules was collected, however, by the same enumerator, at the same time as those for the population schedule.

Use of Sampling in the 1940 Census. The 1940 sample was a representative cross-section of the entire population. Tabulations made from the sample would be as nearly as possible the same as if information concerning every person had been obtained. The sample enlarged the scope of the census and facilitated tabulations in the following ways:

- Since the supplementary questions were asked only 1/20th (5-percent sample) as often as they would have in a complete census, the speed of field work was increased and carried out at a reduced cost, thus making it possible to carry more questions on the schedule.

- Tabulations based on the sample could be completed months ahead of the regular tabulations prepared from the general population—an especially important feature in times of national emergency and for obtaining quick preliminary counts of the distribution of the labor force by area, sex, age, etc.

- The reduced cost of sample tabulations permitted the publication of data that otherwise would not be possible.

- Sample cards could be stored for subsequent tabulations not feasible for the entire population as the need arose.

- Sampling helped to adapt the census to newly developed needs, and to maintain continuity from one census to another.

Participants were selected for the sample by designating 2 of the 40 lines on each side of the schedule as sample lines and instructing the enumerators to ask the supplementary questions for each person whose name happened to fall on these lines. This method resulted in a 5-percent sample of all the lines in each geographic area. The actual percentage of persons drawn from the sample from any district would vary by chance, depending on how the names happened to "line up" as the enumerators proceeded with their enumeration.

The Seventeenth Census: 1950

As in 1930 and 1940, the 1950 Census was conducted according to the terms of the Fifteenth Census Act. The enumeration began on April 1, 1950, with 90 percent of the population having been enumerated by the end of the month (weather delayed enumeration in some areas until mid-May). All but 1 percent of the population had been enumerated by the end of June 1950.

The 1950 census encompassed the continental United States, the Territories of Alaska and Hawaii, American Samoa, the Canal Zone, Guam, Puerto Rico, the Virgin Islands of the United States, and some of the smaller islands and island groups within the United States' possession.[28] The census also made special provisions for the enumeration of American citizens living abroad (and their dependents), including the armed forces of the United States, employees of the United States Government, and the crews of vessels in the American Merchant Marine at sea or in foreign ports.

The census of Americans living abroad was attempted through cooperative arrangements with the Department of Defense, the Department of State, the United States Maritime Administration, and other federal agencies concerned. These agencies took the responsibility for the distribution and collection of specially designed census questionnaires for individuals and households. Other persons living abroad were to be reported by their families or neighbors in the United States; however, the quality of these data was considered suspect and they were not included in the published statistics.

Procedures to improve coverage. Several aids were employed to improve the completeness of the 1950 Census coverage. The most prominent were as follows:

- A longer and better planned period of training was provided for enumerators.

- Each enumerator was furnished with a map of his enumeration district, showing the boundaries of the area for which they were responsible.

- An infant card had to be completed for each baby born after January 1, 1950 (since experience had shown that babies are easily missed).

- A crew leader was assigned to supervise each group of approximately 15 enumerators. The crew leader was responsible for helping enumerators with "problem cases" and for spot-checking a sample of the dwelling units assigned to them.

- A special enumeration of persons in hotels, tourist courts, and other places where transients usually pay for quarters was made the night of April 11, 1950. "Missed Person" forms were published in newspapers at the end of the field canvassing operations so persons who thought they had been missed could complete a form and mail it to the district supervisors.

- District supervisors made preliminary announcements of the population counted so that any complaints concerning the completeness of the enumeration could be submitted before the field offices were closed. If the evidence indicated an appreciable undercount, a re-enumeration of the area was conducted.

---

[28]Although some smaller islands and island groups did not participate in the census, data for their populations were collected from other sources and included in the 1950 census.

- Rates of population change were studied to evaluate the enumeration's completeness.

- Vital and immigration statistics were used in conjunction with census data. (Since the population at a given census should represent the population at the previous census, with additions and subtractions resulting from births, deaths, and immigration, it is possible to calculate the expected population on a given census date and compare the actual total received.)

Following these procedures improved the coverage of the 1950 census over that of the 1940 census.[29] (The components of population change were probably estimated more accurately during the 1940s than for the 1930s because not all states were consistently registering births and deaths until 1933.)

Post-Enumeration Survey. The 1950 census was further checked using a post-enumeration survey, in which a re-enumeration, on a sample basis, was conducted. The Census Bureau recanvassed a probability sample of about 3,500 small areas and compared these to the original census listings to identify households omitted from the enumeration. In addition to the check for omitted households, a sample of about 22,000 households was reinterviewed to determine the number of persons omitted in cases where the household had been included.

The Post-Enumeration Survey interviewers were given intensive training and supervision. Efforts were made to limit respondents to the person who was presumably best informed regarding the information desired, i.e., the person themselves. These precautions resulted in an expense per case in the Post-Enumeration Survey many times that of the original enumeration, and affordable only on a sample-basis.

The Eighteenth Census: 1960

The 1960 census began on April 1, 1960, in accordance with the requirements of an act of August 31, 1954 (amended August 1957), which codified Title 13 of the United States Code. By mid-April, 85 percent of the population of the United States had been enumerated with the count up to 98 percent by the end of the month.
Several notable changes were made in the procedures for taking and tabulating the census. These changes were: 1) the greater use of sampling, 2) the development of procedures enabling most householders an opportunity to consult other members and available records when completing the questionnaire for their families, and 3) the use of electronic equipment for nearly all data processing work.[30]

Sampling. In the 1960 census, a 25-percent sample was used. The greater use of sampling meant that the totals for some of the smaller areas were subject to a moderate amount of sampling variation, the usefulness of the statistics was not significantly impaired. Using a 25-percent sample of households eliminated nearly 75 percent of the processing expenses otherwise required for the items in the sample.

Enumeration procedures. The 1960 enumeration was divided into two stages—the first concentrating on quick coverage of the population and the collection of a few items for every person and dwelling unit, and the second devoted to the collection of the more detailed economic and social information required for sample households and dwelling units. Both stages used questionnaires left at the residence to be filled out by one or more members of the family.

The enumeration began prior to April 1, 1960, when an advance census form was delivered by the U.S. Postal Service to each household. The time between delivery of the form and the arrival of an enumerator to collect the household's information allowed the household to assemble information needed to respond to the census inquiries.

Shortly after April 1, 1960, the second stage of the enumeration began. Enumerators made their rounds to collect the census data and left an additional form—containing the sample inquiries—at every fourth house visited. Households receiving the sample form were asked to complete the form and mail it to their local census office in the postage-paid envelope provided by the enumerator. When these mailed questionnaires were received at the census office, Census Bureau personnel checked the sample forms for accuracy and conducted telephone or personal inquiries to complete unanswered inquiries when necessary.

This two-stage enumeration was believed to be advantageous in that, in the past, enumerators were given only brief special training and were burdened with more instructions and work than they could effectively manage. By creating a two-stage enumeration the field work and training were reduced. Approximately one-third of the enumerator work force was retained for work in the second stage—receiving additional training that focused solely upon the content of the sample questions.
In specified areas (about 15 percent of the total population, characterized as living in areas of low population density and/or having inferior road networks), the two staged enumeration was combined, so that the enumerator collected and recorded sample data in the same interview in which the 100-percent inquiries were recorded.

---

[29]For the decade 1930 to 1940, application of these methods suggests that the total net number of persons missed in the 1940 Census may have been about 1,300,000 more than that missed in 1930.

[30]A. Ross Eckler, "Plans for the 18th Decennial Census," presented at the annual meeting of the Rural Sociological Society, Cornell University, August 27, 1959. Pp. 3-6. Morris H. Hansen, "Procedures for the 1960 Census of Population and Housing," presented at the annual meeting of the American Statistical Association, Chicago, Il, December 1958.

The Nineteenth Census: 1970

When planning for the 1970 census, the need for an accurate count of the population was even greater than in the past because of the increasing tendency for governmental bodies to use population as a basis for distributing funds, and the more general awareness by local government officials and others of the potential effects of census undercounts.

Throughout the 1960s, researchers had reported that the population was increasingly resistant to the census. Studies had shown more alienation and distrust of government, and there appeared to be more organized attempts to protest the census. Furthermore, undercounts following the 1950 and 1960 censuses were blamed upon the enumerators' failure to follow instructions. Hence, stress was placed on simplified procedures, training, and quality control. Analysis of the results of the 1960 evaluation program and studies performed in the 1950s and 1960s indicated that the reasons for the undercounts were more complex. In particular, a substantial part of the undercount appeared to be due to either deliberate attempts by some segments of the population to be omitted from the census or the fact that they did not fit into any households by the "conventional rules" of residence. Even where the undercount was due to complete households being missed, the causes were frequently such that additional enumerator training produced only marginal gains.

This analysis led to a two-phase approach to coverage for the 1970 census. The first phase was the use of a basic census methodology that permitted knowledgeable outside sources to have an offer input into the list of housing units established by the census, and provided for automatic checks that enumerators actually completed a questionnaire for all known units.[31] This was done in areas containing about 60 percent of the population through the creation of an address register independent of the enumeration phase, correction and updating of the register by U.S. Post Office employees familiar with their routes, and checks by Census Bureau employees to ensure that all housing units on the address register were accounted for when enumerators had completed their assignments.

A self-enumeration questionnaire was used in 1970 (as in 1960 for 60 percent of the population). Such questionnaires were believed to provide better reporting within households, because they provided respondents uniform census definitions and rules to follow for unusual household residence situations. In the areas containing the remaining 40 percent of the population, more conventional listing procedures were followed, but with self-enumeration features.

The second phase of the 1970 enumeration was to superimpose on the regular census procedures projects specifically designed to increase coverage. Prior to 1970, studies of the effectiveness of a variety of devices for improving coverage were made, generally as part of large-scale tests conducted during the 1960s, which resulted in several coverage improvement initiatives.

The 1970 coverage improvement program included measures to improve coverage by (1) developing a more favorable public view of the census; (2) increasing the public's understanding of the importance of the census and its confidentiality; and (3) improving the enumerators' performance in hard-to-enumerate areas through intensive training and supervision. The specific changes made included—

- A sharp reduction in the number of questions to be asked of households—the number of inquiries on the questionnaire intended for 3 million households had been reduced from 66 to 23.

- Questions on the adequacy of kitchen and bathroom facilities were reworded to remove any implication that the federal government was trying to ascertain with whom these were shared.

- The Secretary of Commerce increased his supervision of the census and retained independent experts as census advisors.

- A letter accompanied the census questionnaire that explained the need for data requested and emphasized the confidentiality of responses.[32]

Census questionnaires with instruction sheets were delivered by the U.S. Post Office to every household several days prior to "Census Day"—April 1, 1970. In areas with comparatively large populations of Spanish-speaking households, a Spanish-language version of the instruction sheet also was enclosed. Households either received a short-form questionnaire, which contained questions asked of 100 percent of the population (80 percent of the population received this form), or a long-form questionnaire, sent to 20 percent of the population, containing questions asked of 15 and 5 percent of the population.

In larger metropolitan areas and some adjacent counties (approximately 60 percent of the United States' population), households were asked to complete and return the questionnaire by mail on April 1, 1970 (resulting in an 87 percent mailback response rate), which was then reviewed by an enumerator or census clerk. Telephone or personal follow-up was made to complete or correct missing, incomplete, or inconsistent questionnaires. For the remaining 40

---

[31] Throughout the census history, a small percentage of enumerators completed questionnaires by "curb stoning." Curb stoning meant the enumerator completed questionnaires for an individual or multiple households from the curb, without actually conducting an interview or checking the accuracy of their "guesses." This practice was motivated, in part, by the requirement to meet quotas or payment for work done on a "piece-of-work" basis.

[32] *United States Department of Commerce News,* April 18, 1969. P.1.

percent of the United States' population, instructions asked that the householder complete the form and hold it for pick up by an enumerator.

The Twentieth Census: 1980

For most of the United States, "Census Day" for the 1980 enumeration was April 1, 1980.[33] As in past censuses, all questionnaires were to be completed giving information as of that date, regardless of when the form was actually completed.

The 1980 census also included two small surveys—the Components of Inventory Change Survey, which obtained information on counts and characteristics of the housing units that changed or stayed the same between 1973 and 1980; and the Residential Finance Survey, requesting data on mortgages, shelter costs, selected housing characteristics, and owner characteristics.

The use of a mailout/mailback questionnaire in 1970 had proven successful, and eased the follow-up operation burden. Furthermore, tests during the 1970 census indicated the feasibility of administering a mailout/mailback census in rural areas and small towns. As a result, the mail census areas for 1980 covered 95.5 percent of the United States population.

Field Enumeration. The 1980 field enumeration procedures were similar to those used in 1970, with the exception of the greatly expanded use of the mail for questionnaire delivery and return. Households received a questionnaire in the mail, completed it, and mailed it back to their local census district office. In those areas enumerated conventionally (i.e., through enumerator visits to the housing unit), the U.S. Postal Service delivered a questionnaire to each household 4 days prior to Census Day. Respondents were instructed to complete their questionnaires, but hold them until an enumerator visited the household. The enumerators collected the completed short-form questionnaires or helped the head of the household complete the form at the time of the visit, or completed a long-form questionnaire at designated housing units. Enumerators also enumerated individuals living in group quarters.

Publicity. The 1980 census incorporated an extensive advertising and promotion campaign. The focus of the campaign was to increase public awareness and cooperation with the census, i.e., to encourage households to fill out their census forms, and in mail census areas, mail them back to their census district offices.

The campaign was directed by the Census Bureau's Census Promotion Office (CPO), established in the Summer 1978. The CPO secured the free services of the Advertising Council in directing the advertising campaign. The Council, in turn, hired the firm of Ogilvy & Mather to develop the campaign.

The promotion campaign incorporated media advertising, the distribution of information kits to magazines and newspapers and census promotional kits to over 100,000 schools, and the development of an extensive network of partnerships with corporations and private organizations interested in supporting the census. In addition, public relations specialists in the Census Bureau's regional and district offices handled a variety of more localized promotional activities, including obtaining time for public service announcements (PSAs) from local broadcast outlets, advising census managers on working with the press, partnering with local companies, and serving as liaisons with complete-count committees (over 4,000 complete count committees were organized throughout the country in an effort to generate local publicity and support for the census).

The Twenty-First Census: 1990

The twenty-first census of the United States was taken as of April 1, 1990. The census covered the 50 states, the District of Columbia, Puerto Rico, the Virgin Islands, and the Pacific Island territories (American Samoa, the Commonwealth of the Northern Mariana Islands, Guam, and by special agreement, the Republic of Palau.)

The 1990 census used two questionnaires—a short-form containing questions asked of the entire population and a long-form with additional population and housing questions asked of approximately 1-in-6 households.

The content of the 1990 census questionnaire was similar to that for 1980. The short-form questionnaire for households contained the items to be asked of all persons and for housing units. Those items—plus the population and housing questions to be asked on a sample basis—appeared on the long-form questionnaire.

For the 1990 census, the Census Bureau introduced the Topologically Integrated Geographic Encoding and Referencing (TIGER) system, which was developed by the Census Bureau and the U.S. Geological Survey (USGS). The TIGER system documented all streets, roads, rivers, lakes, railroads, and their attributes (names and address ranges, where appropriate), as well as the boundaries, names, and codes of all geographic entities used for data collection and tabulation for the entire United States, Puerto Rico, the Virgin Islands, and the Pacific Island territories. In addition to supporting the geocoding requirement, the TIGER system also provided a means to produce the many different maps required for data collection and tabulation.

---

[33]"Census Day" in northern and western Alaska was January 22, 1980, so the enumeration would be completed prior to the Spring thaw. As part of an agreement with the local governments, Census Day in the Trust Territory of the Pacific Islands (excluding the commonwealth of Northern Mariana Islands) was September 15, 1980, so teachers could be used as enumerators.

With the mapping capabilities of the TIGER system and the use of a master address list, developed jointly between the Census Bureau and U.S. Postal Service, the Census Bureau mailed pre-addressed short- or long-form questionnaires to approximately 86.2 million households. The 1990 census questionnaire packages were mailed to households beginning in February 1990. Most post offices had delivered the initial mailings by March 23, 1990, followed by a mailed reminder card on March 30, 1990. Occupants were asked to complete these questionnaires and return them by mail. Nonrespondents to the questionnaire mailout received a personal visit from an enumerator seeking to complete a census questionnaire for the household.

Publicity. As in 1980, the 1990 census was extensively advertised in television, radio, print, and public advertising. The goal of this advertising was to encourage mail response, reduce differential undercount, and foster a positive atmosphere within which to take the census convincing people that the census was both important and safe.

Promotion activities included "complete count" committees, information kits for schools, churches (the Religious Organizations Project), and the media, workshops, "pro bono" PSAs sponsored by the Advertising Council; local government outreach and partnerships; and the Census Education Project (designed to educate students about the census).

Compared to the estimated $38 million worth of free commercial advertising received in 1980, an audit placed the 1990 figure at about $66.5 million. Local television and radio stations were responsible for 69 percent of that value, followed by 21 percent for ethnic media. The PSA campaign reached a potential audience of 99 percent of the adult-aged population, with an average of 68 exposures to census related advertising per person.

The Twenty-Second Census: 2000

The twenty-second decennial census—Census 2000—enumerated the residents of the United States, Puerto Rico, and the Island Areas, and Federal employees and their dependents living overseas as of Census Day, April 1, 2000. The majority of these households participated in the census through a mailout/mailback operation.[34]

In February 2000, the Census Bureau mailed advance letters to each household within the U.S. informing them that a Census 2000 questionnaire would soon be arriving. The letter also included instructions on how to obtain an in-language questionnaire for non-English speaking households.

Beginning in early March 2000, the U.S. Postal Service began delivering approximately 98 million questionnaires to households throughout the U.S. and its territories. The majority of households (83 percent) received a short-form questionnaire that asked for information on seven subjects (name, sex, age, relationship, Hispanic origin, and race).[35] A sample of 1-in-6 households (17 percent) was selected to receive the long-form questionnaire, which in addition to the short-form questionnaire inquires, also contained 52 questions requesting more detailed information about housing, social, and economic characteristics of the household. The questionnaire mailout was followed by the mailing of "reminder cards" to each household receiving a questionnaire.

In total, 65 percent of households responded to the mailout/mailback census. The remaining 35 percent of households were visited by enumerators who attempted to complete a questionnaire via personal interviews.

Census 2000 Advertising Campaign. Census 2000 featured the first ever paid advertising campaign. So as to reach all adults living in the United States (including Puerto Rico and the Island areas), the Census Bureau awarded a contract to Young & Rubicam, totaling $167 million, for print, television, and radio advertising for its national, regional, and local advertising campaign.

The advertising campaign consisted of more than 250 TV, radio, print, outdoor, and Internet advertisements—in 17 languages—reaching 99 percent of all U.S. residents. By the end of the campaign, the census message—"This is your future. Don't leave it blank."—had been heard or seen an average of 50 times per person. At its conclusion the campaign was ranked the second most effective campaign according to an AdTrack—USA TODAY consumer poll and for the first-half of 2000, the Census Bureau ranked 53rd in spending among all advertisers in the United States.

(For additional information on Census 2000 operations, see "Census 2000 Operational Plan," U.S. Department of Commerce, Economics and Statistics Administration, U.S. Census Bureau, December 2000.)

---

[34]Puerto Rico was enumerated using Update/Leave methodology—enumerators personally delivered a questionnaire to each household, after which the household completed the questionnaire and mailed it back to the Census Bureau.

[35]For the first time, recipients of the short-form questionnaire had the option of providing their information by submitting electronic responses to the questionnaire via the Internet. Although this option was not extensively promoted, approximately 66,000 households chose to respond electronically.

Appendix A.
United States' Population and Census Cost

Census year	Population	Census cost
1790	3,929,214	$44,377
1800	5,308,483	66,109
1810	7,239,881	178,445
1820	9,633,822	208,526
1830	12,866,020	378,545
1840	17,069,458	833,371
1850	23,191,876	1,423,351
1860	31,443,321	1,969,377
1870	38,558,371	3,421,198
1880	50,155,783	5,790,678
1890	62,979,766	11,547,127
1900	76,303,387	11,854,000
1910	91,972,266	15,968,000
1920	105,710,620	25,117,000
1930	122,775,046	40,156,000
1940	131,669,275	67,527,000
1950	151,325,798	91,462,000
1960	179,323,175	127,934,000
1970	203,302,031	247,653,000
1980	226,542,199	1,078,488,000
1990	248,718,301	2,492,830,000
2000	281,421,906	4,500,000,000

Appendix B.
National Archives and Records Administration Headquarters and Regional Branches

Washington, DC Headquarters
7th & Pennsylvania Ave., NW
Washington, DC 20408
202-501-5400
www.nara.gov

REGIONAL RECORDS SERVICES FACILITIES

Pacific Alaska Region
654 West Third Ave.
Anchorage, AL 99501-2145
907-271-2441
E-mail: archives@alaska.nara.gov

Pacific Region (Laguna Niguel)
24000 Avila Rd., 1st Floor-East Entrance
Laguna Niguel, CA 92677-3497
P.O. Box 6719
Laguna Niguel, CA 92607-6719
949-360-2641
E-mail: archives@laguna.nara.gov

Pacific Region (San Bruno)
1000 Commodore Dr.
San Bruno, CA 94066-2350
650-876-9009
E-mail: archives@sanbruno.nara.gov

Rocky Mountain Region
Building 48, Denver Federal Center
West 6th Ave., and Kipling St.
Denver, CO 80225-0307
P.O. Box 25307
Denver, CO 80225-0307
303-236-0804
E-mail: center@denver.nara.gov

Southeast Region
1557 St. Joseph Ave.
East Point, GA 30344-2593
404-763-7474
E-mail: center@atlanta.nara.gov

Great Lakes Region
7358 South Pulaski Rd.
Chicago, IL 60629-5898
773-581-7816
E-mail: archives@chicago.nara.gov

Northeast Region (Boston)
380 Trapelo Rd.
Waltham, MA 02452-6399
781-647-8104
E-mail: archives@waltham.nara.gov

Northeast Region (Pittsfield)
10 Conte Dr.
Pittsfield, MA 01201-8230
413-445-6885
E-mail: archives@pittsfield.nara.gov

Northeast Region (New York)
201 Varick St.
New York, NY 10014-4811
212-337-1300
E-mail: archives@newyork.nara.gov

Central Plains Region (Kansas City)
2312 East Bannister Rd.
Kansas City, MO 64131-3011
816-926-6272
E-mail: archives@kansascity.nara.gov

Central Plains Region (Lee's Summit)
200 Space Center Dr.
Lee's Summit, MO 64064-1182
816-823-6272
E-mail: center@kccave.nara.gov

Great Lakes Region
3150 Springboro Rd.
Dayton, OH 45439-1883
937-225-2852
E-mail: center@dayton.nara.gov

Mid Atlantic Region (Center City Philadelphia)
900 Market St.
Philadelphia, PA 19107-4292
215-597-3000
E-mail: archives@philarch.nara.gov

Mid Atlantic Region (Northeast Philadelphia)
14700 Townsend Rd.
Philadelphia, PA 19154-1096
215-671-9027
E-mail: center@philfrc.nara.gov

Southwest Region
501 West Felix St., Building 1
Fort Worth, TX 76115-3405
P.O. Box 6216
Fort Worth, TX 76115-0216
817-334-5515
E-mail: archives@ftworth.nara.gov

Pacific Alaska Region (Seattle)
6125 Sand Point Way, NE
Seattle, WA 98115-7999
206-526-6501
E-mail: archives@seattle.nara.gov

The following materials are all at Archives headquarters; information about these should be directed to the appropriate unit:

Material	Record Group	Branch
Census field maps and enumeration district maps	29	Cartographic & Architectural Branch 8601 Adelphi Road College Park, MD 20740-6001 301-713-7040
Census schedules and administrative records	29	Old Military and Civil Records Branch (NWCTB) 202-501-5395
Indian records	75, 279	
Immigration records	36, 85	
Military records	Various	
Homestead records	49	
Ordering microfilm, catalogs, finding aids, and publications		Customer Service center (NWCC2) National Archives at College Park 8601 Adelphi Road College Park, MD 20740 1-800-234-8861 FAX: 301-713-6169 www.nara.gov
Ordering free publications		Customer Service Center (NWCC1) National Archives 700 Pennsylvania Avenue, NW Washington, DC 20408 1-800-234-8861 FAX: 301-713-6169

Appendix C.
Availability of Records for the
Eleventh Census of the United States, 1890

ELEVENTH CENSUS OF THE UNITED STATES. 1890

M407, 3 rolls

Most of the 1890 population schedules were badly damaged by fire in the U.S. Department of Commerce Building in January 1921. The extant schedules are numbered and noted at the end of rolls 1-3 below.

- Roll 1. Alabama, Perry County (Perryville Beat No. 11 and Severe Beat No. 8) [fragments 1-455]

- Roll 2. District of Columbia, Q, 13th, 14th, R, Q, Corcoran, 15th, S, R, and Riggs Streets, Johnson Avenue, and S Street. [fragments 456-781]

- Roll 3. Georgia, Muscogee County (Columbus), Illinois, McDonough County (Mound Twp.); Minnesota, Wright County (Rockford); New Jersey, Hudson County (Jersey City); New York, Westchester County (Eastchester); and Suffolk County (Brookhaven Twp.); North Carolina, Gaston County (South Point Twp. And River Bend Twp.) and Cleveland County (Twp. No. 2); Ohio, Hamilton County (Cincinnati) and Clinton County (Wayne Twp.); South Dakota, Union County (Jefferson Twp.); Texas, Ellis County (J.P. No. 6, Mountain Peak, and Ovilla Precinct), Hood County (Precinct No. 5), Rusk County (No. 6 and J.P. No. 7), Trinity County (Trinity Town and Precinct No. 2) and Kaufman County (Kaufman). [fragments 782-1, 233]

INDEX TO THE ELEVENTH CENSUS OF THE UNITED STATES, 1890
M496. 2 rolls, 16-mm

This name index covers the few extant 1890 population schedules. Numbers on the cards match those listed at the end of rolls 1-3 of M407 above.

1. A-J
2. K-Z

SPECIAL SCHEDULES OF THE ELEVENTH CENSUS (1890) ENUMERATING UNION VETERANS AND WIDOWS OF UNION VETERANS OF THE CIVIL WAR
M123. 118 rolls

An act of March 1, 1899, provided that the eleventh census should "cause to be taken on a special schedule of inquiry, according to such form as he may prescribe, the names, organizations, and length of service of those who had served in the Army, Navy, or Marine Corps of the United States in the war of the rebellion, and who are survivors at the time of said inquiry, and the widows of soldiers, sailors, or marines." Each schedule requested the following information: name of the veteran (or if he did not survive, the names of both the widow and her deceased husband): the veteran's rank, company, regiment or vessel, date of enlistment, date of discharge, and length of service in years, months, and days; post office and address of each person listed; disability incurred by the veteran; and remarks necessary to a complete statement of his term of service. Practically all of the schedules for the states Alabama through Kansas and approximately half of those for Kentucky appear to have been destroyed, possibly by fire, before the transfer of the remaining schedules to the National Archives in 1943.

The surviving Kentucky records, and the records for the remaining states (Louisiana through Wyoming), and the District of Columbia, are available on 118 reels or microfilm at the National Archives.

Appendix D.
Bibliography

Eaton, George B., ed., *The Handy Book for Genealogists.* 9th ed. Logan, UT: The Everton Publishers, Inc., c. 1999. 619 pp. ISBN 1-890895-03-2.

Kyvig, David E., and Marty A. Myron. *Nearby History: Exploring the Past Around You.* Nashville, TN: The American Association for State and Local History, c. 1982. xiii, 300 pp. ISBN 0-910050-59-7

National Archives and Records Administration. *Federal Population and Mortality Schedules, 1790-1910, in the National Archives and the States.* Special List 24. Washington, DC, 1986. xvi, 140 pp. (microfiche only) .

____ *The 1900 Federal Population Census, Revised.* Washington, DC, 1996. ISBN 0-911333-14-2

____ *The 1910 Federal Population Census, A Catalog of Microfilm Copies of the Schedules.* Washington, DC, 1982. 44 pp.

____ *The 1920 Federal Population Census, Revised.* Washington, DC, 1992. 96 pp. ISBN 0-911333-86-X

____ *The 1790-1890 Federal Population Censuses, Revised.* Washington, DC, 1997. ISBN 0-911333-63-0

____ *Cross Index to Selected City Streets and Enumeration Districts, 1910 Census.* National Archives Microfiche Publication M1283. N.d., 50 fiche.

____ *Our Family, Our Town: Essays on Family and Local History Sources in the National Archives.* Washington, DC, 1987. xvi, 233 pp. ISBN 0-911333-50-9.

National Archives and Records Service. *Cartographic Records of the Bureau of the Census.* Preliminary Inventory No. 103. Washington, DC, 1958. v, 108 pp.

____ *Federal Population Schedules, 1790-1890. A Catalog of Microfilm Copies of the Schedules.* Washington, DC, 1977. 90 pp.

____ *Guide to Genealogical Research in the National Archives, Revised.* Washington, DC, 1985. xiii, 304 pp. ISBN 0-911333-00-2.

____ *List of Free Black Heads of Families in the First Census of the United States.* Special List 34. Washington, DC, 1974. 44 pp.

Luebking, Sandra H., ed., and Szucs, Loretto D. *The Source: A Guidebook of American Genealogy.* Salt Lake City, UT, Ancestry Publishing Co., 1997. 846 pp. ISBN: 0-916489-67-1.

Thorndale, William, and William Dollarhide. *Map Guide to the U.S. Federal Censuses, 1790-1920.* Baltimore, MD: Genealogical Publishing Co., 1992. ISBN 0-806311-88-6.

U.S. Bureau of the Census. *A Century of Population Growth.* Baltimore, MD, Genealogical Publishing Company, 1970

____ *Factfinder for the Nation.* CFF No. 4, "History and Organization." Washington, DC, 2000. 12pp.

____ *Heads of Families at the First Census of the United States Taken in the Year 1790 [state].* Washington, DC, 2001.

____ *The 1950 Censuses—How They Were Taken.* Washington, DC, 1955. 222 pp.

____ *Principal Data Collection Forms Used in the 1950 Censuses.* Washington, DC, 1952. 41 pp.

____ 1960 Censuses of Population and Housing: Procedural History. Washington, DC, 1966. 387 pp.

____ *Principal Data Collection Forms and Procedures.* Washington, DC, 1961. 62 pp.

____ *Survey of Components of Change and Residential Finance. . .Principal DataCollection Forms and Procedures.* Washington, DC, 1962. 36 pp.

____ *1970 Census of Population and Housing: Data Collection Forms and Procedures.* Series PHC (R)-2. Washington, DC, 1971. 115 pp.

____ *Procedural History.* Series PHC(R)-1. Washington, DC, 1976. 674 pp.

____ *Survey of Components of Inventory Change and Residential Finance: Principal Data-Collection Forms and Procedures.* Series (PHC(R)-4. Washington, DC, 1972. 38 pp.

____ *1980 Census of Population and Housing: History.* Series PHC80-R-2. Washington, DC. Issued in parts, 1986-1989.

____ *Twenty Censuses: Population and Housing Questions, 1790-1890.* Washington, DC, 1979. 91 pp.

____ *100 Years of Data Processing: The Punchcard Century.* Prepared for the Hollerith Centennial celebration, June 20, 1990.

____ Working Paper 39. *Population and Housing Inquiries in U.S. Decennial Censuses, 1790-1970.* Washington, DC, 1973. 179 pp.

_____ *1990 Census of Population and Housing: History.* Series CPH-R-2A-D. Washington, DC. Issued in parts, 1993-1996.

_____ *Census 2000 Operational Plan.* Series DMD/01-1419, Washington, DC. December 2000.

University of Wisconsin-Madison, Center for Demography and Ecology. *Procedural History of the 1940 Census of Population and Housing.* Prepared by Robert Jenkins. Madison, WI, 1983. 200 pp.

Wright, Carroll D. and William C. Hunt. *The History and Growth of the United States Census.* Prepared for the Senate Committee on the Census. Washington, DC, 1900. (Covers 1790-1890.)

For further information about topics in this guide or to request application forms (BC600) for a search of census transcripts, write, call, fax, or E-mail—

U.S. Census Bureau
History Staff
Washington, DC 20233
301-457-1167
301-457-3005 (Fax)
genealogy@census.gov